The Feast of Our Lives

The Feast of Our Lives

Re-imaging Communion

June Christine Goudey

THE
PILGRIM
PRESS
Cleveland

To
Roger, Andy, Millie, and Annie
For their abounding hope.

And to the Holy One
who calls me to the feast.

Deo Gratias

The Pilgrim Press, 700 Prospect Avenue, Cleveland, Ohio 44115-1100
www.pilgrimpress.com

Printed in the United States of America on acid-free paper

08 07 06 05 04 03 02 5 4 3 2 1

Library of Congress Cataloging-in-Publication Data

Goudey, June Christine, 1946-
The feast of our lives : re-imaging communion / June Christine Goudey.
p. cm.
Includes bibliographical references and index.
ISBN 0-8298-1479-5 (pbk. : alk. paper)
1. Lord's Supper. I. Title.

BV825.2 .G58 2002
264′.36 – dc21

2002019590

Contents

Preface vii

1. Turning the Tables 1

2. Thinking outside the Empire 13

3. Imagining and Imaging Communal Well-Being 37

4. Praying as Believing 63

5. Deliver Us from Fear 90

6. What Price Forgiveness? 113

7. The Embodied Soul 134

8. Holy Communion Indeed! 153

Appendix A: Paradigm Shifts to Encourage Well-Being 177

Appendix B: Communion Prayers 179

Index 191

Preface

"Lift up your hearts!" With simplicity and power these ancient words call us to hope in the context of Holy Communion. These words also call us to re-image the sacrament in ways that instill, rather than diminish, a true sense of communion. Our capacity to lift our hearts and minds to God and feed on hope has often been compromised by the Reformed tradition's Achilles heel — its liturgical fascination with sin and guilt. As a consequence, many believers abstain from this rite or take and eat with ambivalence.

My own ambivalence coupled with my scholarly interest in imagination and liturgy encouraged me to take the imagery of Holy Communion and its theological associations seriously, especially the strong association with Jesus' sacrificial death for our sins. Over time as I continued to receive the bread and cup and to deepen my knowledge of the theological history of communion, my own ambivalence was transformed as the steadfastness of the Spirit and the healing power of ritual opened my heart to the greater hope within us all — a hope larger than life itself. In turn, this hope has moved me to write this book for all who are burdened by the liturgical excesses of sin and guilt. Seeking a "picture of grace" for our time, as Luther did for his, I have sought to free the eucharist from its *medieval captivity.* In doing so I have re-imaged the eucharist from funeral to feast while transcending the imagery of fear that underlies atonement imagery in the Reformed tradition.

The book unfolds as follows. Chapter 1 explores the meaning of communion and community and identifies the main reasons for re-imaging the eucharist and transforming the self-sacrificial imagery that plagues the "celebratory nature" of Holy Communion. Chapter 2 presents alternative values in the context of imperial Christianity and encourages the deepening of human imagination. Chapter 3 offers new ways of understanding and experiencing our imaginative powers, the power of symbols, and the role of imagination as the infinite locus of soul. Chapter 4 reviews significant historical shifts in eucharistic practice and traces the evolution of sacrificial imagery in Reformed liturgies. Chapter 5 demonstrates the influence of apocalyptic imagery in Christian thought and its particular impact on the eucharistic image of the eschatological banquet within Christian practice. Chapter 6 addresses the role that fear, guilt, and shame have played in the development of a punitive god-representation via persecution, atonement, and penitential practices. Chapter 7 looks at the embodied nature of fear as well as contemporary insights into the role emotions play in cognitive thinking and liturgical practice. Lastly, Chapter 8 presents my conclusions as to why Jesus' welcoming table-fellowship was overturned by exclusive and punitive practices. I then offer a constructive understanding of Holy Communion and suggest how we might loosen the liturgical hold sacrificial imagery and the words of institution presently have on our ability to enact thanksgiving within a liberating imagination. Within the appendixes, I offer a sampling of communion prayers as well as several paradigm shifts necessary to make eucharist outside the confines of imperial Christianity, yet within the grace-lines of Christ Jesus. My greatest hope is that by engaging this work imaginatively, clergy and laity alike will discover, here and in their communities, a Holy Communion worthy of their lives.

Having arrived at this stage, I owe a profound debt to the many women and men who have wrestled with angels for the sake of naming their truths and living their theology within a wide spectrum of liturgical expression. Likewise the gratitude I feel toward those who have mentored me through my own wrestling is deep and abiding. Foremost among them is Roger Hazelton, former Abbot Professor of Theology at Andover Newton Theological School, without whose wisdom and witness my own views on imagination and faith might never have seen the light of day. As a scholar and friend, Roger shared my questions and encouraged me to live them *in the church,* regardless of the resistance I was bound to meet. He was a gentle and wise soul whom grace had greatened and whose imaginative faith lightens my life even now.

In addition to Roger, I have had the great good fortune of being intellectually challenged by Phyllis Trible, Elizabeth Bettenhausen, Robert Neville, and Horace Allen. Indeed, Horace's liturgical insights during my doctoral work at Boston University proved invaluable in shaping my view of the Reformed tradition and its eucharistic rite. At the same time, I am enormously grateful to Margaret Wiborg and the board of the Anna Howard Shaw Center at BU's School of Theology for naming me as the first Anna Howard Shaw Scholar, an honor that enabled me to grow as a scholar during a difficult time of transition. My continuing associations within the Feminist Studies in Liturgy Seminar of the North American Academy of Liturgy profoundly bless me as well. The encouragement and challenge provided in particular by Marjorie Procter-Smith, Janet Walton, Heather Murray Elkins, and Kathy Black have sustained me through many moments of uncertainty.

Within a pastoral context, there are numerous women and men, both in Arizona and Massachusetts, who have sharpened my thinking on the eucharist. I owe special thanks, however, to the members and friends of the

Old South Church in Boston, where in the early 1990s the foundational aspects of this book found expression and acceptance. The same is true for the members and friends of East Milton Congregational, UCC in Milton, Massachusetts, who allowed their interim pastor in 1993–94 to preach new paradigms of faith, celebrate Holy Communion, and practice resurrection with thanksgiving!

In recent years, I have been blessed by former students and colleagues at Bangor Theological Seminary in Bangor and Portland, Maine, who sharpened my thinking and teaching on eucharist, imagination, and liturgy. Most recently, a grant from the Wabash Center for Teaching and Learning allowed me seven uninterrupted weeks in the summer of 2000 to begin transforming my dissertation into a more accessible work. Several scholars have graciously read portions of this material and offered critical feedback; for their generosity and insights I offer deep thanks to David Trobisch, Glenn Miller, Janet Walton, and Eckehart Stöve. Likewise, I have been blessed by the research and editorial efforts of Brenda Wesselink Leclerc, whose friendship, humor, and steadfast encouragement strengthened both writer and writing. Special thanks and blessings too to Phil Porter and Cynthia Winton-Henry, the founders and co-directors of *InterPlay,* whose philosophy, bodywisdom practices, and personal integrity revitalized my ability to write creatively and play seriously in the final stages of "book-birth." Lastly, but never least, I offer heartfelt thanks and sighs too deep for words to Andy Canale, Millie Goudey, and Ann Feaver, whose steadfast faith, compassionate love, and abounding hope will forever en-courage me to make eucharist with enthusiasm!

ONE

Turning the Tables

> It is not too much but too little imagination that causes illness. ...Like hope itself, it will always suppose that there is a fact and a possibility that is not yet in. The imagination will always be the enemy of the absolutizing instinct and the ally of hope.
>
> —*William F. Lynch*[1]

> Indeed, heresies are themselves instigated by philosophy [by asking questions]....Let our "seeking," therefore, be in that which is our own, and from those who are our own: and concerning that which is our own, — that, and only that, which can become an object of inquiry without impairing the rule of faith.
>
> —*Tertullian*[2]

The scene was familiar, a small congregation in the suburbs of Boston gathered for Sunday worship in the Reformed tradition.[3] Yet the woman knew something was different. Perhaps it was the warm greeting for her and her partner when they entered. Perhaps it was the hymn of praise accompanied by drummers that filled the space where the Gloria Patri (Glory to the Father) was once intoned. Perhaps it was the children singing, ushering, and leading prayers. Perhaps it was the warmth and ease so evident between the worship leaders or the dancing procession that all were invited to enter as the celebrants moved to the communion table. Surely it was all these things and more. She had settled into a stoic numbness as the service proceeded, knowing that as usual she would pass the elements by when they were offered. Too many times this simple act of eating and drinking had conjured up pain rather than promise, reminding her of personal unworthiness rather than divine belovedness.

---

1. William F. Lynch, *Images of Hope: Imagination as Healer of the Hopeless* (Notre Dame, Ind.: University of Notre Dame Press, 1974), 243.

2. Tertullian, *The Prescription against Heretics,* chapters 7 and 12, trans. Rev. Peter Holmes, available at *www.webcom.com/gnosis/library.html.*

3. Jane Dempsey Douglass, "What Is Reformed Theology?" *Princeton Seminary Bulletin,* n.s., 11, no. 1 (1990): 3–10.

She had come out of respect for the friends they were visiting, politely going through the motions asked of her. Until something shifted within and she heard the congregation say, "*Christ has died, Christ is risen, Christ is with us now. Alleluia!*" Gently, resistance gave way to new possibilities. She had expected the celebrant to somberly intone the ancient words of institution, reminding all of Jesus' "broken body" and "saving blood." And she had steeled herself for the all-too-familiar "fencing of the table," the proclamation that only certain people were welcome. But no fence appeared. Instead something stirred and shifted for her as words of welcome and forgiveness filled the sanctuary. The woman began to notice the joyful faces of those who stood and went forward to receive the bread and juice as "bread of life" and "cup of blessing." Something was happening that was hard to resist. Children and adults received alike. Quietly, the spirit of acceptance embraced her too, nudging aside the protective detachment she had long ago donned in desperation. It would take several more visits to this place before she would trust the promises made here; but, for the time being, a door had been left ajar. The possibility lingered that true feasting might one day break the fast she now endured at Christ's table. As the benediction rang out, words of thanksgiving began to dance in her heart.

The Tensions of Interpretation

Far from simply describing one woman's hope for renewal, this imaginative scene touches a chord among many believers in exile[4] who have voted with their feet to leave behind the tradition of their birth. My words are meant to offer them hope and to encourage those who remain active in traditional faith communities to trust the *lived truths* of their lives. If these believers challenge their faith communities to take their truths seriously, especially on Sunday morning, then all of us may yet witness the reformation we long to see. Without these efforts, however, little will happen to bring the renewal many seek.

Death is surely afoot in many a mainline (some would say sideline) church today. Where its symptoms have yet to surface, a lack of wholeness cries out to be remedied. This is most clearly the case with the intransigence that surrounds Holy Communion. Orthodox Christianity remains unwilling to entertain the wonder of divine mystery at the very place where God's mystery resides in its fullness — the love that welcomes all to God's table in Jesus' name. Instead, the mystery that surrounds Holy Communion has more to do with the mystification of bread and cup through

4. John Shelby Spong, *Why Christianity Must Change or Die: A Bishop Speaks to Believers in Exile* (San Francisco: HarperSanFrancisco, 1998), 20.

sacrificial-atonement imagery. In the midst of this sacrament, believers could open themselves to divine mystery and experience the immediacy of incarnation and resurrection in their communal relations. Nevertheless, too few know the truth of this holy meal. In the place of presence, they touch an enormous absence that need not be. Indeed, the somberness and stiltedness with which many enact this meal often seem more funereal than feastlike.

I will argue that the fear instilled by a punitive *god-image* (a misrepresentation of God), coupled with a misplaced sense of mystery, has led us to value ritual elements more than sacred community. I will also demonstrate how misguided fear, arising from the church's embrace of the "Judgment Day" of apocalyptic thinking and its imagery of heaven and hell, now burdens and distorts the simple acts of eating and drinking. The mystification of the eucharist/Holy Communion has involved years of theological controversy and numerous detours from the meals of Jesus that welcomed outcasts and sinners. Contributing factors include the shock of Jesus' death, coupled with Roman persecution; the influence of the Emperor Constantine's conversion and his sanctioning of Christianity as the religion of the Roman state; the creation of a penitential system for sinners; and the ongoing social fears and traumas of medieval Christianity.

The complex layering effect of these shifts means that we have lost sight of the diversity of expression that once marked the liturgical practice of the early church. Once heresy — the freedom to question church doctrine and clerical authority — was named as an offense against the state as well as the church, the mystification of Holy Communion took on the force of law. To imply that the sacrifice of Jesus is one way, *not the only way,* to understand why we say what we say and do what we do in Holy Communion has become a heretical act. The freedom to choose for oneself what one will believe is not the only thing at stake in this inquiry. Equally at risk is the human capacity to imagine more than one way of being and believing. In the context of orthodoxy's rigid thinking, "making choices is evil"[5] because it undermines unity. Heretics are not true Christians, Tertullian claims, because their views are not the views of those whose authority has been passed down from the apostles. Only the "true" church can interpret rightly.

In contrast to Tertullian, I will argue that if imagination is constrained, so too is hope; and if hope is constrained, so too is faith. Lastly, if faith is constrained, so too is our capacity to be fully human. Orthodox thinkers do

5. Elaine Pagels, *The Origin of Satan* (New York: Vintage Books, 1995), 163, 164; Heresy Microsoft® Encarta® Online Encyclopedia 2001 *http://encarta.msn.com* © 1997–2000 Microsoft Corporation. All rights reserved.

not just fear that our choices may differ from theirs; they also fear the very act of making choices — imagining new possibilities. It is time to reclaim the *capacity to make choices,* which has been castigated as heretical, and expose the variations in practice that are part and parcel of our heritage. Having read this far, I hope you have the courage — the imagination — to join me as I live the questions I have always known I must ask.

The Heresy of Hope

Voices of change and challenge continue to speak forcefully. Bishop John Shelby Spong has argued that "Institutional Christianity seems fearful of inquiry, fearful of freedom, fearful of knowledge — indeed, fearful of anything except its own repetitious propaganda, which has its origins in a world that none of us any longer inhabits."[6] Spong's words resonate with my own experience. After twenty years of ordained ministry in the United Church of Christ, as both a pastor and a seminary professor, I continually witness how laypersons are far ahead of most clergy in understanding the pastoral function of Christian doctrine. Women and men, young and old, long for truth-telling. Compared to the truths they live daily, the faith they were baptized into has taken on the cultural nuances of a foreign country. Many of them go through the liturgical motions presented to them as their only option; yet something is missing. Words fail them even as their pastors swallow similar inklings and appeal to an unchanging "tradition" that in fact is ever changing.

The Christian faith has always celebrated a variety of worship expressions related to cultural paradigms. The Gospels provide one example. Each arises out of a different liturgical setting that demonstrates the diversity that once existed. The same is true for Protestantism, whose Reformation beginnings had everything to do with differing views of the Roman mass. Nevertheless, the weight of "orthodoxy," a third-century phenomenon that arose in response to doctrinal controversies, has allowed the richness of liturgical diversity to become captive to the notion of "validity." Evidence for this can be seen in the fact that the changing liturgical sensibilities and sacramental understandings of the twentieth century have yet to be fully realized in most Reformed liturgies. The perceived "norm" remains tied to the insights of certain reformers, even though their own renewal efforts were often subject to their particular civil authorities.

The liturgical renewal movement, sparked in the 1920s by the energies of Benedictine groups in France and Germany, reached its fullness in the

6. Spong, *Why Christianity,* 4.

Second Vatican Council (1961–64). In addition to an increased participation of the laity in Roman Catholic liturgy, a fuller sense of Christ's presence in the mass, and a deeper appreciation of scripture, the lectionary reforms of Vatican II profoundly influenced Protestant worship and preaching. Liberation movements also had an impact, particularly in the lives of women. Drawing inspiration from Latin American theologians who addressed the plight of the poor, theologians reflecting from feminist, womanist, mujerista, and Asian perspectives sought to articulate the experiences of women as being vital to the interpretive process of theology and its liturgical expression. Whether they claim the notion of "defecting in place" or a spirituality of survival,[7] women who remain in the church continue to name the differences that distinguish their spiritual needs and theological perspectives. In so doing their stories challenge and redefine how faith is enacted.

While I refer throughout this book to women's experience, I do so only to use the lens I know best in order to identify the particularities of the problems that beset us all. My primary concern, however, is larger than gender. I hope that you, the reader, will find your own points of connection and name your own truths more powerfully than you have done before. By reclaiming the truths of our personal lives and engaging in public theology we ensure that our communal lives will move toward the salvation — well-being — of the world for whose sake Jesus lived and, yes, even died.

Imagination and Liturgy

Although imagination is a critical component in working for the renewal of Holy Communion, imagination has often been viewed negatively. From the perspective of scripture, *imagination* gets poor press. We are told in Genesis 8:21 (RSV) that "the imagination of [the human heart] is evil." In Luke 1:51 it is a source of sinful pride, and in Acts 17:29 a source for idolatrous art. On the other hand, there are occasions when it appears that human beings are being chastised for not using their imaginations wisely and as a result resisting God's ways. Stiffening of the neck and hardening of the heart (Exod. 32:9; Acts 7:51) are biblical metaphors for the human condition of resistance. For some people, these conditions reveal a positive defensive response to a threatening situation and the knowledge that resistance to evil is imperative. Yet used too often and unreflectively, these responses become locked in place by fear and turn

7. Miriam Therese Winter, Adair Lummis, and Allison Stokes, *Defecting in Place: Women Claiming Responsibility for Their Own Spiritual Lives* (New York: Crossroad, 1994); Susan Brooks Thistlethwaite, *Sex, Race, and God: Christian Feminism in Black and White* (New York: Crossroad, 1989), 108.

against the very ones that rely on them. Very soon their imaginations no longer liberate.

In the Gospel of Mark (8:17), Jesus appears to name the problem while encouraging his disciples to think differently: "Do you still not perceive or understand? Are your hearts hardened?" Over time scholars and poets have resisted these negative viewpoints and demonstrated that imagination is as necessary as breathing. Imagining involves perceiving, sensing, interpreting, re-presenting things via memory, creating symbols, sharing meanings, and expanding our understanding. Imagination thus expands *the possible* by revealing multiple meanings and infinite connections. Likewise, imagination is essential for human becoming, for it has to do with our openness to the new and our receptivity to the Spirit. Imagination is not just a facility of human reason; it is also the divine heart beating within us, the divine breath flowing through us, a lifeline from the Holy Spirit to the soul. Imagination is the embodied interaction of thought and emotion — an open heart-mind — that allows us to create meaning for our lives and offer meaning to one another. As Martin Buber so eloquently reminds us, God "needs [us] for the very meaning of [our] lives."[8]

While the Protestant reformer John Calvin shared scripture's suspicion of human imagination, he believed that "the faculties of the soul are situated in the mind and the heart." He also argued that "the way to the Kingdom of God is open only to [the one] whose mind has been made new by the illumination of the Holy Spirit."[9] Imagination allows us to create inner worlds of our own making and live in them for good or ill. Nevertheless, each of us is called by God to transcend our inner worlds and embrace God's realm — a realm of radical inclusivity, openness, and generosity, where well-being and abundant life reside. In this sense, Jesus' restatement of the Hebraic injunction to love your God "with all your heart, and with all your soul, and with all your mind, and with all your strength... and your neighbor as yourself" (Mark 12:29–31) is the essence of the Christian gospel. An imagination nurtured by divine grace and compassion allows the fruit of the spirit, particularly love, joy, peace, patience, kindness, generosity, faithfulness, gentleness, and self-discipline (Gal. 5:22–23), to reshape the images and symbols by which we live in a complex world.

It is customary to speak of worship as "liturgy," the work of the people — which draws its meaning from the Greek word *leitourgía:* a work (service)

---

8. For Wang Yang-Ming's concept of heart-mind see Robert C. Neville, *Reconstruction of Thinking* (Albany, N.Y.: SUNY Press, 1981), 65; Martin Buber, *I and Thou,* trans. Ronald Gregor Smith (1937; reprint, Edinburgh: T. & T. Clark, 1947), 82.

9. John Calvin, *Institutes of the Christian Religion,* ed. John T. McNeill, trans. Ford Lewis Battles, Library of Christian Classics (Philadelphia: Westminster Press, 1960), 20:256–57, 279.

performed by the people "for the benefit of the city or state."[10] However, I imagine liturgy in a larger context. Liturgy is worship activity — work — engaged in for the benefit of God's commonwealth. Within this commonwealth, the notion of common health (communal well-being) is central to the Spirit's liberating presence. Liturgy is emancipatory activity:[11] the enactment of God's realm here and now rather than the reenactment of things the way they never were. Performed regularly, a rite becomes the "disciplined rehearsal of right attitudes."[12] Nevertheless, our meditation upon significant religious images within the disciplined rehearsal of liturgy becomes problematic when certain images come to dominate the basic structures in which the world appears. Mary Daly made just this point in regard to the "biblical and popular image of God as a great patriarch in heaven, rewarding and punishing according to his mysterious and seemingly arbitrary will."[13]

Performed in the context of a liberating imagination, liturgy communicates the fullness of divine mystery. Narrowly conceived, however, liturgy limits the horizons of possibility — both divine and human — that life offers. Liturgical scholar Margaret Kelleher defines "horizon" as a "dynamic and flexible boundary that changes during the course of [one's] life," as one experiences changes in one's "interests, questions, self-image, range of knowledge, decisions, and actions."[14] One's personal horizon can be understood to be the outer limits of one's imaginative capacity; and just as we now know that the personal is political, we know that personal horizons are shaped by the social horizons of race, ethnicity, gender, and class.

Liturgy is never neutral. Performed justly it evokes hope; narrowly conceived, it perpetuates injustice. Memory and imagination are gifts of the spirit that many consider dangerous. To understand why the act of *re-imaging* in a liturgical context appears dangerous to those in power, one need only experience the power of liturgy itself. Yet oppressed peoples know the Spirit works for justice and fear its power not. Issues of liturgical transformation thus transcend gender, for all of us benefit from communal well-being ritually enacted.

---

10. James F. White, *Introduction to Christian Worship*, rev. ed. (Nashville: Abingdon Press, 1990), 31.

11. Marjorie Procter-Smith, *In Her Own Rite: Constructing Feminist Liturgical Tradition* (Nashville: Abingdon Press, 1990).

12. Susanne K. Langer, *Philosophy in a New Key: A Study in the Symbolism of Reason, Rite, and Art*, 3d ed. (Cambridge, Mass.: Harvard University Press, 1957), 153.

13. Mary Daly, *Beyond God the Father: Toward a Philosophy of Women's Liberation*, 2d ed. (Boston: Beacon Press, 1985), 13.

14. Margaret Mary Kelleher, "Liturgy and the Christian Imagination," *Worship* 66, no. 2 (March 1992): 132.

Gender and Communion

The term "eucharist" refers to the Christian sacrament where consecrated bread and wine are received by communicants in the name of Jesus' body and blood. It may also be called the Lord's Supper, the Last Supper, or Holy Communion. Among contemporary Christians more and more women fail to experience Jesus' body and blood as healing images. They find little comfort in a God who uses crucifixion to express the fullness of divine love. Moreover, they believe any theory that claims Jesus' suffering is intrinsically redemptive masks the depths of human suffering. Through faith, they find redeeming value in the integrity of Jesus' life and ministry, and most clearly in his risen presence. For these believers, clearly no Second Coming will do. In its place, deepening incarnations of resurrection find expression in the joyous proclamation: "Christ has died, Christ is risen, Christ is with us now."

Under the scrutiny of various critiques, the ritual activity of communion/eucharist has come to be seen as a sign of hospitality gone awry. In contrast to the welcoming table-fellowship of Jesus that shattered exclusionary boundaries, the eucharist, in the hands of early Christian fathers, became the primary expression for the excommunication of sinners as well as the subordination of women. Believing women to be inferior as well as unclean, the fathers denied them the ability to preside and thereby consecrate the elements. Contemporary denials of women's ability to serve as deacons and distribute the elements stem from the same biased thinking. For these reasons the sacrament of Holy Communion has often taught women to ignore and repress their own gifts and graces.

Despite the increasing presence of those who call for liturgical change, a significant number of women and men fervently believe change is ill-advised; they have been washed and cleansed in the "blood of Jesus" and they know themselves to be saved. Those who believe that "Christ died for our sins" see any deviation from this norm as heretical. Those who know themselves to be Christian yet experience salvation through Jesus' *life and ministry* find it equally impossible to come to a meal hosted by a "forgiving victim."[15] The range of these positions within the liturgical spectrum makes earthly communion difficult.

I will argue that different understandings of the role of imagination in human formation — not unfaithfulness to Jesus — are at the root of this divergence. I will also demonstrate how fear shapes our imagining capacities and undermines communal well-being. Why is it that Jesus' suggestive image of loving one's enemies has proven to be the hardest pill

15. James Alison, *Raising Abel: The Recovery of the Eschatological Imagination* (New York: Crossroad Herder, 1996), 178.

for many believers to swallow? Moreover, why is it that Christian leaders have often sought to grow the church through fear rather than love? These are critical questions for faith-making in our day, and our ability to answer them has everything to do with our ability to chart new directions for Christian praxis. Far from being aberrations of an earlier time, we must look beyond the violence of the Crusades, the Inquisition, and the witch-hunting tendencies of the Middle Ages to see how easily the church in the name of love abused its power. We must also recognize how easily human beings, under the guise of faith, abdicate personal power and perpetuate systems of oppression.

The Justice of Communion

As symbol-making creatures, we human beings construct our own realities. We create worlds of meaning and live in them. As a consequence, we both shape and are shaped by the imagery we use. What is at issue in the differing interpretations of Jesus' death is nothing less than our respective "picture of grace."[16] All of us rely on our inner worlds of thought — rooted in our social, cultural, and ethnic identities — whenever we interpret our everyday experiences. Consequently, what each of us brings from our inner world to an external image or symbol creates the meanings we attach to it. It is at this point that the image is transformed into a positive or negatively charged meaning and takes on a life of its own, even though in truth the image is always subject to the particularities of our experience.

Sacrificial theories of atonement and sacrificial interpretations of the eucharist share a common history, for each is the fruit of social, cultural, or psychic trauma that shaped Christian imaginations. Although each presents a theology primarily fed by hope, each subtly re-presents a secondary theology driven by fear, which was reinforced by the sacrament of penance, the penitential eucharists of the reformers, and the social influences of unique literary genres such as the Tours of Hell and the Penitentials. Historian Timothy George has noted that "death, guilt, and loss of meaning resound with jarring dissonance in the literature, art, and theology" of the Middle Ages.[17] When one then factors in the prevalence of death that preceded modern medical advances, one can easily appreciate the refuge men and women sought in penitential practices. One cannot

16. Martin Luther, "A Sermon on Preparing to Die," in *Luther's Works,* vol. 42, *Devotional Writings I,* ed. Martin O. Dietrich, trans. Martin H. Bertram (Philadelphia: Fortress Press, 1969), 104.

17. Timothy George, *Theology of the Reformers* (Nashville: Broadman Press, 1988), 23.

assume, however, that this imagery has little bearing on today. Historian Philip Greven gives ample evidence of its continuing impact in his study of the religious roots of punishment.[18] In tracing the connection between apocalyptic fears of judgment and hell and fundamentalist child-rearing practices Greven confronts the harmful consequences that arise from the use of physical punishment cloaked in the heresy of a punishing god — the very image I believe atonement theories shelter under the guise of love.

At the heart of sacrificial theories the notion that God's love is a suffering love (John 3:16) has become sacrosanct. Nevertheless, this interpretation of God's saving work in Christ has consequences that deserve closer scrutiny. In examining these consequences, I suggest that compassionate love — a love that enables us to *interrupt* human suffering — might serve humankind and all of creation as a more just "picture of grace." Compassionate love also leads us to redeem — to re-present, to reclaim, and to recover — the person of Jesus and the liberating actions of his life. Redemption occurs when we choose the relational life God reveals to us through the life-work of Jesus. When we understand that healing has to do with our interconnectedness with creation and solidarity with others, we know redemption equally as freedom in community and a gift of God.

Matters of language and issues of justice — how we speak of God and human experience — have moved many of us to modify our common speech and reimagine our relationship with God and one another. While numerous Christians regularly protest these re-formational changes, my own experience of these momentous shifts is far from despair. Indeed, I experience the tensions we face as clear movements of the Spirit and unmistakable signs of new life. Life is multivalent, and the multiplicities of meaning that surround every human being call forth an imaginative engagement with past, present, and future. Wherever we place ourselves on the theological and liturgical continuums of our time, there are ancient truths to be savored and new truths to be discerned. Worshiping in a Christian context is a multidimensional experience where imagination, liturgy, and gender call forth a trinity of possibility — a new creation that leads to new hope for all who imagine resurrection this side of heaven. It is time to turn the tables on apocalyptic fears, sacrificial altars, penitential eucharists, and punitive gods. Christ is with us now. Indeed!

---

18. Philip Greven, *Spare the Child: The Religious Roots of Punishment and the Psychological Impact of Physical Abuse* (New York: Alfred A. Knopf, 1991; New York: Vintage Books, 1992); Greven, *The Protestant Temperament: Patterns of Child-Rearing, Religious Experience, and the Self in Early America* (New York: Alfred A. Knopf, 1977).

From Feminism to Redemptionism

My own strivings for communion liturgies that refresh and renew are rooted in a *redemptionist* theology[19] — a Trinitarian way of worshiping God that honors God's creation of women in God's own image, the diversity of women's experience, and the worthiness of every woman's life. In this context, I juxtapose the term "Christa" with "Christ" throughout this book. This practice is not meant to trivialize the Christ symbol but to give it a wider birth in our imaginative understanding. Jesus was male. Christ is not. Without the Christa connection we too easily make the symbolic title Jesus the Christ into the proper name Jesus Christ. *Christ* is the Greek word used to translate the Hebrew word *messiah*. Both *messiah* and *Christ* mean the anointed one. Christianity's use of *Christ* applied to Jesus confirms him as the incarnate one, the word (*logos*) who became flesh (*caro*) and lived among us . . . full of grace and truth . . . whose glory revealed the glory of God (John 1:14).

Redemptionism is for women *and* men who seek fresh images of God to express the deepest truths of their worshiping selves and for those who seek to live faithfully amid the complexity and multiplicity of contemporary human experience. Redemptionism is also an invitation to explore new perspectives in faith, for the creation of redemptive communities that will nurture justice, grace, and well-being for all. Redemptionism is not about exclusivity or subordination. Its proponents, having experienced the misogyny and androcentric oppression of dominarchy, have no stomach for domination. Their aim is quite genuinely a re-visioning of Christianity, a revisioning that turns the tables on "rituals of self-hatred."[20]

In offering this perspective on redemptionism and Holy Communion, let me be clear from the outset that I am not seeking validity for a reimagined eucharistic rite. I simply state what is already being enacted in a variety of communal settings and offer one theological rationale for its practice. What then does redemptionism seek? It seeks nothing less that an honest orthopraxy, not just a right practice, but a justly right practice, one that is faithful to Christ-Christa, the incarnate one within us all.

The goal of turning tables back aright in a eucharistic context also extends to the doctrine of incarnation. The Ecumenical Council of Chalcedon (451) transformed the mystery of incarnation revealed in John's prologue into an irrefutable teaching. In so doing, the council fathers and

---

19. "Redemptionism" is not "Junism" or any variation of "Sheilaism" as described by Robert N. Bellah and others, eds., *Habits of the Heart: Individualism and Commitment in American Life* (Berkeley: University of California Press, 1985), 221–35. "Redemptionism" is my own expression of Christian feminism.

20. Adrienne Rich, "Turning the Wheel 4: Self-Hatred," in *A Wild Patience Has Taken Me This Far* (New York: W. W. Norton, 1981), 55.

the Roman emperors Marcian and Valentinian promulgated the "mystery of incarnation" while condemning contrary christological formulations. Those with differing views were opposed, rejected, expelled, and damned to hell to provide an airtight defense of Jesus' divinity. Under imperial pressure the council decreed in essence that God was incarnate only in Jesus. Because this view counteracts the theology of God's presence in all things that is being developed here, I *choose* to differ from (my) neighbors in the doctrines of orthodoxy so that the proclamation of divine truths may be shown forth in a more just manner.[21] Christ-Christa is the expression I use to speak constructively of the incarnation of divine love present in all persons, male and female.

We are accustomed to citing Jesus' words at the Last Supper as his "words of institution" and using them as primary interpreters for understanding Jesus' self-giving love on our behalf. We also look to these words in order to model Jesus' command to "do this in remembrance of me." Thanks in large measure to the reformers, the use of these words attributed to Jesus at the table has become something of a litmus test for Protestant celebrations of Holy Communion. Yet "tradition" has many faces, and even scripture gives us variations on a theme as far as these institutional narratives are concerned. Bryan Spinks and John Austin Baker in separate studies have suggested that the essence of the eucharistic prayer is properly thanksgiving. Their insights thus open the door for today's liturgists to approach the traditional "words of institution" differently in the context of the eucharistic meal. In Baker's words, "what we say should be composed of the faith by which we live, as we see it, and as we wish to express it, bringing out of our treasures things new and old."[22] With these scholarly musings to guide us, I invite you to join me on a journey of the heart, which is always and everywhere a journey into the imaginative world of the Spirit.

---

21. Elisabeth Schüssler Fiorenza, *Jesus: Miriam's Child, Sophia's Prophet: Critical Issues in Feminist Christology* (New York: Continuum, 1994), 20; Rita Nakashima Brock, *Journeys by Heart: A Christology of Erotic Power* (New York: Crossroad, 1988), 113, chap. 3, n. 2; Norman P. Tanner, ed., *Decrees of the Ecumenical Councils;* available at *www.piar.hu/councils/ecum04.htm.*

22. John Austin Baker, quoted in Donald Gray, "Hands and Hocus-Pocus: The Manual Acts in the Eucharistic Prayer," *Worship* 69, no. 4 (July 1995): 309; Bryan D. Spinks, "The Institution Narrative in the Eucharistic Prayer," *News of Liturgy* no. 157 (January 1988): 4.

TWO

Thinking outside the Empire

> There is no life that is not in community, and no community not lived in praise of God. —*T. S. Eliot*[1]

> There is a communion of more than our bodies when bread is broken and wine is drunk. —*M. F. K. Fisher*[2]

The conversion of the emperor Constantine in the fourth century gave rise to creedal forms of Christianity that may be termed imperial Christianity. While imperial Christianity touts the value of communion and community, both communion and community suffer when emperors require allegiance to their way of thinking. By silencing dissenters as heretics and stamping out ritual forms that diverged from the emperor's notions of right practice, imperial Christianity came to value uniformity over diversity, allegiance over experimentation, domination over shared power, and right practice over just practice and communal well-being. Imperial Christianity still exists today. We are told that if we are to be good subjects, we should bow our heads as the emperor passes and accept the emperor's worldview or else. Thinking outside the empire thus requires imagination, courage, and perseverance. Living outside the constraints of the empire also requires a community where discipline (accountability) is balanced with nurture (grace), for the work is hard and the living far from easy. Without such community, thinking outside the empire becomes unimaginable!

This chapter offers alternative values to those of the empire and lays the foundation for re-imaging communion — Holy Communion and the communion of all things divine. Terms such as dominarchy, the relational self, communal well-being, and compassionate love must be woven into the fabric of our consciousness before any appreciation of a re-imaged eucharist can be seriously entertained. In presenting new ways of thinking, I invite us into deeper incarnations of being.

1. T. S. Eliot, "Choruses from the Rock," in *Selected Poems* (New York: Harcourt Brace & Co., 1934, 1936), Part 2, 114.

2. M. F. K. Fisher, *The Art of Eating*, with an introduction by Clifton Fadiman and an appreciation by James A. Beard (New York: Collier Books, Macmillan, 1990), xv.

Communion and Community

T. S. Eliot and M. F. K. Fisher remind us that life thrives in community and communion. For the Christian church, gathered and scattered as the body of Christ, no greater truth exists. Divine life is the source of community, and eucharistic action — thanksgiving — its reason for being. From the family of origin we inherit, to the multiple worlds or relations we choose to enter, the connections we make and keep have a profound impact on our ability to fully achieve the human potential that is uniquely ours through the gift of God's creative love. In community, we know ourselves as extended beings. We also drink from deep reservoirs of hope that nurture and nourish us within the vast magnificence of this beautiful, yet deeply dangerous, world.

In the communion of life with life (measured poetically, not scientifically), we experience a deep sense of bonding, whether it be with our Creator, the earth, other persons, other creatures, or other dimensions of the universe. For Christians that can only mean the divine life at the heart of life itself, for faith begins in awe — in the imaginative feeling that we live on the edge of mystery, yet only rarely grasp its wonder. Communion is indeed a moment of awesome connection and "radical amazement" that gifts us with the larger truth of our existence — we are one with all of which we are in awe. Even so harsh a critic of humankind as John Calvin spoke of our "primal worthiness," our "original nobility," and our instinctual "awareness of divinity" as "beyond controversy."[3]

Nevertheless, in the Reformed tradition, the sacrament of Holy Communion rarely inspires awe-filled connection. I use exaggeration for effect, of course, but there is more truth than untruth here. There will always be individuals who know a different reality. Still there is evidence enough that many people have misgivings — from the infrequency of the rite's celebration, to lower attendance on communion Sundays, to the generalized confusion as to what Holy Communion means. Likewise, instances of disconnection and distrust abound. With allowances in name only, political and familial divisions, racial and ethnic rivalries, economic disparities, and ecological disintegration play havoc with the church's quest for communion and community.

Megachurch approaches may feed a deep hunger for connection temporarily, and celebratory worship may feed our entertainment needs, but where will we turn for deep communion and community of the kind that

---

3. John Calvin, *Institutes of the Christian Religion*, ed. John T. McNeill, trans. Ford Lewis Battles, Library of Christian Classics (Philadelphia: Westminster Press, 1960), 20:43, 242, 244; Abraham J. Heschel, *Between God and Man: An Interpretation of Judaism*, ed. Fritz A. Rothschild (New York: The Free Press/Macmillan, 1959), 40–54.

requires more from us than simply showing up whenever it suits us? In order to strengthen communities of faith with greater well-being, we can take a cue from liberation theologians who have brought revitalization by taking seriously Christianity's role in the concealment and perpetuation of suffering — both human and nonhuman. The Reformed church observes only two sacraments, baptism and Holy Communion; nevertheless, penitential imagery affected eucharistic practice dramatically in the context of how one prepares to receive Christ's body and blood in a worthy manner. In mild cases, Christianity has touted the lessons suffering teaches. In severe cases, it has used the sacrament of penance punitively and exacerbated the suffering of "sinners."

With the advent of liberation theology, the call of revisionists and reformers to practice solidarity with the poor and marginalized and alleviate their suffering has shifted the emphasis of theology from theory to praxis. The process of praxis thus moves from reflection on past practices to a more informed future practice — a process of reflection on one's actions as to their credibility and appropriateness. Consequently, theology can be deemed inadequate if it fails to occasion reflection on human practices, and in particular liturgical practices.[4] Because of its performative nature and reliance on multiple symbol systems, liturgy/worship is one of the most powerful ways we enact our theological convictions. Thus the liberating activity of solidarity through theological reflection includes the denunciation of oppressive structures, including the ecclesiastical structures of the church, and the education of the oppressed. Such education encourages the oppressed to "speak [their] pain and imagination within history" with "words that are full of the reality they are meant to represent, words that help students [and believers] develop critical consciousness."[5]

In making the activity of the community central to Christianity, liberation theology embraces the personal in the context of the communal. Christianity is thus converted into an "interruption," for it interrupts any system, structure, or theory that denies the existence of suffering and that thwarts transformation by the denial of hope. Likewise, I offer this work as an act of hope, for liturgy — the praxis of praise — is not an afterthought of religious activism but a powerful instrument of personal and social transformation. Ultimately the goal of this work is demystification. Men and women need to be able to discern when "mystery" is a humanly constructed effort to retain power and when divine mystery

---

4. Rebecca S. Chopp, *The Praxis of Suffering: An Interpretation of Liberation and Political Theologies* (Maryknoll, N.Y.: Orbis Books, 1986); Pamela Dickey Young, *Feminist Theology/Christian Theology: In Search of Method* (Minneapolis: Augsburg Fortress Press, 1990), 114.

5. Bradford T. Stull, *Religious Dialectics of Pain and Imagination* (New York: SUNY Press, 1994), 96–97.

seeks their well-being. An example of the former is found in a letter written March 11, 1516, to Pope Leo X from Paris de Grassi: "I respond above all to those who think that religious ceremonies should be made accessible to the majority of mortals.... If the secrets of worship are revealed and the ceremonies are made accessible, there will result immediately a loss of prestige."[6] Elaine Pagels makes a similar point in discussing Augustine's (ca. 354–430) challenge of Pelagius's views on baptism. The North African bishop of Hippo and his supporters feared that by appeasing the Pelagians the Catholic Church would lose its "vast authority" as "the only force that could 'liberate men' from themselves."[7] At the heart of such fear lay the motivation to retain power at all cost.

In this context, our goal is to examine doctrinal concerns and attitudes of domination that have captured our liturgical imaginations and allowed the liberating power of the eucharist to be disguised and diminished. The time for the eucharist to be freed from the politics of "anesthetization" and "evasion" is long overdue. It must truly become "the seed of revolution that awakens the mind to what is possible, to what is not yet achieved, to what has not yet been contemplated by the creative imagination."[8] And what would this mean? Among other things, the eucharistic prayer and the symbols of the eucharist itself must help the participants forge mutual involvement with one another and solidarity with the world's suffering people. Moreover, the participants — as relational selves in communion with God and one another — must come to understand their potential role of incarnating the presence of Christ-Christa in community. To enable this true act of communion to occur we must forge a new understanding of the relationship between human nature and divine grace.

In contrast to the language of self-denial that is often directed toward the powerless more than those in power, I suggest that self-transcendence — the full attainment of our divine and relational nature — and imaginative creativity are truer paths to well-being and freedom. Carl Jung and Paul Tillich shared a central critique of Christianity: that "the development of Christian theology since the introduction of Aristotle through Aquinas has been one leading consistently to the loss of the inner sense of God."[9] I am convinced that our natural (ontological) connection with God has never been severed. On the contrary, human fears that influence our imaginative

6. Cited in Rafael Avila, *Worship and Politics*, trans. Alan Neely (Maryknoll, N.Y.: Orbis Books, 1981), 63.

7. Elaine Pagels, *Adam, Eve, and the Serpent* (New York: Vintage Books, 1989), 125.

8. Avila, *Worship and Politics*, 90–91.

9. John P. Dourley, *The Illness That We Are: A Jungian Critique of Christianity* (Toronto: Inner City Books, 1984), 33.

engagement with the world obscure our original communion with God—the divinity within our humanity.

Conversation, Not Convergence

In thinking about new ways to understand and re-image the eucharist, we need to consider the 1982 convergence document of the World Council of Churches, which remains influential. *Baptism, Eucharist, and Ministry* (*BEM*)[10] describes the eucharist as an act of community, wherein the faithful commune with God in Christ and with one another. *BEM* also states that the church, as the body of Christ, receives the eucharist as a gift of God in Jesus Christ and, through its eucharistic practice, expresses its thanksgiving for all that God has done in Christ through the power of the Holy Spirit. While many in the ecumenical community have hailed *BEM* as a sign of ecumenical progress toward Jesus' prayer "that they may all be one" (John 17:21), not everyone finds the eucharist as it is represented in this document to be an act of communion, let alone community. The greatest concern expressed by women is the relationship of the eucharist to the doctrine of atonement and Jesus' once-for-all sacrifice (Heb. 10:10).

The reformers made thanksgiving for the free gift of God's grace the central proclamation of their eucharistic theologies, in contrast to the Roman rite's preference to speak of the offering of Christ by the priest on behalf of the church. In both instances, the interpretation of Jesus' death as a sacrifice for sin was never questioned. This carryover from a medieval worldview is the very issue that occasions today's great divide. The sacrificial imagery perpetuated in the praxis of the eucharist advocates an *inner disposition of obedience* on the part of the believer, even in suffering, so as to follow Christ's example and be united with him in love. The individual believer who *denies self,* takes up the cross (Mark 8:34; Matt. 10:38; Luke 9:23), and follows Jesus receives the bread and wine as Christ's body and blood, broken and shed "for you."

Likewise, the image of the "Lamb for sinners slain," an image related to the eucharistic use of the Agnus Dei chant, also reinforces a self-sacrificial motif that many women experience as detrimental. They resist the argument that women must sacrifice themselves to be saved. They recognize that the world has been structured by precepts in which women are viewed as natural servants who are denied the power to order their own lives and give priority to their own well-being. They also see through the lie that somehow Jesus' once-for-all sacrifice did away with the need for future

10. *Baptism, Eucharist, and Ministry,* Faith and Order Paper no. 111 (Geneva: World Council of Churches, 1982).

ritual sacrifices. Rather, they see how in this context women must forever serve the needs of others, to the detriment of their own self-identity. In this context, then, any theology that promotes Christ's death on the cross as a saving image becomes suspect. The same is true for the message that suffering is redemptive. In Catherine Keller's words: "Suffering may be redeemable, but it is not intrinsically redemptive."[11] Suffering, by itself, even Jesus' suffering, harms more than it heals.

The Erosion of Eucharistic Grace

While a corrective to a heavy penitential view of the eucharist has been launched through the work of *BEM* and other contemporary liturgical tracts, the practice of the eucharist remains heavily individualistic. This is true by virtue of its theological emphasis on the assurance of the forgiveness of sins (related to Matt. 26:28) and its pledge of eternal life *for each believer* (related to John 6:51–58). Moreover, the penitential nature of the eucharist, closely associated with the Reformed stress on forgiveness of sins, remains a formative part of local church practice, despite contemporary insights on resurrection.

When the remembrance of Jesus' death, not the healing power of his life, became the primary premise of the eucharist, our attention turned in upon the elements and away from the table-fellowship of those gathered. As a result, a powerful, celebratory, and communal meal began a steady evolution into an individualistic and penitential rite. Over time, as the language and form of this rite laid greater stress on the salvation of each believer rather than the well-being of the community and its members, the community's capacity to be in solidarity with the world's suffering people was seriously compromised. A rite of survival turned from resistance to acquiescence. Rather than offering a clear alternative to the "twin faces of evil — sin and suffering"[12] — the theology of the eucharist now offers the mixed message of a loving and merciful God who somehow relies on suffering as a tool for right behavior. Such theology deceives the believer into accepting a rupture in the divine-human relationship because of the presence of human sin. However, any rupture that may exist has more to do with human suffering than sin and more to do with the wounds in our imagination than the wounds of Jesus.

11. Catherine Keller, "Scoop Up the Water and the Moon Is in Your Hands: On Feminist Theology and Dynamic Self-Emptying," in *The Emptying God: A Buddhist-Jewish-Christian Conversation,* ed. John B. Cobb Jr. and Christopher Ives (Maryknoll, N.Y.: Orbis Books, 1990), 112.

12. Wendy Farley, *Tragic Vision and Divine Compassion: A Contemporary Theodicy* (Louisville: Westminster/John Knox Press, 1990), 11.

Perhaps my own reflections can clarify this assertion. My earliest memory of Holy Communion takes me back to the Congregational church where I was raised. I remember the event as having a somber and decidedly penitential nature. If the words themselves did not register fully in my mind, the slow and somber music surely did. For many years my experience of communion retained this penitential cast. More often than not the event seemed tied to the experience of Maundy Thursday and Jesus' crucifixion rather than the Easter joy of resurrection. More importantly, I could never reconcile my personal experience with the words that Jesus had died for us . . . for our sins. An assurance of pardon from the United Church of Christ's *Services of the Church* lays out this theology quite clearly: "Beloved, God has promised us his mercy and has given us his Son, Jesus Christ, to die for our sins that we may live in newness of life, obedient to his will. Therefore, I announce, in the name of Christ, that your sins are forgiven according to his promises in the gospel."[13]

What I could not articulate then but now know to be true for myself is that the use of the eucharistic images of body and blood, which suggest the trauma of Jesus' violent death on the cross as well as the identification of his death as a means to new life, strikes many believers as a denial of their pain and a re-traumatizing of their personal lives. If memories of one's own blood being spilled or one's body being bruised are stored in one's body, then it is difficult to have God's presence associated with victimization. Even if one's own memories are not conscious memories, the verbal association alone may be enough to turn people away. To suggest that the "redeeming narrative" of Christianity lies in the "power of the stripped and tortured One on the Cross,"[14] and not in the resurrection power of God, is to dismiss the symbolic power the imagery of death has when continually rehearsed in our liturgies.

F. W. Dillistone has argued that the "ultimate principle" of human existence — "the highest that we can conceive" — is a movement "*through-death-to-life,*" by way of the "womb of death."[15] However, to name death as a symbolic womb denies the evil of suffering and makes illusory the real forces that contend with us. In addition, the womb by which we make our way from death to life is not the womb of death, but the Womb of God, which is the womb of life and the womb of compassion. The Hebrew word embracing compassion, mercy, and love is the plural noun *rah^{a}mîm.*

13. United Church of Christ Commission on Worship, "Service of Word and Sacrament I," in *Services of the Church,* vol. 1 (Philadelphia: United Church Press, 1966, 1969), 6.

14. Robert J. Schreiter, *Reconciliation: Mission and Ministry in a Changing Social Order* (Maryknoll, N.Y.: Orbis Books, 1992; Cambridge: Boston Theological Institute, 1992), 79.

15. F. W. Dillistone, *The Christian Understanding of Atonement* (Philadelphia: Westminster Press, 1968), 410–11.

Its singular form, *rehem*, means "womb" or "uterus," an organ unique to women but one that does not exclude men from the journey of compassion.[16] The womb of compassion — from which we are birthed and by which we are called to "choose life" continually — provides the context for well-being to happen. Knowing that many have chosen to leave the church because of its shortsighted view of salvation, I am moved to ask, How can we teach salvation — newness of life — differently?

As a young child, quarantined during the tuberculosis epidemic of the late 1940s and 1950s, I was significantly shaped by a theology that emphasized God's punishing judgment over and above God's compassion. Under the influence of this theology, the physical and emotional suffering I experienced as a result of this disease and its consequent impact on my family functioned to confirm my fears that I was at fault for being ill. I believed (mistakenly) that my illness (I) was responsible for changes that took place in my family and thus in the only world that mattered to me. Consequently, the death of Jesus has never been a consolation to me, despite the argument that he had died for my sins and for the forgiveness of many.

His resurrection, on the other hand, was always a mystery to me, and in that mystery I found the hope to work out my own salvation, relying on God's grace at work within me (Phil. 2:12–13). Despite my negative responses to segments of the communion liturgy, the rite has always held a certain fascination for me. No doubt the isolation of my confinement in a TB sanatorium fed my wonderment about an event where people ate and drank together, some even from a common cup. Though my physical stay in the sanatorium lasted but fourteen months (a veritable lifetime for a four-year-old), I lived there psychically well into adulthood because I carried deep within me an unconscious image of myself as a contagious person who could still prove dangerous to the health of others. Because of the fears that existed within society in the early 1950s toward those diagnosed with TB, I was made to feel unclean at the core of my being. The stain that marked my outcast existence remained out of reach to my conscious self and thus impenetrable. On the surface, however, I remained vulnerable to periodic attacks of sheer panic that I might somehow cause the death of others. These unreachable fears remained in control until, in a moment of grace, a close friend identified these deep fears for what they were. The exhilaration of liberation mediated through her loving presence would require much reinforcement in the years that followed, but her deep psychic touch was indeed a critical turning point in my personal journey toward well-being.

Nevertheless, communion remained an experience of mixed messages. It promised life — eternal life! Yet it often dwelt on death, the death

16. Phyllis Trible, *God and the Rhetoric of Sexuality* (Philadelphia: Fortress Press, 1978), 33.

of Christ for the sake of my sinful self. Such ambiguity has never been a comfort to me, for my suffering self has always resisted the prevailing notion that suffering and sin are causally related. As I grew older and tried to understand the suffering that I experienced as a child and that I continued to carry, I did not feel forgiven; nor did I accept the view that my suffering was related to my inherent sinfulness. The young child within me has always resisted the theological notion that she was a worthless sinner in need of special dispensation from God. "Saved from sin?" she would ask herself. "Why not from pain?"

Only recently have I come to realize that my deepest resistance to the penitential dimensions of the eucharist coincides with the images of death and hell so prominent in my childhood. Raised as the daughter of a third-generation mortician, my first home was literally a funeral home. Though multicolored floral arrangements delighted and comforted me in the midst of this house of death, it was the haunting refrains of funeral dirges, along with the muffled sobs and anguished cries of the bereaved, that seeped into my consciousness. Before I knew what was happening, the fear of death had become a subtheme of my interactions with the world. My subsequent banishment to a sanatorium reinforced these fears and added the element of punishment to my psychic worldview. Though many years would pass, images of this psychic trip to hell, replete with a powerful vision of the devil running through the woods that bordered the hospital, haunted my childhood. Even though I later came to the awareness that this demonic vision had been occasioned by fever, it was real enough to keep me fearful.

My awareness of how fear shapes imagination has caused me to question the images that dominate Christian theology and wonder what role suffering and fear played in the development of eucharistic imagery. This questioning became all the more compelling for me as I traced the transformation of my own thought from depression to hope. In many ways liturgy has been a lifeline for me, bringing me out of the depths of despair by pulling me to new life. At the same time I have often experienced liturgical moments as millstones dragging me into the abyss of alienation, by treating my presence (as well as that of other women) as no presence at all. Holy Communion bears the greatest burden. Whenever it has been acted out with funereal solemnity, I have found myself stifling a cry of protest. Tom Driver makes a similar but more general observation in *The Magic of Ritual:* "I noticed, as I so often do, that Christian communion services have become funereal."[17]

My turn from liturgical leadership in the church to the academic arena of theological and liturgical studies is not accidental. I have been seeking

17. Tom Driver, *The Magic of Ritual: Our Need for Liberating Rites That Transform Our Lives and Our Communities* (San Francisco: HarperSanFrancisco, 1991), 198.

answers to the ritual boredom that permeates much of Christian liturgy today. But boredom is merely a symptom of a deeper discontent. I also know from pastoral experience that many individuals have ambivalent feelings about communion/eucharist and numerous questions they hesitate to raise for fear of appearing ignorant. While I understand the saying "the personal is political," I do not claim that my own experiences offer universal insights. Instead, I hope that the particularities of my journey will offer new clues for understanding why arguments critical of sacrificial theories of atonement must be taken seriously.

In a direct challenge to the notion that Christianity promotes the well-being of women, Rosemary Radford Ruether speaks of the eucharistic famine from which many women suffer: "They are starved for words of life, for symbolic forms that fully and wholeheartedly affirm their personhood and speak truth about the evils of sexism and the possibilities of a future beyond patriarchy." By calling women "to incarnate the community of faith in the liberation of humanity from patriarchy in words and deed, in new words, new prayers, new symbols, and new praxis," Ruether clarifies the choices before us.[18]

Patriarchy as Dominarchy

When one takes seriously the pervasive abuse that women and children suffer in many areas of the globe, the argument that Christianity has been a primary force in shaping many women's acceptance of abuse gives one pause.[19] The power of domination rules through internalized oppression (internalized self-hatred in the minds of the nondominant) and lies deeper in one's psyche than "rational thought or even mere insight can reach."[20] On one's own, isolated from the truths of one's own life, any person is hard-pressed to experience liberation from self-hatred, even within a Christian context.

Feminists have named patriarchy as the comprehensive pattern of oppression held in place by the "power of the fathers." The term "kyriarchy" has also been used to refer to the rule of emperors, lords, and masters over social and familial institutions. Under these systems women's freedom is constricted through the power of domination experienced in "ritual, tradition, law, language, customs, etiquette, education, and the division of

18. Rosemary Radford Ruether, *Women-Church: Theology and Practice* (San Francisco: Harper & Row, 1985), 5.

19. Joanne Carlson Brown and Rebecca Parker, "For God So Loved the World?" in *Christianity, Patriarchy, and Abuse: A Feminist Critique*, ed. Joanne Carlson Brown and Carole R. Bohn (New York: Pilgrim Press, 1989), 2.

20. Demaris S. Wehr, *Jung and Feminism: Liberating Archetypes* (Boston: Beacon Press, 1987), 22–25.

labor."[21] Because the use of these terms is invariably misinterpreted as implying an antimale bias, I use the term "dominarchy" to point to the subtext of oppressive power. Dominarchy is the rule of domination that requires the subordination of others, while "dominology" refers to the body of knowledge that allows us to demystify its presence. Through gaining this critical wisdom we come to see that dominarchy is a sociocultural phenomenon that threatens men as well as women.

Dominarchy supports a zero-sum mentality — an erroneous notion that shared power leads to the loss of power for the one who gives it away. Mutuality, on the other hand, demonstrates that when control is lifted and power is shared, power increases. In a dominarchal worldview, control — "power-over" — is the dominant motif and is held in place by the love of order and obedience and the threat or use of violence. Using the language of laws, rules, and generalized abstractions that tend to ignore the concrete particularities of lived experience (particularly that of women), power-over "motivates through fear."[22] Relying on violence and physical force to keep subordinates obedient to the will of the dominant, the power-over system creates false divisions and fosters a sense of individual isolation and powerlessness in order to conquer others through fragmentation and manipulation of their innermost self.

In the power-over system of dominarchy, conflict inevitably leads to violence, because violence drives the system to devalue life itself. "Cruelty and injustice become possible where men and women are treated as less than human. In that process of dehumanizing his victim, the moral consciousness of the perpetrator atrophies, the imagination withers, the ability to empathize is encased in bonds of iron."[23] Cruelty and fear perpetuate violence in the power-over context. We shall soon see that they are also at the heart of the doctrinal teachings on atonement that transformed the eucharist from a revolutionary act into an evasion of the true challenge of Jesus' all-embracing love.

For almost two thousand years the Christian representation of the dominarchal worldview has been secured in place by an imaginative concept of the divine that elevated one metaphorical image of deity, the all-powerful and all-knowing Lord and King, to a definitive and incontestable status. In *The Politics of Worship,* William Johnson Everett argues that Christian

---

21. Adrienne Rich, *Of Woman Born: Motherhood as Experience and Institution* (New York: W. W. Norton, 1976, 1986), 57; Elisabeth Schüssler Fiorenza, *Jesus: Miriam's Child, Sophia's Prophet* (New York: Continuum, 1994), 13–18; Riane Eisler, in *The Chalice and the Blade: Our History, Our Future* (San Francisco: HarperCollins, 1988), xxvii.

22. Starhawk, *Truth or Dare: Encounters with Power, Authority, and Mystery* (San Francisco: Harper & Row, 1987), 8–16.

23. Michael Walker, "The Atonement and Justice," *Theology* 91 (May 1988): 186.

worship is still beholden to this "nostalgic relic of feudal monarchy and empire."[24] This model, in which God is distant from the world yet controls the world through domination and benevolence, has been a powerful source of inspiration for many. Yet it also has an underbelly of fear. In his survey of hymns on God's nature in *Hymns and Psalms — a Methodist and Ecumenical Hymnbook,* Brian Wren found that of the main metaphors used in 328 texts, the most frequent metaphor was of God as a dominant male, a King who rules and gives commands. "Approximately 190 hymns (60 percent of those giving G-d [*sic*] images) have strong imagery of rule and many others presuppose it. Thus, though there are other rich metaphors, the dominant metaphor system is KINGAFAP — the King-G-d-Almighty, Father-Protector."[25] In light of the Reformed tradition's insistence on the sovereignty of God, which emphasizes God's omnipotence, Everett appeals to more democratic imagery — a republic — as a way to address the ethical integrity of worship and allow our rituals to "rehearse" God's creative justice more fully. Likewise my own use of the term "commonwealth" (commonweal, common health) to reference God's redemptive realm is meant to suggest the sharing of power that supports communal well-being and justice-making love.

In contrast, an omnipotent sovereign offers love of a very different kind. Benevolent Father/King imagery demands a high price not only from its rebellious children but from loyal subjects as well. When we honor a God who has no need of us, as Augustine believed, we are encouraged to worry more about what God thinks of us than about our own needs and feelings in relationship to this God. This God may be emotionally distant from us (having no need); nevertheless, this same deity demands psychic allegiance/obedience at all costs. Because this deity *conquers us from within* (heart, soul, and mind), our ability to be ethically responsive is undermined. As Beverly Harrison rightly notes, the moral question is not so much, What do we feel? but, What do we do with what we feel?[26]

The Nature of God

The theological tenet at the heart of my reflections on the divine is "panentheism" — meaning that God is in all things and all things are in God, but no one thing is equal to God. As Creator, God is source of all things, yet does not separate Godself from creation in the act of creating. God is

24. William Johnson Everett, *The Politics of Worship: Reforming the Language and Symbols of Liturgy* (Cleveland: United Church Press, 1999), 4.

25. Sallie McFague, *Models of God: Theology for an Ecological, Nuclear Age* (Philadelphia: Fortress Press, 1987), 63–69; and Brian Wren, *What Language Shall I Borrow? God-Talk in Worship: A Male Response to Feminist Theology* (New York: Crossroad, 1990), 119.

26. Beverly Wildung Harrison, "The Power of Anger in the Work of Love," in *Making the Connections: Essays in Feminist Social Ethics,* ed. Carol S. Robb (Boston: Beacon Press, 1985), 14.

thus infinite, not finite. Panentheism is not to be confused with pantheism, which asserts that "everything that exists constitutes a unity and that this all-inclusive unity is divine."[27] Panentheism is also distinct from classical theism, which stresses God's transcendence and ignores the quality of immanence. From my perspective, the transcendence (beyondness) and immanence (withinness) of God are inseparable.

As Calvin acknowledges the incomprehensibility of God that "fills the earth itself,"[28] so I use the term "panentheism" to speak of the mystery of God whose Spirit transfuses all creation and breathes into it the divine essence, life, and movement. This mystery is always many in terms of the names by which we discern it and always one in terms of the unifying presence we experience. As Christians we speak of God's manyness as triune. Nevertheless, despite nods to Trinitarian thinking, the relationship of Father and Son often takes center stage in Western theological discourse while the Holy Spirit is more often than not marginalized (theologically, not liturgically). To appreciate a communal (nonindividualistic) eucharist, one must give the Spirit her due, particularly in terms of her influence on the connecting power of human imagination.

In using the term "God," which has a history of being identified as masculine, I am not abdicating my belief that the divine mystery at the core of our being and universe is beyond gender. The use of hybrid nouns such as "God/ess" or "G*d" to signify this metaphorical truth has limited value. Indeed these hybrids may have inadvertently undermined the cause of justice in liturgical language by creating resistance more than understanding. Liturgically and devotionally I use the phrase "Father-Mother God" (as well as nonanthropomorphic images) to symbolize the finiteness of human words in the context of infinity. I prefer to shift the pronouns used for God rather than the noun because it is the pronoun "he" attached to the noun "God" that so dominates our imaginations, in the form of "he" and "his" and "him." God is always "neither male nor female, nor a combination of the two."[29] Until we have the courage to speak of God more freely than we have, our experience of the *is-ness* of God, which is always more verb than noun, will seem to us as absence more than presence.

The Relational Self

My use of the image *relational self* is based on an understanding that the self is a social being, constituted by a multiplicity of relationships over

27. Alisdair MacIntyre, "Pantheism," in *The Encyclopedia of Philosophy,* ed. Paul Edwards (New York: Free Press/Macmillan, 1967), 6:34.

28. Calvin, *Institutes,* vol. 20:121, 138.

29. Trible, *God and Rhetoric,* 21.

time. The self does not *have* relationships; it *is* its relationships. The multiple networks of family, friends, and acquaintances with whom we come to know ourselves in relation — however intangible those connections may be — are always transforming the self we know. Unlike the atomistic selfhood or "separative selfhood" of dominarchy, the relational self exists with permeable boundaries that allow the self both to receive from and to give to the other.[30] A significant dimension of the relational self is its capacity for empathy, the ability to enter and understand another's experience. Within relationships which are mutual, "where empathy and concern flow both ways, there is an intense affirmation of the self and, paradoxically a transcendence of the self, a *sense of the self as part of a larger relational unit.* [This] interaction allows for a relaxation of the sense of separateness; [so that] the other's well-being becomes as important as one's own."[31]

In authentic relationships of mutual empathy, being seen (or received) for whom one is allows the individual to develop a sense of response/ability rather than agency or autonomy. Thus the feeling of being "received"[32] is actively transmitted to everyone involved in the relational encounter. Being conscious of these connections allows the relational self to experience a greater sense of well-being in contrast to the "separative" self who, in a world where all things are ultimately interrelated, seeks independence and self-sufficiency in the illusion of living as a separate self.

In a relational worldview that values interdependency, violence is not a tool for ordering life but a power to be reckoned with and resisted. At the same time, a compassionate deity encourages empathy and mutuality while judging us with tender care and healing mercy for the sake of *the world's well-being.* Through the image of a loving judge, rather than a divine punisher, God chooses blessing over punishment and well-being over violence. This God also calls us to communal well-being in contrast to the childlike dependency so often touted in orthodox spirituality. As we relate to God through the paradigm of friendship, divine grace gives birth to earthly well-being. Likewise, Alfred North Whitehead's poetic image of God as the great companion — the fellow-sufferer who understands — evokes the metaphor of companionship that guides my own re-imaging.[33]

30. Catherine Keller, *From a Broken Web: Separation, Sexism, and Self* (Boston: Beacon Press, 1986), 7–46; Judith Jordan, et al., *Women's Growth in Connection: Writings from the Stone Center* (New York: Guilford Press, 1991).

31. Jordan, *Women's Growth,* 82; emphasis added.

32. Nel Noddings, *Caring: A Feminine Approach to Ethics and Moral Education* (Berkeley: University of California Press, 1984), 30–35.

33. Robert C. Neville, *A Theology Primer* (Albany: SUNY Press, 1991), 120; Alfred North Whitehead, *Process and Reality,* corrected ed., ed. David Ray Griffin and Donald W. Sherburne (New York: Free Press, Macmillan, 1978), 351.

Salvation — Well-Being — through Grace

The word "therapeutic" so easily thrown about to trivialize and dismiss the modern critique of Christianity, need not be seen as pejorative. Therapeutic is an adjective whose synonyms imply something that is healing, beneficial, curative, and restorative. In this sense the gospel — *good news* — has always been therapeutic. Jesus was a healer, a physician to the sick in Mark (2:17) and "the kind physician" in the words of Ephrem the Syrian. The eucharist, described as the "medicine of immortality" by Ignatius of Antioch, also has therapeutic associations.[34] Indeed, reconciliation, forgiveness, and penance all deal with the restoration of right-relation and the healing of communal ties. What needs to be addressed, however, is how easily the notion of healing has been distorted in Christianity by the fear of hell and eternal damnation.

Though Reformed theology stresses the atoning work of Jesus' death as the mark of salvation, the theology presented here takes note of the linguistic roots of salvation — Greek *sōtēria* and Latin *salus* — that have to do with *healing in this life.*[35] The authority that Jesus claimed for himself put him at risk, precisely because he dared to speak human words of forgiveness and grace in a religious context where before only God could enact such power. As John Dominic Crossan observes, "If sickness is a divine punishment for sin, then the one who cures sickness has forgiven sin and manifested divine power."[36] The fruits of Jesus' ministry clearly point to well-being as being the primary mark of his loving engagement with life. But what exactly is meant by the term "well-being"?

I understand well-being to be a state of health whereby persons are able to integrate all dimensions of their embodied selves (physical, emotional, and spiritual) and engage in loving relationships that foster mutuality. This state of health does not imply perfection, as though an individual achieves pain-free existence; rather, it honors the realities of past and present fragmentation in one's life, as well as one's ability to live with psychic and bodily limitations, which are representative of human finitude. I have purposely tried to avoid the wholeness/brokenness dichotomy because this language has been so insensitive to the experience of many individuals who are differently abled. Language that equates sin with bodily limitation

---

34. *Ephrem the Syrian: Hymns,* trans. Kathleen E. McVey (Mahwah, N.J.: Paulist Press, 1989), 424, 425. Ignatius of Antioch, "To the Ephesians," in *Early Christian Fathers,* ed. Cyril C. Richardson (New York: Macmillan, 1970), 93.

35. Jaroslav Pelikan, *The Melody of Theology: A Philosophical Dictionary* (Cambridge, Mass.: Harvard University Press, 1988), 106; Paul Tillich, *Systematic Theology,* vol. 2 (Chicago: University of Chicago Press, 1957).

36. John Dominic Crossan, *The Historical Jesus: The Life of a Mediterranean Jewish Peasant* (San Francisco: HarperCollins, 1991), 324.

does much harm, as Valerie Jones Stiteler has rightly cautioned: "Disability is part of human experience and should not be judged by theological categories."[37] Suffering and sin are not causally related.

Well-being is always communal and always loving. Individuals who experience well-being are able to act in their own behalf, to express their own creativity, and to be fully conscious of their personal responsibility to promote the well-being of all. In this context, power is experienced as *power-from-within* and *power-with*. Power-from-within has to do with our consciousness of and connectedness to the deeper mysteries of life, including our own abilities and potential. Power-with has to do with social power, "the power we wield among equals."[38] Both are rooted in the life of the Spirit and honor the diversity that lies at the heart of God's creative embrace of the world.

Communal Well-Being

Being "received," feeling accepted by others, is critical to personal well-being and our active engagement with the world. Our personal well-being influences others and is influenced by those around us, just as our lack of well-being affects our ability to experience and encourage relational mutuality. If our own sense of self-worth has been nurtured early on by a profound positive regard, experienced in and through our significant relationships, we develop a healthy dose of self-respect, as well as respect for the dignity and worth of others. We also welcome a communal criterion of well-being. Any community that embodies interdependency becomes a "redemptive structure," where the well-being of one individual encourages the well-being of many and the well-being of many encourages the well-being of the individual.[39] Community and the quality of freedom experienced in community are thus essential to one's experience of the gospel.

Catherine Keller enlarges upon this theme in arguing for a "connective" selfhood that seeks "connection that counts" rather than disconnection. As a connective self, "I become who I am in and through and beyond the particular activity of connection."[40] In order to live and love as a

37. Howard Clinebell, *Well-Being: A Personal Plan for Exploring and Enriching the Seven Dimensions of Life: Mind, Body, Spirit, Love, Work, Play, Earth* (San Francisco: HarperSanFrancisco, 1992); Valerie C. Jones Stiteler, "Singing without a Voice: Using Disability Images in the Language of Public Worship," *Anna Howard Shaw Center Newsletter* 8 (fall 1991): 3.

38. Starhawk, *Truth or Dare*, 8–16; Bernard M. Loomer, "Two Conceptions of Power," *Criterion* 15, no. 1 (winter 1976): 12–29.

39. Marjorie Hewitt Suchocki, *The End of Evil: Process Eschatology in Historical Context* (New York: SUNY Press, 1988), 72, 123, 133.

40. Keller, *Broken Web*, 3, 200, 248.

becoming self, in Keller's view, our personal boundaries must be permeable, shifting, and coextensive with the boundaries of our universe. The essence of the connective self is thus a "radical world-openness" that thrives on its connectedness to all of life. Divine love calls us to participate in the binding of wounds and the reconnection of worlds, for love, as ethicist Beverly Harrison has argued, "is the power to act-each-other-into-well-being."[41]

Theologian Mary Grey concurs: grace nurtures in us a "wide fellow-feeling" — "a sensitive awareness of one's own bodiliness, personal strengths and strengths in relationship"[42] — that encourages us to reach out beyond our own pain and oppression to unite in solidarity with others for the sake of mutuality and love-in-relation. Because God is the source of our relationality, a relational theology of the eucharist views the world as sacramental. The world is a "bearer of God" and an "epiphany of salvation."[43] In becoming filled with the fullness of God through grace, the self is not sacrificed but "greatened" through an inner strengthening, a "being-made-new," as we participate more deeply in the life of God.[44] While native peoples intuitively understand what it means to view the world as sacred, many Christians have little sense of the symbolic nature of sacraments. Yet the sacraments have their primary connection with simple elements of nature and the ordinary moments of human experience — eating and drinking, bathing, and anointing with oil.

Sacraments Anew

Defining and distinguishing what a sacrament is has been complicated by the realization that the word "sacrament" is nowhere found in the Christian Scriptures, the uncertainty of the term itself, and the assumption that the sacramental rites were instituted by Christ.[45] Despite its legalistic bias, the Latin word *sacramentum* (from *sacrare,* to consecrate) was chosen to represent the Greek *mysterion,* meaning mystery or secret. *Sacramentum* originally carried various meanings, but the most popular was a military oath of allegiance to the emperor. Today, the ritual elements of this "sacramental oath ha[ve] found expression in worship through practices

41. Ibid., 114, 218; Harrison, *Making the Connections,* 40.

42. Mary Grey, *Feminism, Redemption, and the Christian Tradition* (Mystic, Conn.: Twenty-Third Publications, 1990), 39, 220.

43. Leonardo Boff, *Sacraments of Life, Life of the Sacraments: Story Theology,* trans. John Drury (Washington: Pastoral Press, 1987), 4.

44. Roger Hazelton, *Ascending Flame, Descending Dove: An Essay on Creative Transcendence* (Philadelphia: Westminster Press, 1975), 122.

45. For further treatment of the material in this section, see June C. Goudey, "The Sacraments," in *An A to Z of Feminist Theology,* ed. Lisa Isherwood and Dorothea McEwan (Sheffield, England: Sheffield Academic Press, 1996), 209–10.

of kneeling, the laying on of hands, bowing, and clasping hands together in prayer."[46]

While it lacked the depth of *mysterion,* one of the earliest liturgical usages for the term "sacrament" appeared in the writings of Tertullian (ca. 160–225). Later Augustine developed the first theory of sacraments based on the conjunction of word and physical element. In general a sacrament has been understood to be an "outward and visible sign of an inward and spiritual (invisible) grace." These sign-acts or "visible words" have celebrated God's loving self-disclosure in Christ, but little agreement has existed as to how many of the church's sign-acts are truly sacraments. While the Eastern Orthodox and Roman Church have recognized Peter Lombard's (ca. 1100–1160) designation of seven sacraments — baptism, confirmation, eucharist, penance, extreme unction, ordination, and marriage — most Reformation churches acknowledge baptism and the eucharist as the only true sacraments.

John Calvin kept close to Augustine's thought that the word plus an external sign make a sacrament; however, he joined this "outward and visible sign" to "an antecedent promise." Nothing in the material element — neither the baptismal water nor the bread and wine — makes it sacramental. The sacraments thus became a visible *seal* of God's pledge of grace in Christ Jesus that could only be received "with firm faith." For grace to be present, the elements require the divine Word.[47] Today, many liturgical scholars and theologians, influenced by modern physics and considerations of lived experience, stress the relational dimensions of the sacraments in community and perceive them as profound symbols of God's dynamic presence in all of creation. There is also movement in some circles to experience the sacraments as "rites of passage or intensification" whereby prior commitments such as confirmation become renewed whenever one partakes of the communion meal.

When Women Set the Table

This sea change in sacramental theology remains largely a scholarly exercise, lacking a full appreciation of women's experience and having little influence on actual church practice. For this reason feminists continue to question the basic nature of sacramental thought. Mary Daly called the Roman Catholic notion of transubstantiation an exercise in "swallowing the lie" because it distances us from the truth of our bodily senses and

46. Everett, *Politics of Worship,* 63.
47. Calvin, *Institutes,* 21:1279–83.

makes us believe that the "Elemental acts" of eating and drinking are not what we think.[48]

Early critiques of the sacraments confined themselves to focusing on the use of inclusive language and the exclusion of women from the priesthood. In the 1990s, however, this critical agenda broadened. Catholic feminists, noting that the "sacramental principle" in their tradition affirms that God is revealed in all of creation, argued that the sacraments must be reconnected with ordinary biological life and grounded in an incarnational theology that honors human embodiment and the bodily experiences of women as well as men.

Protestant feminists, acknowledging their debt to the insights of their Catholic sisters, have focused their call for reform on baptism and eucharist. Marjorie Procter-Smith argues that since baptism and eucharist are acts that both bring into being and sustain the church, the ecclesial context of the sacraments as well as the rites themselves must be rigorously challenged. Because the sacraments have functioned to reinforce male clerical power, the recognition of their social and political context is a crucial step in moving to an emancipatory praxis that will make the church value women's experience of the real. For the sacraments to be "true revelations, true *mysteria*," she argues, they must witness to "God's self-disclosure in women's lives." Sacraments laden with dominarchal inequities thus give the lie to the church's promise of baptismal equality and dignity (Gal. 3:27–28). Procter-Smith also notes that the dependence of the eucharist on sacrificial language and imagery is a continuing problem for women. Such language, she argues, must be rejected as an "inadequate understanding of the meaning of suffering," for any understanding of suffering must encourage the "possibility of resistance and struggle."[49] With this critique we come face-to-face with atonement.

Communion vs. Atonement

"Atonement," as it has functioned historically in Christian theology, has referred to the saving or redeeming work of Christ brought about through his incarnation, sufferings, death, and resurrection. Western theology, however, has too often dropped the significance of the resurrection by stressing crucifixion. Among the many views of atonement, the principle proponent of an individualistic eucharistic worldview has been the penal substitutionary theory, whose imagery is still conveyed in traditional hymns, such as

48. Mary Daly, *Pure Lust: Elemental Feminist Philosophy* (Boston: Beacon Press, 1984), 51, 53.

49. Marjorie Procter-Smith, *Praying with Our Eyes Open: Engendering Feminist Liturgical Prayer* (Nashville: Abingdon Press, 1995), 133.

"O Sacred Head Now Wounded." The belief that Christ died for our sins has functioned as a liberating motif for many, particularly the oppressed. Nevertheless, substitutionary atonement, in whatever guise it appears, places limits on who has access to the well-being Jesus offers, especially those who have little power or who find the concept of substitutionary atonement troubling.

While some wish to redefine atonement as "at-one-ment" to mean a "setting at one," an act of reconciliation with God within community, I no longer find the term "atonement" adequate. Instead, I suggest that well-being is preferable to "setting at one," and the image of communion truer than atonement. While the image of sacrifice may have validity in the context of how the powerful may come to act justly through voluntarily sacrificing their power, it has no such weight in the lives of the oppressed. While many will continue to use the image of sacrifice/atonement to understand Jesus' death, my point is this: Jesus' death should in no way be narrowly understood as a sacrifice . . . *for our sins.*

Redemption as Freedom

Redemption means here a reclaiming and recovery of the person of Jesus and the liberating actions of his life, rather than the traditional understanding of redemption as salvation from sin through the sacrifice of Jesus. Redemption occurs when we choose the relational life God reveals to us through the life-work of Jesus. We participate in God's work of redemption even though God is the initiator of the redemptive process. When we understand that healing has to do with our interconnectedness with creation and solidarity with others, we know redemption as freedom in community — a gift of God and a faith-choice to be celebrated. Those who insist that we never contribute to our own salvation in the face of Christ's atoning work deny the very relationality at the heart of creation.

The Bible Urges Christ

In promoting relational selfhood as a truer model of human well-being in community, I rely on the relational ethic of pre-exilic prophets such as Hosea, Micah, Amos, and Jeremiah. When the choice between life and death is set before us, I believe God's word to us is "choose life" — by giving glory to God and embodying relational grace. Choosing life also encompasses prophetic exhortations to build houses, work the land, and bear children even when in exile or captivity (Jer. 29:4–7). The grace of God embodied in Jesus of Nazareth embraces not only our liberation from sin, but also our liberation from social and political oppression. Hence, in distinction to those parts of the Bible that urge dominarchy (such as the household codes in the Christian Scriptures), I use the criteria of well-being and healing to identify the points at which the Bible "urges Christ." Luther understood scripture to be authoritative "insofar as it bears witness to Christ," for Christ, in Luther's words, is "nothing other than sheer life."[50] Just so I rely on scripture's witness to guide my own life choices.

Compassion and Suffering

Suffering can take many forms; yet all of them raise troubling questions about the goodness of God. For centuries God's role in human suffering and God's capacity to suffer (or not) have been hotly contested. One way that Christianity has attempted to make sense of Jesus' suffering on the cross is to interpret his death as a sacrifice. In so doing, Jesus' suffering becomes an expression of divine love and a model of human love, as in the words Jesus utters to his disciples in the Gospel of John: "No one has greater love than this, to lay down one's life for one's friends" (John 15:13). Laying down one's life voluntarily to save another is a profound act of heroism and love for neighbor, even when the one being saved is a total stranger. Individuals who respond in moments of crisis to traumatic and tragic events, as well as everyday acts of courage performed by the likes of police, firefighters, and medical personnel, can move us deeply. Without such self-transcendent acts humankind would be the poorer.

Whereas many frame the essence of atonement as a suffering "for" the sake of others unto death, the true nature of compassion is an empathetic *being with* others to bring them into well-being. "To receive compassion is to receive respect. . . . Compassion identifies suffering as an affront to [the sufferer's] integrity. . . . [I]t identifies the wretchedness of her situation as alien to her." Compassionate love, not suffering love, is the truest sign of God's grace, for compassion embodies divine love "as redemptive power against the domination of evil."[51] Compassion, unlike suffering, is an imaginative act, for it is an act of openness to the life-situation of others. Far from condoning a glorification of suffering, I am arguing that a theology of communal well-being recognizes the reality of suffering and the context in which the one suffering can be understood to be encountered by the compassion of God. Though many people will continue to merge the two,

50. Dorothee Sölle, *Thinking about God: An Introduction to Theology* (Philadelphia: Trinity Press International, 1990), 76; B. A. Gerrish, *The Old Protestantism and the New: Essays on the Reformation Heritage* (Chicago: University of Chicago Press, 1982), 65; Martin Luther, "A Sermon on Preparing to Die," in *Luther Works,* vol. 42, *Devotional Writings I,* ed. Martin O. Dietrich, trans. Martin H. Betram (Philadelphia: Fortress Press, 1969), 104.

51. Farley, *Tragic Vision,* 79, 115.

suffering must be understood to be larger than the presence of life's "labor pains." "Making sense of suffering means resolving it. To do so . . . we have to seek and determine its causes today in order to prevent its recurring tomorrow."[52]

Sunday Morning Blues

Stark questions stand before us. How are we to sing God's eucharistic song in the land of dominarchy? Is the eucharist a moment of confusion wherein theological inconsistencies foster alienation and abuse? Or is it in fact a rite of communion wherein the relational self commits itself to the community-forming power of God's commonwealth, for the sake of a more just creation? Perhaps it's time to sing the "blues" on Sunday morning and allow our worshiping selves to voice their true needs. In the African American tradition the "blues and spirituals" convey hope. They are songs that "tell it like it is" and resist despair. Spirituals transform the singer and keep the community's song alive. Surely that is what many of us desire for Holy Communion, a moment in time to sing songs that tell it like it is, resist despair, and unleash the power of hope, rather than the "funeral dirges" that too often accompany this sacrament.

My experience of pastoral ministry has confirmed that many individuals abstain from this rite for at least two reasons. On the one hand, they may have a sense of personal worthiness that the performance of the rite denies. In order to participate, these individuals must, ironically, disregard an intrinsic truth regarding their own well-being. Others, unfortunately, fail to participate because they have a profound sense of unworthiness that the rite reinforces. Thus, a rite that is meant to strengthen one's participation in the body of Christ more often serves to fracture the work of this body, by fostering self-reflection more than communal identity.

On the other hand, the dramatic increases in attendance that take place at Christmas and Easter services cannot be explained away by simplistic notions attributing this phenomenon to the unwillingness of laity to be faithful in all seasons. Might it not be that the symbolic messages of incarnation and rebirth through resurrection, and not merely the celebration of these events as past, speak to the heart of most people in search of a meaningful faith? After all, we now see more and more Christians who are fundamentally illiterate when it comes to their knowledge of scripture and tradition; yet they experience these symbols as full of life. That the church has inadequately articulated the demands of faith can hardly be the fault

52. J. Konrad Stettbacher, *Making Sense of Suffering: The Healing Confrontation with Your Own Past* (New York: Dutton, 1991), v.

of those who look to the church for clear direction. Salvation is not only a function of deliverance — it also involves a state of well-being.[53] Over time, as my own consciousness has been raised to see the fragmenting power of dominarchy at work, this fundamental question has taken root in me: Must the eucharist always be understood — misunderstood — in this way? Or is there a way to reclaim the relational (community-forming) power of the eucharist and experience communion as "holy" indeed?

Ritual involves repetitive actions of a symbolic nature that both shape and express one's beliefs. When we reflect on the messages a particular rite conveys, we learn a great deal about our faithfulness to past traditions as well as the truthfulness these messages have for our own situation. Ritual reveals the convictions a society or group has about itself; thus, how we worship becomes an expression of what we value and what we care about. In light of the gospel's proclamation of new life and its prophetic call to fashion a just society in God's name, the public horizon of any ritual activity cannot avoid scrutiny.

Ritual can be transformative and life-changing, but as Amos and First Isaiah point out so well, ritual can also serve the status quo (those in power) and fail to honor God's justice-seeking love. For the church to be faithful to the gift of God's Spirit and the proclamation of Christ Jesus' message, one must be able to discern the social and theological meanings symbolically mediated in ritual actions. Failure to do so is to deny the world-making power of ritual. As James Cone reminds us, "through the power of human imagination [in song and ritual] defined by their struggle against slavery and segregation, blacks created a separate world for themselves — a world defined by justice and peace, where women, men, and their children can freely love and be loved."[54]

Liturgical Theology as Practical Theology

Since it is well established that the institutional church is pervasively dominarchal and hierarchical, any hope for change will require an analysis of the symbol systems that lie at the heart of dominarchal power. Living in a world where children and adults too often become detached from their own humanity under the lure of drugs and glorified violence, our communal salvation cries out for a communion rite that "expands the sense of

---

53. Claus Westermann, *Blessing in the Bible and the Life of the Church*, trans. Keith Crim, Overtures to Biblical Literature (Philadelphia: Fortress Press, 1978).

54. James H. Cone, *The Spirituals and the Blues: An Interpretation* (New York: Seabury Press, 1972; reprint, Maryknoll, N.Y.: Orbis Books, 1991), 129.

the possible"[55] by opening the future for us all. When informed by creative imagination, good liturgy liberates the participants not only to expand the possible but also to act each other into well-being. Such liturgy also opens individuals to the transforming power of a *communal eucharist,* for it builds solidarity among those who partake of this eucharist and helps them to identify themselves as citizens of the world.

Countless women and men have experienced profound healing within Christianity. Still, we must ask ourselves whether sacrificial theology has re-imaged the eucharist from a faithful milestone to a dominarchal millstone. Does a theology of self-transcendence and creativity, unlike a theology grounded in the obedient and sacrificial self of dominarchy, nurture a relational sense of self? More importantly, can Christianity endure and flourish separated from its long-standing proclamation that the cross is the symbol of redemptive suffering? I would answer, Yes. Arguing for the constructive dimensions of the relational self and a eucharistic rite that promotes a relationality of care and connection does not ignore the truth that relationality also can bring with it death and destruction. Not all relationships are inherently good, as women who have lost themselves in relationships for the sake of the other (or have been beaten and killed by the other) know too well. Our desire to find connections that count — that value our experience as women — speaks to our understanding of potential dangers as well as future possibilities of grace.

Misplaced fear violates the relationality of God, while the constancy of fear ensures the constancy of injustice. This is why we must find the courage to critique our ritual interactions and ask whether they do justice and promote love and kindness (Mic. 6:8) within the communal life of the church, the body of Christ-Christa. As Elisabeth Schüssler Fiorenza argues so passionately, "How can we point to the eucharistic bread and say 'this is my body' as long as women's bodies are battered, raped, sterilized, mutilated, prostituted, and used to male ends? How can we proclaim 'mutuality with men' in the body of Christ as long as men curtail and deny reproductive freedom and moral agency to us?"[56] New light must be shed on such questions. To do that, we turn then to imagination and its role in human becoming and divine redeeming.

---

55. David Tracy, *The Analogical Imagination: Christian Theology and the Culture of Pluralism* (New York: Crossroad, 1981), 108.

56. Elisabeth Schüssler Fiorenza, *In Memory of Her: A Feminist Theological Reconstruction of Christian Origins* (New York: Crossroad, 1983), 350.

THREE

Imagining and Imaging Communal Well-Being

Imagination is a necessary component of all profound knowing and celebration; all remembering, realizing, and anticipating; all faith, hope, and love. When imagination fails doctrines become ossified, witness and proclamation wooden, doxologies and litanies empty, consolations hollow, and ethics legalistic. —*Amos Wilder*[1]

A Conversation with Myself

Long ago, I know not when—
My imagination died
A silent death
That no one came to mourn.

Yet I have mourned ever since,
Mostly in silence—
Then again,
With tears that only God can see.

Still I ask,
"What does God do with my tears?"

(I use them . . . I use them.)
—*June C. Goudey*, 1987[2]

Liturgy is an imaginative act. Whenever we celebrate the eucharist we enact and rehearse images and symbols that influence community formation as well as self-identification. In order to understand how and why the imagery of the eucharist evolved from the table-fellowship of Jesus to the "marriage feast of the Lamb," we must deepen our understanding of symbols and explore the role of imagination in human experience. We do so

1. Amos Niven Wilder, *Theopoetic: Theology and the Religious Imagination* (Philadelphia: Fortress Press, 1976), 2.

2. From an unpublished paper, "Acting on Our Deepest Yearnings: A New Vision of God."

to discover not merely a new way of understanding how to make eucharist but also a new way of becoming human. As the images of table-fellowship evolved so too did our awareness of one another at table. To ignore this liturgical turn away from communal celebration would be to ignore the power of images to make and unmake the world. After setting forth my understanding of the process of imagination and how symbols function, I will explore the necessary function of judgment in imagination as well as the necessary function of praise and thanksgiving in the life of faith.

Imagination as Process

Imagination is essential to life and to resurrection living. Yet what exactly is imagination? How do we get it? How do we use it? And what does it mean to have one and have it die? Perhaps you are an artist, a poet, or a theologian (or a combination thereof) and have a ready answer to these questions. If, on the other hand, you are at a loss to define imagination, let me offer some clues. Imagination is intimately involved with the notion of vision and dreams, both of which are deeply valued in scripture as unique vehicles for God's revelation to humankind. One passage often cited as an example of this is 1 Samuel 3:1: "Now the boy Samuel was ministering to the LORD under Eli. The word of the LORD was rare in those days; there was no frequent *vision*" (RSV).

It is possible to read biblical texts as warning of the evil of human imagination; and it is equally possible to watch Jesus use his own imagination for good, by way of the stories and parables he used to communicate the gospel of divine love. What are we to make of these two scenarios? One tack would be to argue that because Jesus was human and divine, and knew no sin, his imagination was free of human fallibility. One could also conclude that without Jesus, human beings are hard-hearted and stiff-necked people, who turn away from God's salvation. In so doing, they permit evil rather than good to shape their imaginations. The Reformed doctrine of the Fall of Adam and Eve bodies forth this logic. This way of thinking, however, does little to clarify the process of imagination that all human beings rely on to navigate and re-create their worlds.

Imagination is a complex phenomenon with two necessary components: an action (imagining) and an image (the imagined object). What we imagine thus comes "to consciousness as an image."[3] To be conscious of an image does not mean that other images are not influencing us. It simply means that we are free to work with these images more readily and de-

3. Margaret Mary Kelleher, "Liturgy and the Christian Imagination," *Worship* 66 (March 1992): 127.

termine whether they are true for us. Perhaps they were once true but are no longer, or perhaps they never were true and someone else's will imposed them on us. The former awareness usually evolves through the process of maturity and self-evaluation while the latter demonstrates undue influence. The distinction is critical since the process of imagination constitutes what it means to be human. Imagination is the point of consciousness "at which experience begins."[4] *Imagination shapes experience and experience shapes imagination.* Without imagination we can neither interpret nor express what we encounter through our physical senses. At the same time, the experience of others has the potential to shape our imaginations positively or negatively. Teachers, mentors, loving parents, and role models are instrumental in helping us expand our minds and gain self-confidence. In contrast, under conditions of subordination, those who are constrained imaginatively by their own fears have the power to dramatically *dominate* how we receive and interpret information. Imagination thus functions at the levels of ordinary perception and of universal insight.

Imagination allows us to perceive the world, to re-present objects in their absence, to create symbols and share their meanings with one another, and to "see into the life of things" — to see into the heart of the matter and to know that all matter is sacramental.[5]

Newtonian physics and the seventeenth-century Enlightenment's emphasis on reason convinced many that God's creation was separate from God. The theological perspective of deism imaged the world as a machine that God created and left to its own devices. Without a sense that God was immanent in (within) nature, humankind came to treat the earth as something to be manipulated and dominated rather than respected. With the advent of Einstein's relativity theory and a recovery of mystical thought, the twentieth century offered a much-needed corrective.

From the perspective of panentheism, which accepts God as being in all things and all things as being in God, God's immanence and transcendence are one. The unfathomable, infinite, and inexpressible mystery that can never be contained by any one finite reality is present in all things, including humankind. Relying on Calvin's view of divine power, Paul Tillich saw that the sacramental power of nature comes from God's sovereignty over nature. As Creator, God uses natural elements as sacramental expressions of God's mercy and faithfulness. Likewise, Christian mystics perceive every creature as a word of God.[6]

---

4. Robert C. Neville, *Reconstruction of Thinking* (Albany: SUNY Press, 1981), 258.

5. William Wordsworth, "Tintern Abbey," quoted in Mary Warnock, *Imagination* (Berkeley: University of California Press, 1978), 117.

6. On Tillich, see Donald M. Baillie, *The Theology of the Sacraments and Other Papers* (New York: Scribner's and Sons, 1957), 44–45; John Calvin, *Institutes of the Christian Religion*, ed. John T.

Colonizing the Imagination

Our capacity to think symbolically is essential to viewing the world sacramentally — taking the physicality of our world and our humanity seriously as revealers of divine mystery. Yet strong forces within and without conspire against us. Because our unconscious minds fail to distinguish between image and reality, all images are treated as real, as are their consequences. Negative images limit our active engagement in the world by limiting our capacity to love. They also undermine our immune system and distort our relationships with others; in essence they restrict our ability to build well-being. Positive images, especially positive images of the self, world, and God, function as healers and promote well-being.[7] Consider a recent study aimed at understanding the current shift from the classic New England commons, around which our forebears gathered, to the diverse and complex global commons created by today's technologies of travel and international communication. The study identifies patterns of images that help us meet new challenges:

> *[I]mages that give form to a positive, connected, and centered sense of self* enable people to withstand personal, commercial, and political assaults on their self-esteem; *images that reveal the world as it is* along with images of "what should not be so" fuel the strength to engage the complexity and moral ambiguities of the new commons; *images that convey the overcoming of obstacles and discouragement* engender hope; and *images that hold a sense of paradox and mystery* enlarge the mind and sustain energy and spirit over the long haul.[8]

Human interconnectivity flows in more than one direction simultaneously. Just as external images affect our well-being, our lack of well-being affects the way we image the world. What happens to us during our lifetime, even what happens to us within the womb (as in fetal alcohol syndrome), may have a lasting effect on our capacity to be expansive in our relationships with others, particularly in relationship to love and fear, the two strongest emotions human beings know. In *The Body in Pain,* Elaine Scarry explores how extreme pain gives rise to fears that destroy inner worlds of meaning: "World, self, and voice are lost, or nearly lost,"

McNeill, trans. Ford Lewis Battles, Library of Christian Classics (Philadelphia: Westminster Press, 1960), 20:51–53; Matthew Fox, *Meditations with Meister Eckhart* (Santa Fe, N.Mex.: Bear & Company, 1983), 14.

7. Howard Clinebell, *Well-Being: A Personal Plan for Exploring and Enriching the Seven Dimensions of Life: Mind, Body, Spirit, Love, Work, Play, Earth* (San Francisco: HarperSanFrancisco, 1992), xi.

8. Laurent A. Parks Daloz et al., *Common Fire: Leading Lives of Commitment in a Complex World* (Boston: Beacon Press, 1996), 145–46.

she argues, "through the intense pain of torture"[9] as it attacks the very bonds of trust that are essential for the formation of relationship. In the act of torture, as others deny the very pain that we know to be true, our ability to "imagine the real" is undermined. We no longer trust our own senses.

Speaking in the context of the repression experienced by the people of Chile under the Pinochet regime (1973–90), William Cavanaugh details the isolation and fragmentation that were systematically put in place. In attacking individual bodies through random acts of violence the regime succeeded in its primary goal, which was the use of torture to capture the soul of the Chilean people. In effect the Pinochet regime effectively dominated the collective imagination of Chile by manufacturing the very threat the people needed the state to save them from. At the same time the "atomizing" effect on individual bodies stifled the creation of social bodies capable of challenging the state's abuses of power. The church also acquiesced in the creation of an imagined enemy of the state. Cavanaugh argues that the ecclesiology (the doctrinal self-identity) of the Chilean Catholic Church initially kept it from resisting the regime's power.[10]

The coercive tools of dominators are fear and violence, and both are most effective when they complete the dominator's goal of "conquering from within." When internalized oppression is in place, the victims are no longer a threat because they in effect "police" themselves. Although released from prison, the individual remains captive to the regime. As one exiled Chilean writer put it: "Yes, I was free. Free to see and hear and even to walk within the occupied city. But I could hardly speak. My movements had been restricted. I knew that I should stay far away from the street and people and be seen as little as possible. . . . I was now a branded, muted man. I remained inside the house. That's all—nothing else."[11]

Unlike forced isolation, pain is not evil. In a healthy body pain draws attention to itself and allows the painful area to be cared for and eventually healed. This is a critical way our body communicates with us, if not a pleasant one. When something happens to keep us in pain, through accident or illness, the healing mechanisms of the body—the immune system and its white blood cells, as well as the process of grief—weigh in to counter the disruption pain occasions. Nevertheless, the healing mechanisms of the body become vulnerable when trust is absent and hope succumbs to hopelessness—to the sense that help is unavailable and nothing will change.

9. Elaine Scarry, *The Body in Pain: The Making and Unmaking of the World* (New York: Oxford University Press, 1985), 35.

10. William T. Cavanaugh, *Torture and Eucharist: Theology, Politics, and the Body of Christ* (Oxford: Blackwell, 1998).

11. Cited in ibid., 42.

Our ability to imagine new alternatives counters hopelessness and occasions healing — but only when we are able to draw from many wells of renewal and trust that the natural "labor pains" of life have not been superseded by the more serious consequences of suffering. For victims of torture a critical well is the regaining of their voice; for victims of hate crimes a critical well is a community of affirmation; for abused children a critical well is one adult who believes them; for recovering alcoholics a critical well is Alcoholics Anonymous. In every instance, the road to well-being requires a network of relations to aid us in the difficult work of regaining a sense of safety and selfhood in community. Interdependence is essential to being and becoming more fully human.

Influences and Resources for Imagining

In its English use, "imagination" (that which touches the real) is often confused with "fantasy" (that which is unreal or make believe). However, Dorothee Sölle argues that the German word *Phantasie* represents a more positive understanding of imagination than "fantasy." *Phantasie* includes the "dimensions of imagination, inspiration, inventiveness, flexibility, freedom and creativity." Thus Sölle argues for the revival of the Old English form — "phantasy" — as the "free play of creative imagination." Phantasy then becomes the "creative faculty to imagine that which we know [Shelly]."[12] It is this use of imagination that leads me to suggest that women and men who willingly follow Jesus' imaginative (and receptive) ways promote and sustain the formation of redemptive communities centered in the well-being of all creation. The heart of this well-being requires nothing less than our willingness to become *icons* (windows) for God, gracious symbols of divine love *in* the world and *for* the world. The primary tools for discerning well-being through an imaginative engagement with the world have to do with our physicality and the interaction of our bodymind. These tools include:

- *Our physical senses*
  - ~ Touch, taste, smell, hearing, sight, spatial perception, kinesthetic movement, and intuitiveness
- *Our emotions*
  - ~ What we feel and our awareness of our feelings

12. Translator's Preface in Dorothee Sölle, *Beyond Mere Obedience: Reflections on a Christian Ethic for the Future*, trans. Lawrence W. Denef (Minneapolis: Augsburg Publishing House, 1970), 10.

- *Our sexuality*
  - ~ Our comfort with our bodies
  - ~ The physical expression of love
  - ~ The cultivation of tenderness
  - ~ The ability to experience intimacy
- *Our freedom in community*
  - ~ Our ability to live in a peaceful, just society where mutual respect is honored and interdependency encouraged

Drawing from a variety of sources, a lively imagination comes from being open to one's fully embodied self, from trusting others to tell you the truth in love, from an active encounter with the gifts of the Spirit, and from actively seeking well-being in community. Well-being, in turn, relies on several interconnecting spheres of influence that create a sense of integrity for the embodied soul. Like well-being, integrity functions as a relational power, allowing us to make connections with one another for the common good. The integrity of our embodied spheres of influence affects our capacity to be well and depends on an interactive system of multifaceted resources:

Spheres of influence (in-flowing energy) that aid our imagining:[13]

- *Psychic integrity*
  - ~ One is able to imagine oneself beloved by God and worthy of that love
  - ~ One possesses confidence and competence in one's own agency—ability to act
  - ~ One strives to "exorcise" obsessive passions and idolatrous thoughts
  - ~ One practices a devotional life that offers oneself to God in friendship
  - ~ One lives with a sense of safety and selfhood
- *Emotional integrity*
  - ~ One is aware of one's emotions
  - ~ One is able to manage one's emotions

13. Robert C. Neville, *A Theology Primer* (Albany: SUNY Press, 1991), 119–20; Daniel Goleman, *Emotional Intelligence* (New York: Bantam Books, 1995); Al J. Mooney et al., *The Recovery Book* (New York: Workman Publishing, 1992).

- ~ One is able to motivate oneself
- ~ One is able to identify other people's emotions rightly
- ~ One is able to form healthy and joyful relationships
- ~ One is able to live with conflict

- *Physical integrity*
  - ~ One likes one's body
  - ~ One listens to one's body — one knows when hunger, anger, loneliness, and fatigue are present
  - ~ One exercises regularly and plays
  - ~ One provides one's body with proper nourishment
  - ~ One gets sufficient rest
- *Spiritual integrity*
  - ~ One prays or meditates regularly
  - ~ One belongs to a life-giving community that honors divine mystery
  - ~ One is open to wonder
  - ~ One appreciates beauty
  - ~ One cares for creation
  - ~ One is compassionate toward all
- *Relational integrity*
  - ~ One cultivates humility and rejects all forms of humiliation
  - ~ One practices kindness and befriends all creatures
  - ~ One cultivates open communication and respect among family members
  - ~ One cultivates friendships with others and acts justly toward all

All of the above networks influence well-being. However, psychic integrity, emotional integrity, and physical integrity are critical to the full expression of spiritual and relational integrity. The mind is both "embodied" and "embrained," and our emotions are its "primary architect."[14]

While a variety of wounds may rend the fabric of wellness in one or more of the above spheres, it is the overall integrity of the soul that allows each

14. Stanley I. Greenspan with Beryl Lieff Benderly, *The Growth of the Mind and the Endangered Origins of Intelligence* (Reading, Mass.: Addison-Wesley, 1997), 1; Antonio R. Damasio, *Descartes' Error: Emotion, Reason, and the Human Brain* (New York: Avon Books, 1994), 118.

of us to be responsive to the Spirit's saving activity in our midst. Wherever networks of integrity exist (however imperfectly) we are strengthened by grace to overcome the dominarchal forces that intend us harm. As we consider the role of imagination in liturgy, we will surely need to consider the performative nature of liturgy: That is, to what extent are participants free to move and express themselves in common worship?

A Saving Power: Imago Dei

One of the central tenets of scripture is that human beings are created "in the image of God" (Gen. 1:26–27). However, one of the central tenets of Western Christianity is that human beings fell from grace and so marred the image of God through sin (disobedience) that only through Christ and our acceptance of his sacrifice *for us* can this image be restored. Likewise, Augustine's thought on "original sin" contributed to a "reviling of human nature" in the West. This way of thinking reinforces firm boundaries between human beings and God, very much in keeping with the Reformed belief in the sovereignty of God. In contrast, Eastern theologians offer a more positive attitude. Although they concur that humankind is sinful, they more readily praise human nature by making reference to the divinity of our humanity. Eastern theologians appeal to the "changeless truth" of the prophets, the Gospels, and the apostolic fathers, as do Western theologians. At the same time they lean toward a "symbolic and sacramental interpretation of scripture," which allows them to offer differing views on ancient teachings. The Eastern understanding of salvation is thus dependent on the premise that "God became human in order that man might become divine."[15] Furthermore, the Eastern Church holds that images — in the form of icons — serve as vehicles of grace by helping believers meditate on the holy presence being symbolized. The icon functions as a window to the divine. It is not, as Western Christianity once feared, an idol to be worshiped.

I define imagination as a saving power, a gift from God that is essential to our humanness. Foundationally theocentric — God-centered — this power gives us access to the "more-than-human humanness"[16] that is the mark of God's incarnational presence. Nonetheless, human experience can alter this God-centeredness and colonize imagination with fear. Whenever it allows hopelessness to capture the hope within us, imagination

15. Jaroslav Pelikan, *The Spirit of Eastern Christendom (600–1700)*, vol. 2 of *The Christian Tradition: A History of the Development of Doctrine* (Chicago: University of Chicago Press, 1974), 11, 17.

16. Roger Hazelton, *Ascending Flame, Descending Dove: An Essay on Creative Transcendence* (Philadelphia: Westminster Press, 1975), 46.

experiences the tyranny of the *im*-possible. No longer able to experience the possibilities of God, a colonized imagination begins to undermine the very community it needs for wellness. Constricted by fear and rooted in self-centered isolation, imagination soon becomes incapable of compassion — though, as we shall see, when dominarchal forces threaten one's very being, what others choose to call self-centeredness more than likely is a generous dose of self-protectiveness.

Imagination is ultimately a function of the imago Dei — the image of God at work in us by the power of the Holy Spirit. When our imaginations are liberated from fear (real or unfounded), we become receptive to the new and expansive in our witness to hope. Because we are rooted in divine love, we are able to build well-being for ourselves and others. Yet it is only in community that we experience the divine connectedness of the image of God in us. Because the imago Dei is a relational truth, no one person can be understood to image God or have the fullness of God's image within by virtue of a particular trait, such as reason, will, or love.[17] However, each of us can become a symbol of the divine self-expression (an icon of divinity) by sharing in the liberating activity of the imaginative mind of God — not just in ethical terms (by what we do) but in terms of who we are. Since we are made in God's image, we never lose the iconic power of that image, despite our frailty and failures. At the same time, no one icon, symbol, or image can claim to be the full expression of God. Indeed, the breadth, length, height, and depth of God are as much hidden as they are revealed in the *event* of Christ (Eph. 3:18).

A Feeling for Infinity

I speak of the salvific power of imagination because I understand imagination to be the infinite locus of soul: the inner birthplace of divine revelation and a reservoir of hope. The soul is not a substance that can be located, tagged, and identified; rather it is an *infinite point of contact* that resists formal demarcation. One cannot say, "Behold, here is the soul," but one can say to what degree imagination broadens the soul and nourishes its relational capacities. Imagination is the "point of contact" between the human spirit and divine Spirit. Divine revelation happens through our imagination and in our imagination.[18] When imagination comes into play,

17. Ellen M. Ross, "Human Persons as Images of the Divine: A Reconsideration," *Ad Feminam, Union Seminary Quarterly Review* 43, nos. 1–4 (1989): 93–111.

18. *Whatever Happened to the Soul? Scientific and Theological Portraits of Human Nature,* ed. Warren S. Brown, Nancey Murphy, and H. Newton Malony (Minneapolis: Fortress Press, 1998); Garrett Green, *Imagining God: Theology and the Religious Imagination* (San Francisco: Harper & Row, 1989), 5, 40.

functions fruitfully if you will, grace happens and the embodied soul at the heart of our humanness is moved to pray and sing, "It is well...it is well!" Imagination is also inseparable from eros — the life-energy God endows us with. Imagination participates in this life-power as it opens us to what moves us inwardly and outwardly, to what motivates us to engage the world.[19] Free movement of the body also contributes to the elasticity of imagination, whether that means freedom to move in space or freedom to be moved from within. Indeed, studies have shown that the body remembers what it experiences even when the individual cannot articulate what has happened (as in the preverbal child).[20] Feeling and thinking are thus cocreative faculties of human becoming and imaginative being. To imagine rightly — truthfully — one must be able to feel honestly. Again, to imagine the real we must be capable of knowing the truth of our embodied presence.

Lest I be misunderstood, let me offer a word of caution. The Spirit opens us to the infinity of life and calls us into loving relationships where grace abounds. We are healed, therefore, not because we possess imaginative powers but because we open ourselves to the power of God. The Spirit of God working through our imaginations, through the images and symbols that sustain us, evokes healing power. When the "wider fellow feeling" occasioned by well-being takes hold of our heart and mind, we experience the healing power of imagination as self-transcendence and embrace the Spirit's call to community. Imagination is a process, and yet it is also an attitude, an attitude toward living that — at its best — bears the fruit of openness to the Spirit. While many religious leaders restrict the work of imagination to the hearing of the Word in scripture and tradition, others are more open to the depths of human experience and the interconnections of nature and grace. Thus Mary Catherine Hilkert distinguishes between the "dialectical imagination" and its emphasis on the Word of scripture and tradition and the "sacramental imagination" with its openness to the depths of human experience. Likewise, dancers and other artists know that the human body is intricately designed to communicate with God in more ways than one.[21]

Imagination is thus a multidimensional power: it allows us to transcend (move beyond) the present existential situation of the self as well as to embrace a "feeling of infinity," a feeling that there is "always *more*

---

19. Neville, *Reconstruction*, 254, 255; Rita Nakashima Brock, *Journeys by Heart: A Christology of Erotic Power* (New York: Crossroad, 1988), 25–49.

20. Robin Karr-Morse and Meredith S. Wiley, *Ghosts from the Nursery: Tracing the Roots of Violence* (New York: Atlantic Monthly Press, 1997).

21. Mary Catherine Hilkert, *Naming Grace: Preaching and the Sacramental Imagination* (New York: Continuum, 1997); Phil Porter with Cynthia Winton-Henry, *Having It All: Body, Mind, Heart, and Spirit Together Again at Last* (Oakland: Wing It! Press, 1997); see also on the Internet *www.bodywisdom.org*.

to experience, and *more in* what we experience than we can predict."[22] Imagination is an inner spontaneous source of life that opens us to — and engages us with — the world beyond our inner world. As a relational power, it encourages the making of connections where none seemed to exist. Imagination is thus a mind-expansive, world-expansive way of being human — "it intends and extends the realm of 'coming to be.'"[23] Through faith imagination helps us trust the divine "more" within us and experience our more-than-human humanness. This openness to life is what theologian Dorothee Sölle finds missing when faith embraces the imagery of obedient self-sacrifice. To counter the mindlessness of "mere obedience" and the unreality of "fantasy" she appeals to the imaginative spontaneity of Jesus that can set us free to welcome other persons in love. "The phantasy of Christ is a phantasy of hope, which never gives up anything or anyone and allows concrete reversals to provoke nothing but new discoveries.... It is inexhaustible in the discovery of new and better ways. It is ceaselessly at work improving the welfare of others."[24]

Self-transcendence — the awareness of one's interconnectedness — is not separation from our embodied existence but immersion into reality, into the truth of our diverse lives. To experience self-transcendence is to enter into the self-awareness of relationality and to acknowledge the interdependence of all living things. People liberated from unhealthy fears are builders of well-being through generous hospitality. Thus Sölle avers that Jesus practiced a discerning obedience that allowed him to imaginatively engage the world through an open acceptance of others. This acceptance allowed Jesus to transform the world by the grace of compassionate love. Moreover, from those who would follow him he asked the same responsiveness. In this way, the imaginative "mind of Christ," acting in Jesus and *potentially* in us, functions as a saving power, a divine gift accessible to every individual, yet the property of none.

The Function of Symbols

The sustaining of communities where well-being can thrive depends on a full appreciation of human interconnectivity, the sense that we are all members of one body. However, women and men whose imaginations have been conquered by rampant individualism have few clues as to the symbolic nature of community as the body of Christ. The secular individualism so prevalent today keeps these individuals stuck in a *disconnected* world,

22. Warnock, *Imagination*, 202.

23. Ray L. Hart, *Unfinished Man and the Imagination: Toward an Ontology and a Rhetoric of Revelation* (New York: Herder and Herder, 1968; repr., Atlanta: Scholars Press, 1985), 135.

24. Sölle, *Obedience*, 78.

one that speaks far more of divine absence than presence. That is why our human capacity for symbolic living is an essential dimension of our ability to imagine the real, to intuit the unspoken "more." With his usual elegance, Roger Hazelton wrote,

> Unless we live by symbol, song, and story we do not live at all; we merely vegetate or react, and these too are metaphors for a nonmetaphorical existence. Our very bodies serve as metaphors in which, by a transfer or carry-over of meaning, we express what takes place in "the mind's eye" of imagination. Metaphor, indeed, may be one of the principal means by which human beings "hold body and soul together" — that is, insist upon giving expression to our humanity.[25]

Like symbols, metaphors have a connecting function. They allow us to bring more than one world together — to connect what is seen, known, and familiar with that which is unfamiliar. Yet, paradoxically, as soon as we use a metaphor to say *what is* (as in God is a rock, God is Father), we also say *what is not* (God is more than a rock, God is more than a Father). Today, the inability to understand this paradoxical function of metaphor is at the heart of much religious discord. Playing havoc with the language of our hymnody and our progress toward inclusivity, diversity, and justice, "nonmetaphorical" existence prevails in too many communities of faith. As a consequence too many believers are out of touch with their own humanity and their innate capacity for divine communion.

Symbols are essential to our becoming selves. We are symbol-making and symbol-using beings. We think symbolically and "out of signs and symbols we weave our tissue of 'reality.'"[26] We perceive the world imaginatively by constructing meanings out of raw experiences and communicate these meanings to one another through symbolic discourse. By means of suggestion, association, and relation, symbols move us to think and thereby stimulate our imaginations. They open our inner worlds of meaning to alternative possibilities. Most importantly they open up aspects of our selves that are often hidden. Symbols connect us with ourselves and with one another; they also connect us with the world of mystery that transcends all human experience. "Within the sacred universe there are not living creatures here and there, but life is everywhere as a sacrality, which permeates everything and which is seen in the movement of the stars, the return to

---

25. Hazelton, *Ascending Flame*, 42–43; Sallie McFague, *Metaphorical Theology: Models of God in Religious Language* (Philadelphia: Fortress Press, 1982).

26. Susanne K. Langer, *Philosophy in a New Key: A Study in the Symbolism of Reason, Rite, and Art*, 3d ed. (Cambridge, Mass.: Harvard University Press, 1957), 53–78, 280; Paul Tillich, *Dynamics of Faith* (New York: Harper & Row, 1958), 41–43.

life of vegetation each year, and the alternation of birth and death. It is in this sense that symbols are bound within the sacred universe."[27]

Symbols function; they do something. They evoke and invite something new to come into being. They also do something to the person encountering them, even as we do something to them by means of interpretation. We bring our histories to the symbol; that is, we bring potentialities of meaning to the symbolic encounter, and depending on what we bring, by virtue of who we are, the symbol evokes meanings. A symbol may also mean one thing to me, even as it means another thing to you. In our pluralistic world, we find ourselves confronted by a multitude of symbols and a variety of interpretations. Invariably, the life of any symbol is emotionally charged by virtue of its interconnectivity with the cultural value systems it embodies. A Brooklyn, New York, exhibition (spring 2000) of a Madonna smeared with elephant dung became a political minefield and a religious headache. Why? Because of the emotional energies unleashed by those who felt their religion and they themselves were under attack. Flag burning in the protest years of the 1960s commanded broader national attention for similar reasons. Likewise, in the aftermath of September 11, 2001, the presence of the American flag on cars, civic buildings, and homes provided a strong emotional witness for those who felt they had to do something in response to terrorist attacks on "America."

Symbols live and die by virtue of the meanings attached to them. Meanings, as the named value of something, also evolve. The cross remains a living religious symbol. Yet not everyone interprets its meaning in the same way. The cross was once a common symbol of torture and Roman oppression, but Christianity transformed its meaning into a symbol of hope and new life after Jesus' resurrection. Yet the cross can still be seen as an oppressive symbol to those whose religious sensibilities find Christian beliefs unacceptable. After Pope John Paul II visited a death camp in 1979 and called it the "Golgotha of the modern world," a group of Carmelite nuns established a convent nearby to offer prayers for Christian martyrs who had died in the Holocaust, what Jews call the Shoah. The worldwide protests that occurred from 1984 to 1998 in response to the nuns' actions led to the erection of several small crosses and one very large one. The protests also occasioned several of the nuns' supporters to label Jews who protested as "Christ killers." The Catholic Church and contemporary Christians of conscience have rightly rejected this haunting indictment—fed throughout history by many Christian leaders, Martin Luther among them. Nevertheless, anti-Semitic sentiment continues to have a strong

27. Paul Ricoeur, *Interpretation Theory: Discourse and the Surplus of Meaning* (Fort Worth: Texas Christian University Press, 1976), 61.

foothold in the minds of many. To the Catholics who erected the cross, it became a symbol of their atonement and hope for redemption before the horror that marked the death camps; but to the Jews who remember the Shoah as genocide, any suggestion that meaningful suffering took place there is unacceptable.[28]

The simple cross of Golgotha, whether presented in the form of a crucifix or two wooden beams, remains a potent symbol of Jesus' death. Yet interpretations of his death evolve from generation to generation. Today, Jesus' death on the cross is a point of scholarly contention and the crux of the matter is this: Did Jesus die as the ultimate expression of divine love or the ultimate expression of Roman oppression? How we choose to answer this question will depend on a sound analysis of scripture and tradition as well as the personal histories we bring to the cross *as symbol*.

Everything in life is a potential symbol. By conveying meaning that is larger than the thing itself, symbols participate in — bring close — the reality to which they point. The stone I routinely carry in my pocket may be just another stone to someone else, but to me it symbolizes the beauty of Iona, Scotland, and the profound faith-experiences I had there in the late 1980s. Images — like my stone — become symbols when they become storytellers, calling us to remember who we are as we look below the surface of our everyday lives for new understanding. The key to being open to the life-energy symbols convey, however, is the recognition that our lived experience forms the interpretative matrix from which our symbol-stories arise.

Our communication with each other depends heavily on our ability to respect the storytellers among us as well as the diversity of our stories. When we recognize that our own lived truths may not be universally true, and that another's story, though not relevant to us, contains its own truths, then we are able to bridge our differences and form communities where unity exists even in the midst of our diversity. At the same time, if we forget the prophetic words of Micah and fail to walk humbly with God (and all of God's creation), then our communities quickly become breeding grounds for intolerance. Likewise our churches can become enclaves where difference is feared rather than honored.

Mindfulness in the Service of Faith

Distinctions between mindfulness and mindlessness may allow us to see why miscommunication stalks our symbol-making and symbol-sharing

28. James Carroll, *Constantine's Sword: The Church and the Jews, a History* (Boston: Houghton Mifflin, 2001), 3–12.

connections. Mindfulness is one way of naming the gifts of a liberated imagination open to the diversity of lived experience. Mindfulness is a form of attentiveness to the present moment. All mystics cultivate mindfulness in opening themselves to the immanence of divine presence. But one need not be a mystic in the traditional sense to cultivate awareness. In Christian worship attentiveness allows us to experience the presence of Christ, in the Word, in the presider, in sacramental elements, and in the community. Likewise, our attentiveness to the Spirit's presence in the ordinary moments of life matters more than we know.[29] Mindfulness makes one

- open to new information
- willing to create new categories of thought
- open to more than one perspective
- able to foster differing points of view

When we are mindful, we live in the present moment, not the past. As such we are better able to receive new information. We are also able to take the new information on its own terms rather than plugging it into outdated categories. As a result new paradigms such as the Copernican view that the earth revolved around the sun and not vice versa could come to consciousness years before it could ever be supported by Galileo's observations. Mindfulness allows us to consider more than one perspective, such as light being made of particles and waves. Likewise it allows us to entertain differing viewpoints, rather than reject outright what we cannot understand.

Mindfulness also encourages an appreciation of context and an awareness that attributes need not be seen as absolutes. Depending on the context, then, something may be a disability, a liability, or an asset. When mindfulness is present, individuals focus on process rather than outcome — on the game, not the score; they also think beyond their present context and entertain new ways of looking at difficult issues. In contrast, mindlessness demonstrates a lack of awareness or faulty imagining that manifests

- a narrow and inhibiting self-image
- unintended cruelty toward others
- a loss of control in our lives that prevents us from making intelligent choices

29. Ellen J. Langer, *Mindfulness* (Reading, Mass.: Addison-Wesley, 1989); Peter E. Fink, "Perceiving the Presence of Christ," *Worship* 58, no. 1 (January 1984): 17–28.

- a limited potential (Langer's term is "stunted potential") that keeps us from reaching our fullness of being
- single-minded attitudes
- a reliance on old and often outdated categories of thought

Speculation may be one aspect of the mindfulness process, but a willingness to put one's speculations to the test and question long-held assumptions is what ultimately produces startling innovations. For example, imagine "a biologist looking in scalding hot-springs for clues to the origin of life; an astrophysicist searching evidence of the 'antigravity' force that Einstein once dismissed; and a neuroscientist studying how the brain, despite what all the textbooks said, *can grow* new cells."[30] To be mindful means choosing where to pay attention, embodying new ways of thinking and receiving new information. When we practice mindfulness we receive life's creative fullness.

Nature and Grace

Despite the limited horizons of human thought, there is an intimate union between nature and grace that cannot be undone, for "each creature in its essential or natural being, as itself, is a 'symbol' of the presence of the holy."[31] Accordingly, we become iconic images of God and mediate the mystery of being as we practice mindfulness and live imaginatively. At the same time, we risk being separated in thought *but not in essence* from the truths of our own nature.

At its best, Christian worship ought to awaken the creative and relational energy that is the ground of our being and the source of our creativity. And yet, in its eucharistic expressions, Christian worship often disconnects us from our deepest selves. Archaic language, a heavy focus on sin and guilt, the suggestion of personal unworthiness, as well as a strong focus on the elements of bread and wine as the *only* vehicles of divine presence all function as *anticommunion* representations. By denying our original communion with creation, these attributes keep us focused on individual limitations rather than divine transformation.

Imagination, Judgment, and Social Context

Kelleher argues that our social horizons — the collective meanings we receive from "society, culture, [and] community" — set limits on personal

30. "Postcards from the Edge," Innovators, Time 100: The Next Wave, *Time*, August 7, 2000, 69.

31. Langdon Gilkey, "Symbols, Meaning, and the Divine Presence," *Theological Studies* 35, no. 2 (June 1974): 256.

imagination. Imagination also determines what is made available within the various "corporate worlds of meaning" in which we operate. The positive dimensions of limit-setting allow us to filter out distractions and focus our energies. As a positive censor, imagination functions to help us discern the spirit's presence, order our lives toward well-being, and focus on what is needful. On the other hand, when social and religious forces weight our imaginations with fear, imagination becomes a negative censor.[32] In this guise, sacrificial imagery proves its potency. While frequent rehearsals of sacrificial imagery may function as a positive social censor for those who control the power of the status quo, the same imagery functions differently for subordinate individuals within a dominarchal worldview. When domination prevails, horizons narrow dramatically.

As in the case of Chile, extreme fear functions to reduce our worlds to the narrowest of meanings, where we risk becoming not just the oppressed but the oppressor. In keeping company with our fears we visit them on one another. We also draw firm boundaries between who is welcome and who is not. In the extreme, unfounded and unexamined fear encourages us to deny our relationality by seeing difference where none exists. Hitler's regime could thus sanction "the final solution" for the Jewish problem by re-imaging Jews as vermin. Likewise, the Pinochet regime tortured Marxists, not human beings.[33]

Of the many ways that censorship functions liturgically, Kelleher argues that performance is the most significant, since it is "in performance"—in enactment—that a "horizon is actually mediated."[34] Performance involves creativity and communication. It also involves being active participants rather than passive spectators. However, on the one hand, today, living as we do in a celebrity culture, it is easy to narrow the notion of performance to the field of entertainment and see it as something others do for us. Worshipers then come expecting to be entertained and look to the liturgical leader to do everything. Liturgical leaders, accustomed to such expectations, may crave the attention and power others give them. Yet when performance and leadership narrow, communication narrows too. The world of the liturgical leader can distort as well as enlighten the worldviews of those who seek their solace and direction. On the other hand, when leadership is shared and worshipers are welcomed as full participants in the liturgy, the creative and communicative elements of performance become less restrictive and more fully embodied.

As we participate in liturgical events, we open ourselves to the power

32. Kelleher, "Christian Imagination," 131–35, 144.

33. Cavanaugh, *Torture and the Eucharist,* 188.

34. Kelleher, "Christian Imagination," 135.

toward which symbols point, as well as the limits they impose. This is especially true in the case of a *classic*. Classics, whether they are text, image, ritual, symbol, or person, have the power to disclose truths that expand the sense of the possible and bestow a "realized experience of that which is essential, that which endures."[35] Describing Jesus' life, death, and resurrection as the *classic event* of God's self-disclosure, David Tracy refers to the excess of meaning within the Christ-event as past, present, and future. Nevertheless, scholars continue to designate the "cross-event," which is only one moment of revelation in the event of Christ, as the primary pattern for ethical action, liturgical formation, and self-identity.[36] In narrowing the event of Christ to the cross, however, we allow the full event of Christ to forfeit its liberating power.

Imagination orders our experience by making judgments according to the values we hold. As a socially determined power, influenced by the world around us, it both interprets the world and creates a world of meanings in which we live. The dominant images that shape our lives must therefore be tested in concrete ways to evaluate their impact on the health, vitality, and freedom of our lives and the societies we live in.[37] In order to safeguard itself from forces that would limit its engagement with the world, our becoming self must take responsibility for the imagery that governs our actions. Whenever old images are found wanting, we must be able to entertain alternative imagery for real change to follow. When undertaken in isolation, however, this task becomes daunting. To change our images, we must be willing to change our character — how we are in community — since our character establishes the context for the images we use.[38] This process cannot go forward, however, until we identify what images are true for us.

To know the name of a person in a positive sense means a relationship can be formed. But naming another's experience for them and denying the experience of the other are mechanisms of control. In Hebraic understanding, if you knew the name of your enemy you could divest them of some of their power.[39] Even today, those who critique sacrificial-atonement theories through social analysis, artistic insight, and personal reflection show this to be the case. The collective learning from their self-naming of experience — of what they truly feel and think — has allowed women

---

35. David Tracy, *The Analogical Imagination: Christian Theology and the Culture of Pluralism* (New York: Crossroad, 1987), 108, 305–38.

36. Geoffrey Wainwright, *Doxology: The Praise of God in Worship, Doctrine, and Life: A Systematic Theology* (New York: Oxford University Press, 1980), 21–23.

37. Wilder, *Theopoetic*, 103.

38. Neville, *Reconstruction*, 289, 288.

39. Roland de Vaux, *Ancient Israel*, vol. 1, *Social Institutions* (New York: McGraw-Hill Book Company, 1965), 43–46.

representing a variety of racial and ethnic identities to challenge long-held assumptions about the character of being human, and being women. As a result, more women are now able to name the harm done to them by the paradigm of "self-sacrifice" and claim alternative saving images.

The very act of naming dominarchy as the enemy creates the necessary distance for many oppressed persons to gain enough objectivity that they no longer blame themselves for the actions of others. When victims of sexual abuse reconnect with what was once done to them by another, they may finally be able to reclaim their lives and identify the source of their shame and self-hatred. Only then, perhaps, are they able to refuse to engage in suicidal acts and self-mutilation. This naming power can be ours as well, but more than hoping is required of us. We must come to know the power of praise as the language of hope; yet more importantly, we must embrace the power of praise as the language of resistance. In praising the God who genuinely seeks our well-being we say yes to life and no to dominarchy's subterfuge.

Praise as Thanksgiving and Resistance

In a liturgical context Christians offer praise and thanksgiving to the Spirit who urges them toward abundant interconnectedness. At the same time, they are called to recognize this interconnectedness as a symbol of divine creativity and experience the grace of praise itself:

> Oh speak, poet, what do you do?
> —I praise.
> But the monstrosities and the murderous days,
> how do you endure them, how do you take them?
> —I praise.
> But the anonymous, the nameless grays,
> how, poet, do you still invoke them?
> —I praise.
> What right have you, in all displays,
> in very mask, to be genuine?
> —I praise.
> And that the stillness and the turbulent sprays
> know you like star and storm?
> —since I praise![40]

40. Rainer Maria Rilke's "The Poet Speaks of Praising" is reprinted from John J. L. Mood, *Rilke on Love and Other Difficulties: Translations and Considerations of Rainer Maria Rilke* (New York: W. W. Norton, 1975), 65; printed by permission of W. W. Norton & Company, Inc., copyright ©1975 by W. W. Norton & Company, Inc.

The redemptive power of praise is the power to commune with stillness and star, spray, and storm. It is the power to know the communion of God in Christ-Christa and to be blessed by that knowing with new life. When our worship is grounded in a liturgical theology of praise and thanksgiving, we say yes to God's healing grace and befriending love revealed in the life-work of Jesus. We also open ourselves to the hope-filled presence of God experienced through communion and community. To know the power of praise, one must know the power of the imagination, for imagination opens us to the world of possibilities inherent in God's gift of creation — a world where play, dreams, and poetry unite us with the wonder of God. Fully awakened to the power of God's presence within us and fully conscious of our interconnectedness with all of creation, our liberated imaginations widen our hearts in love and well-being. It is then that self-transcendence destroys the prisons that limit the becoming self and challenge its energies.

If becoming praise-makers were as simple as going to church on Sunday morning, we might all be more praiseworthy beings; but such is not the case. Observing that praise is "not often evident in our Christian worshiping communities," Doris Donnelly suggests five potential "impediments":

- personal lives lacking in affirmation
- the absence of genuine community
- the presence of individuals who distrust emotions
- an inability to manage conflict
- a lack of self-transcendence (her term is "God-groundedness")[41]

These impediments may well be related to the side effects of mindlessness. A lack of affirmation and self-transcendence may reflect a narrow and inhibiting self-image that can undermine one's potential. The absence of genuine community may encourage single-minded attitudes and unintended cruelty. A distrust of emotions and an inability to handle conflict may contribute to a loss of control that prevents us from making intelligent choices as well as communal connections. Lastly, a lack of trust in one's emotions and the inability to deal with conflict may be a symptom of our reliance on old and often outdated categories of thought.

Donnelly rightly sees the importance of praise as "grace to us" and points us to the wisdom of C. S. Lewis, "Except where intolerable adverse conditions interfere, praise almost always seems to be inner health made audible."[42] I would push her good insights further by suggesting that a

41. Doris Donnelly, "Impediments to Praise in the Worshiping Community," *Worship* 66, no. 1 (January 1992): 40.

42. Cited in ibid., 53.

serious lack of praise in our faith communities reflects a serious lack of personal and communal well-being. Moreover, this lack of well-being reflects a serious lack of hope, which, in turn, can be traced to imaginations constrained by fear. Lack of praise thus appears to be hopelessness made visible.

In speaking of the "classic text," Tracy argues that it is produced only when imagination is "at work, in a work" — a process that "frees the creator to express the meaning" within the work itself.[43] It would seem then that our liturgies must honor our imaginative relationality to God and help us free our creative imaginations for even greater work in the service of God's incarnating love. We must be free to honor the divine gifts that we *are,* without denying our capacity to misuse the gift and dishonor the giver. It is in this sense that I speak of liturgy, particularly eucharistic liturgy, as a *classic event.* When informed by the presence of imagination — at work in the work — a liturgy grounded in praise and thanksgiving allows participants to open themselves to the transforming power of the eucharist and the beneficent God who gathers them. Through the power of God's Spirit, God's beneficence is learned in and through communion in the life of Christ-Christa.

When the image of a beneficent God orders our liturgical practices, well-being expands communal horizons. When dominarchy undermines God's beneficence, the horizons of community collapse inward. As our songs of praise ring hollow, our hopes do the same. Reformed liturgies are no exception. Today in many instances a forced solemnity robs the eucharist of the very presence we seek. While the nature of this solemnity varies from setting to setting, common signs may include the singing of slow, self-reflective music, somber-looking deacons engaged in a rigid choreography of distribution, and worshipers who sit quietly and introspectively reviewing their personal sins and praying for their own salvation. Whenever misplaced solemnity censors imagination, individualistic distortions enter our liturgies, constrict our generosity, and reduce communal horizons to self-preservation. As a consequence, God's beneficent presence becomes mired in the limitations of fear rather than the wonder of love.

For those seeking well-being, however, this option is no option. Truly redemptive liturgy makes us "realists."[44] It encourages us to imagine the real and trust our own reality. Good liturgy also enlightens us, for it shows us how we can live communal lives of abundance. Realism falters, however, whenever false and self-limiting images fail to awaken the human spirit and lead it to liberation. Self-limiting images of humanity and god-

43. Tracy, *Analogical Imagination,* 128.
44. Evelyn Underhill, *Worship* (New York: Harper & Brothers, 1936, 1957), 18.

limiting images of the divine are primary social censors that must be attended to in the re-imaging process. The fullness of God cannot be diminished; nevertheless, eucharistic liturgies often diminish our experience of God's beneficence to the detriment of our salvation. This happens through the use of scripture as well as the images that accompany the secondary scripture of our hymns and prayers.

Imago Dei and Human Representation

Our hymns and prayers, shaped as they are by sociocultural, religious, and personal dimensions of experience, convey only partial truths; hence we perceive God in representational images. Likewise, the Bible is "a *representation* of God."[45] Within the limitations of finite existence and the limited representations of scripture, each of us constructs a personal "image" of god that re-presents God for us. In turn this image determines how freely we engage the world. Although we perceive it as real, our god-representation remains an illusion.

In the latter part of the twentieth century, Karen Armstrong presented the *History of God* and Jack Miles gave us *God: A Biography*.[46] While both works are fascinating, Miles engages the representational nature of God with surprising results. Under Mile's skillful hand, the monotheistic God of the Judeo-Christian faith emerges as a cast of characters whose God-like characteristics seem more human than divine. Miles and Armstrong both understand God to be a fusion of deities incorporated by Israel into its own religious consciousness. But Miles finds God's character difficult, compelling, "addictive," and clearly unsaintly. To suit his purpose, which is to liken God to Hamlet, Miles offers a literary analysis of God's development and suggests that God "is trapped as Hamlet is trapped in himself."[47]

Following the work of creation, in Miles's analysis, the divinity of God makes an abrupt transition from a distant, powerful, and generous God to a less powerful and more vindictive character, who remains internally conflicted by good and evil impulses. This God loses interest in himself and humankind because he finds himself trapped in his own contradictions. Likewise, in Miles's view, we remain "the divided image" of "the divided original." In offering this pitiful image, Miles presents a deity many have encountered yet few understand. Thanks to the power of Augustine's

45. J. Severino Croatto, *Biblical Hermeneutics: Toward a Theory of Reading as the Production of Meaning*, trans. Robert R. Barr (Maryknoll, N.Y.: Orbis Books, 1987), 78.

46. Karen Armstrong, *A History of God: The 4000-Year Quest of Judaism, Christianity, and Islam* (New York: Alfred A. Knopf, 1994); Jack Miles, *God: A Biography* (New York: Alfred A. Knopf, 1995).

47. Miles, *God*, 408.

authority in the West, God continues to be understood as "supreme, utmost in goodness, mightiest and all-powerful, most merciful and most just." At the same time, Augustine's representational deity reveals the descriptive elements of dominarchy's separative self. Knowing that this God owes "nothing to any," many fear his wrath, even as they seek his rewards.[48] Yet something seems amiss.

Mirror, Mirror, on the Wall

Jung and Freud believed that god-images emerge from the inner world of the individual.[49] While their differing arguments have undergone critique, their basic insight prevails. Our god-representations (which are not God) are primarily, but not solely, dependent on the parental (female and male) *imagos* of our childhood — the wished-for parent and the feared parent, as well as the social and cultural environment of the child, all make contributions. Additionally, these images respond and change according to the developmental influences of human experience and the enlightening power of the Holy Spirit.[50]

Karl Barth spoke of the paradox of being both *justified* sinners and *sinners* justified through Jesus Christ; he also stressed that any theological talk about "God in man" must be "cut out at the roots."[51] We must come to terms then not only with Reformed theology's emphasis on the unworthiness of human beings *coram Deo,* before God, but also with the image of ourselves that we carry in the depths of our being. For it is both of these images — the god-limiting and self-limiting ones — that affect our ability to praise and give thanks as well as our ability to sit at table with one another and make eucharist.

The question before us is not which image is the fairest one of all. Rather we must ask ourselves how humanity's understanding of itself is influenced by god-limiting representations of God. When we call God "Father" what kind of father do we image and what is our relational experience of this image? Are we strong mature children, or do we see ourselves as small, disobedient children rebelling against God, like those Isaiah chastised? Do we become fearful of how God may treat us, or are we confident that God is ultimately beneficent, seeking only our good? Lastly, are we truly "the divided image" of the "divided original"?

48. St. Augustine, *The Confessions,* ed. E. V. Riev et al., trans. and foreword by R. S. Pine Coffin (London: Penguin Books, 1961), 23.

49. Ana-Maria Rizzuto, *The Birth of the Living God: A Psychoanalytic Study* (Chicago: University of Chicago Press, 1979).

50. Ibid., 46, 52, 78; Ann Belford Ulanov, *Picturing God* (Cambridge, Mass.: Cowley, 1986).

51. Karl Barth, introduction to Ludwig Feuerbach, *The Essence of Christianity,* trans. George Eliot and James Luther Adams (New York: Harper & Brothers, 1957), xxx.

Excavating the Eucharist

As we ask these questions and set about exploring the nature of liturgical images, we soon realize how intertwined liturgical and theological imagery has become. Nevertheless, it is often the case that the imagery of eucharist is treated separately from images of atonement and penance. With the exception of the messianic banquet, the same holds true for apocalyptic imagery. Each of these theological categories, however, has played a pivotal role in the evolution of eucharistic practice. To understand the nature of this evolution, it is helpful to construct a series of *archeological layers* and lay out the distinctive dimensions of each layer, knowing all the while how difficult it is to separate them completely.

First, we have to become aware of the personal dimensions of our own experience. Then we have to consider the archeological layers of sacramental imagery that exist in religious contexts larger than our own heritage. While we may hope to step outside of out own biases, they continue to structure our imaginative horizons. If we were to imagine the numerous theological layers whose imagery influences our views of the eucharist, the archeological strata might look something like this:

Identify one's conscious images of God/self/world
Consider the shaping influences of one's religious heritage
Acknowledge the role of scripture within one's tradition
Consider scriptural legacies regarding the "words of institution" attributed to Jesus
Reflect on the stories of Jesus' table-fellowship and his ministry of forgiveness
Explore imagery related to:
The nature and function of meals in antiquity
Apocalyptic eschatology
Interpretations of the cross-event — atonement
The nature and function of second baptism — the sacrament of penance
Consider the theological distinctions present in Eastern and Western Christianity
Consider medieval influences
Consider the eucharistic arguments of Protestant reformers
Consider the importance of the "convergence document" *BEM*
Explore contemporary scholarship in an interdisciplinary manner
Reexamine the interpretive lenses — of experience, reason, scripture, and tradition — that consciously inform one's beliefs

As we analyze the collective impact of these imagistic strata, *the medieval captivity* of contemporary eucharistic liturgies will manifest itself in greater detail. The primary function of a liberated imagination is to renew inner worlds of meaning by transforming the sensory and social data of lived experience into new patterns of well-being. In the context of a new millennium, then, my task is to demonstrate the limitations of medieval theology, show the ways this theology still shapes liturgy, and offer a constructive proposal for liturgical transformation. To demonstrate these theological limitations with some specificity, we turn now to the eucharistic rite, for within the sphere of religious imagination, the performance of this rite holds primacy of place both as enactment and proclamation.

If we truly want to have the mind (the imaginative heart-mind and soul) of Christ-Christa among us, we must frame our worship lives differently and celebrate divine relationality more intentionally. If we do, I have no doubt that our communal lives will be transformed and our liturgies transforming. Were we to tell the truths of our lives, and enact those truths liturgically, our eucharistic feasts might well be the unique moment where the Spirit comes to make all things new. Imagine!

FOUR

Praying as Believing

> The Lord's Supper in most of our churches... is a solemn affair marked by sad, mournful, even morbid thoughts associated with death. It is more like a fast than a feast.... Could the root cause of our gloomy melancholy services be due to the fact that we have lost the sense of the presence of the risen, living Lord and the sense of his imminent return? —*Arthur C. Cochrane*[1]

> If torture is the imagination of the state, the Eucharist is the imagination of the church. —*William T. Cavanaugh*[2]

Orthodox eucharistic praxis presents itself as being faithful to Jesus' "words of institution" and the imagery of "This is my body.... This is my blood." Remembered as the "Lord's Supper," this event is presented as the cornerstone of a seamless tradition from the "Last Supper" experience of Jesus to our meals of remembrance today. While church bulletins often announce our "celebration" of the sacrament of Holy Communion, Cochrane's observation regarding "gloomy melancholy services" belies the notion of joy and thanksgiving that is *artificially* attached to this memorial meal. We speak of joy and yet many of our "celebrations" are solemn and funereal. Alone in their self-reflections, bound to their pews, surrounded by mournful music, participants receive little encouragement, if any, to understand the relational nature of life and their own role in incarnating God's love. Is this what Jesus meant by the words, "Do this in remembrance of me"? I think not.

Worshipers need to understand the issues that scholars of liturgy and the Christian Scriptures have been engaged in for some time. Uncensored by religious dogma they have asked critical questions: Has the celebration of this rite actually followed a seamless path from Jesus to us? If not, what historical influences have shaped the way it has been "celebrated"?

1. Arthur C. Cochrane, *Eating and Drinking with Jesus: An Ethical and Biblical Inquiry* (Philadelphia: Westminster Press, 1974), 74.

2. William T. Cavanaugh, *Torture and Eucharist: Theology, Politics, and the Body of Christ* (Oxford: Blackwell, 1998), 229.

What images have had a lasting impact? And why do Mark, Matthew, Paul, and Luke have different versions, while John has no last meal ritual? Different names alert us to the presence of liturgical diversity: Lord's Supper, Last Supper, eucharist, and Holy Communion. Each image in turn conjures up a variety of associations. Notions of thanksgiving and remembrance, connection, and presence come to mind. Yet what are we to make of the somberness that many experience? More importantly, why do so many still abstain from the simple acts of eating and drinking together in Christ's name? These are but some of the questions this chapter will explore. We will look at Reformation patterns, lines of convergence in *BEM*, and contemporary postscripts that challenge past assumptions about sacrificial imagery. In particular we will expose the fault lines present in the words of institution, Passover meal imagery, and the much-touted imagery of Christ's messianic banquet. Above all we will identify images that affect our view of bodies — social and human — as well as associations of images that lend themselves to mindlessness and lack of praise. For far too long the eucharist (the practice of *prayer* as thanksgiving) has borne the burden of atonement (the *belief* that God and humankind no longer live in at-one-ment, save for the death of Jesus). Identifying how we got to this point is the focus of this chapter.

Praying and Believing: What Difference Do They Make?

The Latin axiom *lex orandi, lex credendi,*[3] "the rule of prayer orders the rule of belief," refers to how liturgical practice shaped church doctrine. For example, the threefold pattern of baptismal questions (Do you believe in God? Do you believe in Jesus Christ? Do you believe in the Holy Spirit?) illustrates how baptism contributed to the development of Trinitarian doctrine. On the other hand, *lex orandi, lex credendi* can also mean "belief orders prayer." A noteworthy example of this involves the anti-Arian response, when prayers were reformulated to honor the divinity of Christ and guard against any attempts to explain the Son as being subordinate to the Father. The doxology "Glory to the Father through the Son in the Holy Spirit" was transformed in the West to read "Glory to the Father *and* the Son *and* the Holy Spirit."[4] The simple addition of "and"

3. Geoffrey Wainwright, *Doxology: The Praise of God in Worship, Doctrine, and Life: A Systematic Theology* (New York: Oxford University Press, 1980), chaps. 7 and 8.

4. Josef A. Jungmann, *The Early Liturgy: To the Time of Gregory the Great,* Liturgical Series, no. 6, trans. Francis A. Brunner (Notre Dame, Ind.: University of Notre Dame Press, 1959), 192, 193.

put greater stress on Christ's divinity. Unfortunately it had a detrimental effect on the religious mentality of most believers. Worshipers found themselves surrounded by images that stressed their separation from God rather than the more accessible imagery of Jesus their brother. This alteration, as well as the Arian controversy preceding it, severely fragmented the community's ongoing relationship with Jesus' humanity.

As significant as these changes were, however, they followed a greater shift. Luke pictured early Christians as gathering in one another's homes to give thanks and commune with the risen Christ in their midst (Acts 2:42–46). However, several years earlier, the apostle Paul had significantly shifted the imagery of Christianity's communal meal from the *risen* Christ to the *coming* Christ. Using the doctrinal lenses of salvation and the Second Coming to shape the practice of the Corinthian church, Paul instructed his followers that "for as often as you eat this bread and drink the cup, you proclaim the Lord's death until he comes."[5] The importance of this shift lies in its apocalyptic roots.

While Paul's version is the only one to use this exact phrasing, Matthew, Mark, and Luke all point to an eschatological future kingdom where Jesus will once again eat and drink. Significantly, this kingdom comes forcefully, not silently, heralding consequences that still reverberate in Christianity's collective psyche. Cochrane bemoans the lost sense of the presence of the risen, living Lord as well as the lost sense of Jesus' imminent return. The expectation of Jesus' return in glory, which is tied to Jesus' use of the Son of man imagery in Mark 13, is an apocalyptic refrain that is intimately tied to the notion of Christ's sacrifice for our sins — the same sacrifice that became atonement's central pillar.

The variety of images historically associated with the eucharist demonstrates the critical relationship between imagination (belief) and ritual (prayer). These images include:[6]

- a Passover meal
- Jesus' death on the cross
- the atoning and saving death of Jesus imaged as a sacrifice
- our participation in this event as a memorial
- our communion with Christ as a personal encounter
- a somber supper where we recall our past sin and guilt and ponder the cost of salvation

5. Wainwright, *Doxology*, 253.

6. Robert L. Browning and Roy A. Reed, *The Sacraments in Religious Education and Liturgy: An Ecumenical Model* (Birmingham, Ala.: Religious Education Press, 1985), 168; adapted by permission of Religious Education Press.

Having dominated interpretations of the eucharist for centuries, this imagery has been altered dramatically to embrace new meanings:

- the power of resurrection and the presence of the risen Christ
- a foretaste of the feast we will experience with Christ when he returns
- Christ as host of a present celebration
- the future and the coming of God's realm
- communion as fellowship with Christ
- the supper as a feast of thanksgiving

This shift from somberness to joy and from sacrifice to thanksgiving was due in part to the recovery of a sense of joy and anticipation that were present in eucharistic prayers regarding the hope of Jesus' return.[7] Nevertheless, in far too many instances, local church practice continues to be captivated by the earlier images of cross and death.

Likewise, efforts to loosen the stranglehold this imagery has on Christian imagination are hampered by churches that retain the motif of sacrifice for the sake of ecumenical convergence. *BEM* represented a fifty-year process of study designed to demonstrate the extent to which theological differences in doctrine and practice had lessened as a result of Faith and Order's efforts. The commission thus hoped to reflect "the common Christian Tradition on essential elements of Christian communion."[8]

The exploration of theological differences is always a praiseworthy effort, and this one was no exception. Nevertheless, whenever the "teachings of the universal church" remain the criteria for living in communion, orthodox tradition continues to exert undo influence and authority. While no ecclesiastical body was asked to agree with everything being said in *BEM*, the document still affirms a heavy emphasis on Jesus' death as sacrifice, although the manner in which this imagery relates to a particular denominational eucharist may vary.

If a true alternative to sacrificial imagery is to be found, however, ecumenical consensus cannot be our first priority. Theological communion when tied to a unified eucharist seems misguided, since orthodox arguments claiming that only one authoritative tradition exists have been soundly challenged by contemporary biblical, liturgical, and historical scholarship. Many will construe my argument as an impediment to the ecumenical movement, since celebrating the eucharist as "one church" has been a driving force of ecumenism. However, it is not my intent to

7. Geoffrey Wainwright, *Eucharist and Eschatology*, 2d ed. (London: Epworth Press, 1978).

8. *Baptism, Eucharist and Ministry*, Faith and Order Paper no. 111 (Geneva: World Council of Churches, 1982), ix.

undermine the important strides that the World Council of Churches and other ecumenical bodies have achieved in their quest to break down dividing walls of religious hostility. My chief concern has to do with any suggestion that only one particular form of the feast — one rooted in sacrificial imagery — is authentically Christian. Ecumenism is a worthy goal, if, in my view, it fosters an acceptance of diversity rather than conformity. Jesus' prayer "that they might all be one" (John 17:11) does not mean we must all be the same.

The Limits of Convergence

According to *BEM*, the presence of Christ is the center of the eucharist. His presence is mediated to us by the Holy Spirit, which God sends in response to the church's prayers. The bread and wine thus become sacramental signs of Christ's body and blood by virtue of the living word of Christ in the "words of institution" and the power of the Spirit. Yet nourishment comes not only by Christ's presence in the eucharistic bread and wine but also through "communion within the body of Christ which is the church." By virtue of the reconciliation and sharing demanded by our eucharistic celebration, our sharing in the body and blood of Christ radically challenges the injustice present in our social, economic, and political relationships. Having been reconciled in the eucharist, Christians are also to be witnesses of the joy of resurrection and signs of the love of Christ in the world.[9] Worthy goals, indeed! Yet when we push the imagery of the eucharist further, problematic connections arise. While regarded as *one complete act,* the eucharist in its fullness is considered in *BEM* under five distinct but *inseparable* perspectives: thanksgiving to the Father, memorial of Christ, invocation of the Spirit, communion of the faithful, and meal of the Kingdom.[10] Within these distinctions, however, sacrificial imagery takes center stage.

Uniting word and sacrament, the eucharist is fundamentally a "proclamation and a celebration of the work of God" and the "benediction by which the Church expresses its thankfulness for all God's benefits." It is here that the first reference to sacrificial language appears. The eucharist is the "*great sacrifice of praise*" offered through Christ on behalf of the whole creation. The bread and wine are then designated as fruits of the earth and of human labor, presented to God in faith and thanksgiving. Within the discussion of the "memorial of Christ," this memorial is linked primarily with the crucified and risen Christ as the "living and effective sign of his

9. Ibid., 11–16.
10. Ibid., 10–15.

sacrifice, accomplished once and for all on the cross and still operative on behalf of humankind." Here Christ is understood to be the great high priest and intercessor, granting communion with himself, as the church offers itself to God. As members of the body of Christ, we offer ourselves as a "living and holy sacrifice in our daily lives" and are "sanctified and reconciled in love" to be "servants of reconciliation in the world." The self-offering of Christ is thus juxtaposed in the eucharist with the self-offering of the church.[11]

When connected with the Passover memorial of Israel as the "new paschal meal," the eucharist becomes the "anamnesis of Jesus' death and resurrection, and the anticipation of the Supper of the Lamb (Rev. 19:9)." It is also a sign of the kingdom, when viewed in conjunction with the meals Jesus shared in his earthly ministry and those related to resurrection appearances. While many find the meal of the kingdom to be a compelling alternative to sacrificial metaphors, we must not lose sight of the inseparability of these perspectives. It is not the case that we may choose one over the other, thinking that the more distressing imagery of sacrifice will easily disappear.

BEM sought to effect reconciliation in the face of Reformation arguments that pitted the reformers' eucharistic view of "sacrifice proclaimed" over against Rome's more active view of "sacrifice offered." Nevertheless, it has become clear that no single view of the eucharist ever existed. It is also clear that sacrifice is not a primary concept of interpretation. David Power has argued that sacrifice is "not a necessary category for the interpretation of Christ's death, for an interpretation of the life of the Christian reborn in the Spirit, or for an interpretation of the eucharistic action, however rooted it may be in the religious imagination."[12] Robert Daly, on the other hand, has sought to clarify the origins of Christian sacrificial language, arguing that early Christians stressed the ethical dimensions of sacrifice — the inner disposition of obedience and love — rather than the material dimensions. Following the act of Christ's self-giving love, Daly concluded, Christian sacrifice centered not on acts within worship but on the everyday practical life of Christian virtue. In speaking of the sacrifice of Christ, themselves as the new temple, and their own lives as sacrificial, early Christians stressed the value of sacrifice as obedient piety.[13] In the context of an imperial church, however, the efficacy of obedient piety de-

11. Ibid., 12.

12. David N. Power, "The Anamnesis: Remembering, We Offer," in *New Eucharistic Prayers: An Ecumenical Study of Their Development and Structure,* ed. Frank C. Senn (Mahwah, N.J.: Paulist Press, 1987), 165–66.

13. Robert J. Daly, *The Origins of the Christian Doctrine of Sacrifice* (Philadelphia: Fortress Press, 1978), 1–10, 135.

serves to be questioned — Was it a beneficial model for all Christians or only those on the upper echelons of power's hierarchy?

The essential understanding of the eucharist is that it is the "sacrament of the gift which God makes to us in Christ through the power of the Holy Spirit." The gift of salvation received through communion with Christ, in the eating and drinking of the bread and wine, offers each baptized member of the body of Christ the "assurance of the forgiveness of sins" and the "pledge of eternal life."[14] However, these promises have more to do with a theology of fear than grace. When we review the sacrament of penance, it will become clear that these promises refer to the fear of God's wrath and the possibility of eternal punishment — signature marks of a punitive god whose modus operandi is sacrifice.

While contemporary scholarship has sought to dispel the dominant notion that the eucharist was a Passover meal and reclaim the motif of resurrection, the image of the Last Supper and the Gospel accounts of how Jesus died keep sacrificial imagery fully present. This imagery tends to dominate our thinking in part because of the liturgical use of the words of institution and the authority of scripture. Given the weight of history portraying sacrifice as an essential interpretation, many will find it difficult to embrace alternative views. Nevertheless, because *BEM*'s presentation is theological rather than historical, attention to three constellations of imagery can help us uncover the layers that now burden contemporary understandings of Holy Communion. These images are connected with

- the not so "normative" status of the words of institution and the shift from a meal of sacred friendship to sacred food
- the image of a Passover meal and the notion of sacrifice
- the eschatological banquet, the foretaste of the kingdom, and apocalyptic thinking

The Words of Institution

The earliest reference to the supper is attributed to Paul in his First Letter to the Corinthians (chap. 11), but of the four versions attested in scripture (Matthew, Mark, Luke, and Paul), two — Matthew 26:26–29 and 1 Corinthians 11:23–26 — have emerged as the most favored liturgically. And even here diversity is present. Matthew has the only reference to Jesus' blood being shed "for the forgiveness of sins," and Paul is the only one to associate the meal celebration with the proclamation of the "Lord's death

14. *Baptism, Eucharist and Ministry*, no. 10.

until he comes."[15]On the basis of the differences that exist among the four versions concerning the bread and the cup, the omission of reference to the bread and cup in John's Gospel, and the complex Greco-Roman banquet tradition that preceded early Christian meals, the uniqueness of Jesus' last meal with his disciples has undergone major revision. While many argue that we must retain the Passover meal imagery because of its association with Jesus' self-sacrifice (as the Passover Lamb), others argue that a wider context of interpretation exists. The Last Supper, according to the latter group of scholars, must now be understood to share affinities with a common-meal tradition that was adapted by different groups to fit multiple social settings and multiple meal experiences, all of which contributed to the formation of early Christian meal liturgy. Thus the argument is made that there is "no one original meal moment to which the churches can appeal."[16]

Dennis Smith and Hal Taussig argue that each of the eucharistic sayings has a different subtext. Mark emphasizes "the cup of martyrdom." Matthew idealizes "the heroes of the faith" and the sacrificial theology of the Old Testament, and Luke (in his short version) shifts from the emphasis on Jesus' death to "the future consummation" of God's plan. The breaking of bread thus becomes symbolic of unity in Luke's community and the eschatological banquet that awaits all believers. In the Johannine community and in the Pauline documents, the evidence also points to several distinct meal traditions and their adaptation over time. In every instance, however, the communal meal functioned to define social boundaries binding the community together.[17] Within these social boundaries, social rankings were clearly evident. However, even with these distinctions, it is clear that the social dimensions of sharing food and drink, rather than cultic ritual, provided the essential conditions for the celebration of early Christian eucharistic meals. The power of these meals was thus the communication of the Holy Spirit through *a set of relationships* formed and shared with one another when Christians gathered at table.[18]

---

15. Cheslyn Jones, Geoffrey Wainwright, Edward Yarnold, and Paul Bradshaw, *The Study of Liturgy*, rev. ed. (New York: Oxford University Press, 1978), 195–96.

16. Dennis E. Smith and Hal E. Taussig, *Many Tables: The Eucharist in the New Testament and Liturgy Today* (Philadelphia: Trinity Press International, 1990), 74; Willi Marxsen, *The Lord's Supper as a Christological Problem,* trans. Lorenz Nieting, Facet Books Biblical Series, no. 25 (Philadelphia: Fortress Press, 1970).

17. Smith and Taussig, *Many Tables,* 68–69.

18. Elisabeth Schüssler Fiorenza, "Tablesharing and the Celebration of the Eucharist," in *Can We Always Celebrate the Eucharist?* ed. Mary Collins and David Power, *Concilium* 152 (New York: Seabury Press, 1982), 10; Robert Banks, *Paul's Idea of Community: The Early House Churches in Their Historical Setting* (Grand Rapids, Mich.: William B. Eerdmans, 1980), 111, 118; Elisabeth Schüssler Fiorenza, *In Memory of Her: A Feminist Theological Reconstruction of Christian Origins* (New York: Crossroad, 1983), 345.

Fellowship and Food

The importance of the meal as a communal event of transformation and solidarity is also found in the arguments of John Dominic Crossan and Bruce Chilton, both of whom highlight the importance of sharing a meal (commensality) in Jesus' ministry. For Crossan the distinguishing mark of Jesus' saving activity is the *healing* that Jesus occasions through specific acts of healing and exorcism and, most especially, through the fellowship of the meal itself. Through the very act of eating together with those who were considered by society to be sinners and outcasts, Jesus embodied the loving acceptance of God and encouraged others to experience it for themselves. In Crossan's view, Jesus' great transgression was his willingness to challenge the social ranking system of his day, including the Mediterranean system of honor and shame that complemented institutional arrangements for the distribution of power and the creation of order in the Greco-Roman and Judaic world. Combining a strategy of "free healing and common eating," Jesus, according to Crossan, encouraged "a religious and economic egalitarianism" that negated the discriminating "normalcies of Jewish religion and Roman power," as well as "civilizations' eternal inclination to draw lines, invoke boundaries, establish hierarchies, and maintain discriminations."[19] One of the central convictions held by Christians throughout the history of Christianity involves Jesus' welcoming of the outcast and his searching for the lost on God's behalf. In this context, Crossan's views on meal sharing strike a convincing chord.

Chilton rejects Crossan's depiction of Jesus as a "Cynic philosopher" and has his own views regarding Jesus' practice of meals as "celebrations of the kingdom" and as "replacements" of temple sacrifice. Yet he supports Crossan's view that "the nature of [Jesus'] concern [with what was pure] and the character of his meals were distinctive in their inclusiveness."[20] Chilton also makes the case that the experience of the meals as well as the cultural and religious leanings of Jesus' followers generated multiple meanings for the eucharistic celebrations that emerged in a post-resurrection world. Likewise, these multiple meanings were tied to the various identities by which Jesus was imaged and re-membered by the various postresurrection communities:

- For Peter's followers, Jesus was "donor of the Spirit," and the meals became signs of covenant renewal.

---

19. John Dominic Crossan, *The Historical Jesus: The Life of a Mediterranean Jewish Peasant* (San Francisco: HarperCollins, 1991), xii, 14, 303–53, 422.

20. Bruce Chilton, *Jesus' Prayer and Jesus' Eucharist: His Personal Practice of Spirituality* (Valley Forge, Pa.: Trinity Press International, 1997), 58.

- For the circle of James, Jesus was the son of David, and the meals were "Passovers that restored the house of David."
- For Paul, he was the new Adam, and the meals were "festivals of a new Israel."
- For Matthew, Mark, Luke, and John, Jesus was the apocalyptic messenger, the Son of man whose meal became "feasts of salvation."

When we appreciate the role of imagination, we can appreciate Chilton's observation that just as none of these is wrong, "none of them is exclusively right."[21] What we see working, even from the earliest Christian practices, is humans' capacity to "make meanings" consistent with their lived experience and dependent on their social and cultural contexts. The same influences continue to shape our lives today.

Paul made no effort to tie this meal to cultic activity. The setting of the meal was a home, and *no priestly celebrants* are ever in view.[22] Nevertheless, the evolution of the meal's content and the designation of what is holy are fascinating. From Paul's account to John's, the transformation moves from a meal where the participants eat with Jesus to a meal where Jesus is eaten. When we put the two earliest stories of the eucharist together, those recorded in 1 Corinthians 11 and Mark 14, a clear shift emerges. Paul's celebration points to a pre-Pauline actual meal tradition with the emphasis on breaking bread together and its representation of the *cup as the new covenant,* not its contents. The later Markan text reveals that *bread and wine,* not table sharing, are the focus. The final transformation appears in John 6. Where Paul used the ecclesial word *soma* to stand for the bread as the body of Christ, John now uses the fleshly word *sarx.* Thus John has Jesus say: "Whoever eats my *flesh* and drinks my *blood* has eternal life."

The eucharistic transformation from sacred fellowship to sacred food is now complete, and the notion of sacrifice is unmistakable.[23] As Jews ate the Passover Lamb, so Christians eat Jesus. Despite the fact that Jesus offers no allusions to the specifics of a Passover meal in the four accounts of the Last Supper, interpretations of Jesus as the Lamb of God persist. Could it be that sacrificial imagery was reinforced in the collective imagination of Christianity by the influx of those who, though steeped in sacrificial practices, had suffered the loss of their liturgical center — the Temple? Luke's singular reference in Acts 6:7 is worth noting: "And a great many of the priests were obedient to the faith." We shall return to this influx of

21. Ibid., 94–97.
22. Banks, *Paul's Idea,* 84–85.
23. Marxsen, *The Lord's Supper,* 14.

priests in a later chapter; but for now we turn to Passover imagery and its eucharistic relevance.

Passover Meal?

In his classic study *The Eucharistic Words of Jesus,* Joachim Jeremias argues that Jesus' last meal was a Passover meal and that Jesus himself applied Passover theology to an interpretation of his death. Jeremias also argues that the crucifixion could have taken place legitimately on the festival, but on this point few scholars are convinced.

In light of the meal's intimate association with Jesus' return in glory to "judge the living and the dead," I would urge caution in joining the eucharist with the Passover meal. Jeremias is clear in his concluding remarks that when table-fellowship with Jesus is viewed as a Passover meal, it is viewed as "an anticipatory gift of the final consummation."[24] Yet we know that no distinctively paschal features such as the unleavened bread, the lamb, or the bitter herbs were used. Instead Jesus chose only "the bread and cup of normal festal custom."[25]

Scholars also speak to the chronological and linguistic difficulties in making the association of this meal with the Passover. The chronological difficulties relate to the assertions found in Matthew, Mark, and Luke that the meal is a Passover meal, observed on the evening before the festival, while John's Gospel insists that Jesus was crucified before the Passover and died along with the lambs (John 18:28; 19:14, 36). The earliest Christian allusion to Passover is found in 1 Corinthians 5:7–8a when Paul proclaims: "For our paschal lamb, Christ, has been sacrificed. Therefore, let us celebrate the festival." However, scholars argue that this basic image, thrown out with no explanation by Paul, may have been interpreted in two ways. John, without an account of the meal, applies this image to the death while Matthew, Mark, and Luke apply the image to the meal at which the death was interpreted as a sacrifice.[26]

In *Bread of Life and Cup of Joy,* historian Horton Davies supports Passover imagery by suggesting that the elimination of Passover details from Paul and the Synoptic writers relates to their concern that Jewish converts not be confused. On the other hand, Davies also suggests that the details of the Passover, including its acts and prayers, were so familiar

24. Joachim Jeremias, *The Eucharistic Words of Jesus,* trans. Norman Perrin, 3d ed. (New York: Charles Scribner's Sons, 1966), 262.

25. Jones et al., *The Study of Liturgy,* 197.

26. Ibid., 197–98.

to Jewish disciples that they did not need to be reported.[27] I suspect, however, that the silence of these accounts has more to do with what Jesus didn't say than with what he did.

As liturgical scholars have discovered, the ability of sources in the Christian Scriptures to project later liturgical developments is quite limited. For example, it now appears that Passover may not have become a true family meal until after 70 C.E. and that pluriformity outweighed uniformity in early eucharistic gatherings. As Paul Bradshaw concludes: "it seems probable that there was considerable variation not only in the theological emphases within the different traditions but also in the structural details of the rite and perhaps even in the frequency of its celebrations."[28] Bradshaw confirms what Willi Marxsen argued long before women theologians raised the issue of eucharistic interpretation: "There is no *one* Lord's Supper in the New Testament; there are various Lord's Suppers and there is a history of the Lord's Supper."[29] Taken together these observations undermine the primacy of Passover imagery. At the same time they fail to appreciate the impact such imagery has when it is rehearsed liturgically as the dominant motif.

The Case for Sacrifice

As previously noted, Robert Daly believes Jesus' sacrifice fundamentally altered the way Christians ethically ordered their lives. In his view, the full-blown sacrificial theology of Origen in the second century merely elaborates what is already present in Pauline theology and amply reinforced by the Gospels, the Letter to the Hebrews, and other texts in the Christian Scriptures. Daly argues that the later controversial developments, whereby the eucharist is a sacrifice that can be offered only by an ordained priest in a fully cultic sacrifice, are, in fact, preceded by a New Testament soteriology that stresses the life of sacrifice that individual Christian believers offer in the context of their own practical (noncultic) life-experiences.

Sacrificial theology thus reaches far into the mythology of the Hebrew Scriptures, coming to rest at the altar experience of Abraham and Isaac. Daly calls the binding (the *Akedah*) of Isaac the "great 'founding' sacrifice of the Old Testament."[30] The historical origins of the story are obscure, residing only with the Elohist, whose narrative exists in Genesis 22:1–19.

---

27. Horton Davies, *Bread of Life and Cup of Joy: Newer Ecumenical Perspectives on the Eucharist* (Grand Rapids, Mich.: William B. Eerdmans, 1993), 13–16.

28. Paul F. Bradshaw, *The Search for the Origins of Christian Worship* (New York: Oxford University Press, 1992), 54.

29. Marxsen, *The Lord's Supper*, 14, 33.

30. Robert Daly, *Origins*, 47.

However, Daly believes the essential background of sacrificial soteriology in the Christian Scriptures can be found within the Jewish (haggadic) development of the *Akedah* in which the voluntary self-immolation of Isaac, the mature man, emerges as a central construct. Daly thus understands the free consent of Isaac to be a model for the salvation-by-sacrifice doctrine that was developed by Paul and other New Testament writers. Again his primary objective is to make the case that the *inner disposition* of the believer is of central importance, even though Judaism made no such association between the *Akedah* and its liturgical practice.

There is, Daly argues, a spiritualizing trend (regarding internal religious/ethical dispositions) in the development of sacrificial imagery that is superseded by the institutionalizing trend (an actual offering) of the hierarchical church's eucharistic praxis. What Daly has done is demonstrate the potential for embellishment that can take place both in the haggadic development of the *Akedah* and in the Christian interpretation of Jesus' crucifixion. Although he was used as a model for Jews during the Crusades whose choice was convert or die, Isaac is not used as a model for ordinary human behavior in Judaism. Likewise, the Orthodox Jews' tradition of reading the *Akedah* in every morning service started in the thirteenth century C.E., not the first. In contrast, the "sacrifice of Isaac" functioned as a central theme in early Christian art, at least from the time of Constantine.[31]

Gordon Lathrop, following Justin Martyr's metaphoric and purposeful use of the term "sacrifice" to distinguish the Christian meal from ritual killing, agrees that sacrifice is the "wrong word" for what we are about in this meal. Nevertheless, precisely because it is the wrong word, he is convinced it has revelatory power. Christian sacrifice is "no sacrifice at all" (in the literal sense). "It is a meal, a sharing of food in thanksgiving."[32]

Lathrop argues for the continued use of sacrificial terminology in the eucharist while insisting that we must constantly seek to break and convert its power. Yet he is quick to acknowledge that this option is not as easy as it sounds because many people still think Christianity has to do with "giving to God" and "doing violence for God." Insightfully he writes: "For us to newly criticize the pervasive language of sacrifice, requiring its transformation, will be for us to newly open ourselves to transformations in the meanings of Christian worship, of the death of Christ, of Christian

31. Robert J. Daly, *Christian Sacrifice: The Judaeo-Christian Background before Origen* (Washington, D.C.: Catholic University of America Press, 1978), 182–86; conversation with Rabbi Margaret Moers Wenig, March 5, 1993. Robin M. Jensen, "How Jews and Christians See Differently: The Binding or Sacrifice of Isaac," *Bible Review* (October 1993): 46.

32. Gordon W. Lathrop, "Justin, Eucharist, and 'Sacrifice': A Case of Metaphor," *Worship* 64 (January 1990): 43.

ethics and of the human relationship to the created world." Precisely my point! Lathrop fails to carry through with the power of his own insight. *Wrong words* remain, in his view, "stunningly revelatory."[33] It is one thing to say that Justin's use of the term "sacrifice" had revelatory power in the context of other sacrificial acts of worship *in Justin's time,* and another thing entirely to speak of sacrifice as being a "revelatory" word *in our time.* The metaphor of sacrifice now carries with it a history that has witnessed the neglect of the poor, the oppression of women and other nondominant peoples, and, most disturbing of all, a failure on the part of Christianity to recognize its own complicity in the suffering of others.

Chilean bishops who suffered bodily under Pinochet's rule proclaimed proudly: "We give thanks to the Lord for this privileged opportunity to experience in our own flesh the sufferings of so many who cannot defend themselves like a Bishop can."[34] But as Cavanaugh reminds us, by the time the Catholic Church in Chile forcefully resisted the dictatorship and refused to be complicit in the suffering of the Chilean people, its efforts did nothing to alter the thousands of disappearances the regime had already orchestrated. Although the coup began in September 1973, it was not until the late 1980s that the church moved from being the "mystical body of Christ" to the "real body of Christ" and was able to mount any significant resistance to the regime's crimes. While Cavanaugh credits sacrificial imagery as the key to this transformation, one can also wonder if the same imagery obscured the need for transformation in the first place.

Sacrificium Laudis: The Sacrifice of Praise

At first glance it would appear that the critiques of sixteenth-century Protestant reformers opened the door to a full-scale assault on the influence of sacrificial imagery. However, this is not the case. Even as they argued against the priestly repetition of Christ's sacrifice in the mass, Luther, Zwingli, and Calvin presented three distinctive eucharistic views united by their shared interpretation of Jesus' death as a sacrifice. Luther was crystal clear in his denunciation of the mass as a repeated sacrifice, yet he never wavered from the view that *Christ's death* was a sacrifice for our benefit and the sign of a gracious God. Relying on the Letter to the Hebrews, he argued that the only sacrifice present in the Christian Scriptures was the once-for-all sacrifice of the cross (Heb. 10:10) and the sacrifice

33. Ibid., 47, 48.
34. Cited in Cavanaugh, *Torture and Eucharist,* 106.

of praise (Heb. 13:15), although in his commentary on Hebrews he also spoke of "faith in Christ" as a "sacrifice pleasing to God."[35]

Zwingli spoke of the Lord's Supper as a *spiritual memorial* of the death of Christ and a "memorial of thanksgiving." He argued, based on Hebrews 6–10, that "since Christ has suffered only once the death on the cross, thus he also has been sacrificed only once. His dying is his sacrifice for us, and his sacrifice is his dying."[36] Calvin concurred with the sacrifice-of-praise imagery for the eucharist and spoke of the duties of love as *sacrifices of thanksgiving.* He also relied on Hebrews for his understanding that doing good constituted spiritual sacrifices "pleasing to God," a view of Christian life held by Augustine and clearly present in Paul.[37] Each reformer thus honored the memory of Jesus' actions at the Last Supper, which is to say, he "gave thanks." In his specific exegesis of the sacrifice-of-praise motif, Calvin also points us to the Hebrew Scriptures and to Psalm 50 (49 in the Septuagint), verse 23 in particular: "Those who bring thanksgiving (praise) as their sacrifice honor me." There is, however, a subtle yet important distinction that emerges in the thinking of the reformers relative to the nature of the sacrifice that is "pleasing to God": Calvin and Luther distanced themselves from Zwingli's focus on the inner disposition of the believer in the sacrament. Indeed, Luther's major theological battle was against "inner disposition."[38] The believer's attention, he argued, is directed to the certainty of God's gift in the eucharist, not our disposition to it. Luther also argued that the "sacrifice pleasing to God" was "faith in Christ," which was itself a prior gift of God.[39] Thus we are justified not by works but by faith. Despite these insights, the reformers' collective emphasis on the contrite heart brought inner disposition to the foreground of liturgical practice.

Their use of scripture and the Psalms in particular gave the reformers

---

35. Martin Luther, "The Misuse of the Mass," in *Luther's Works*, vol. 36, *Word and Sacrament II*, ed. Abdel Ross Wentz, trans. Frederick C. Ahrens (Philadelphia: Muhlenberg Press, 1959), 162; *Luther's Works*, vol. 29, *Lectures on Titus, Philemon, and Hebrews*, ed. Jaroslav Pelikan (St. Louis: Concordia Publishing House, 1968), 223; Edward J. Kilmartin, "*Sacrificium Laudis:* Context and Function of Early Eucharistic Prayers," *Theological Studies* 35, no. 2 (June 1974): 268–87.

36. Huldrych Zwingli, *Huldrych Zwingli Writings*, vol. 2, *In Search of True Religion: Reformation, Pastoral and Eucharistic Writings*, trans. and ed. Edward J. Furcho (Allison Park, Pa.: Pickwick Publications, 1984), 71; Bard Thompson, *Liturgies of the Western Church* (Cleveland: World Publishing Co., 1961), 149–50.

37. John Calvin, *Institutes of the Christian Religion*, ed. John T. McNeill, trans. Ford Lewis Battles, Library of Christian Classics (Philadelphia: Westminster Press, 1960), 21:1444–45; Bernhard Lohse, *A Short History of Christian Doctrine: From the First Century to the Present*, trans. F. Ernest Stoeffler, rev. ed. (Philadelphia: Fortress Press, 1985), 136–41; Daly, *Origins*, 59–67.

38. Carter Lindberg, "Justification by Faith Alone: *The* Lutheran Proposal to the Churches," *New Conversations* 10, no. 2 (winter–spring 1988): 33.

39. *Luther's Works*, vol. 29, *Lectures on Titus, Philemon, and Hebrews*, 223.

ample reason to focus on sacrifice. Nevertheless, an acceptable sacrifice of praise — faith for Luther and doing good for Calvin — took on ominous overtones in Psalm 51. The progression from Psalm 50 to 51 is striking in itself:

> Offer to God a sacrifice of *thanksgiving,* and pay your vows to the Most High (50:14). Those who bring *thanksgiving* as their sacrifice honor me (50:23). The sacrifice acceptable to God is a *broken spirit;* a broken and *contrite heart,* O God, you will not despise. (51:17; emphasis added)

The notion of a contrite heart and a broken spirit being acceptable to God is a basic supposition of contemporary Lenten liturgies, as the words of Joel 2:12–13a attest: "return to me with all your heart, with fasting, with weeping, and with mourning; rend your hearts and not your clothing." In the postexilic world of Psalm 51, the disposition of obedience — listening to Christ and doing the will of God — seems to merge with the inner disposition of brokenness. But what does a broken spirit have to do with God and why is a broken (contrite) heart an acceptable sacrifice? More importantly, what has brokenness to do with thankfulness?

To use extended hands in the act of prayer and thanksgiving, as the *orans*[40] of catacomb art indicate, is quite a different gesture than wringing the hands in an act of confessing one's contriteness. Indeed, contriteness speaks more of being at the mercy of another's hands than of being the active subject of one's own praise offering. Consider the words of 51:8–9. The psalmist (having already identified himself as one guilty from conception) appeals to God for mercy: "Let me hear joy and gladness; let the bones that *you have crushed* rejoice. Hide your face from my sins, and blot out all my iniquities" (emphasis added). The assumption that God is punitive is disturbing, to say the least, but we shall discover it again and again in the widely held view that God breaks (crushes) bones as well as spirits. The boldness of this assertion is supported by the very words that are translated as "contrite": *dakkâ* means crushed (as in powder) and destruction, and *dâkâh* refers to physical or mental collapse. Another word for contrite, *nâkeh,* refers to being smitten — literally, maimed; figuratively, dejected.[41]

In truth a wide range of meanings associated with the Hebrew roots for

---

40. In the catacomb of Priscilla in Rome there is a representation of a "female orans," a type of figure with hands outstretched in prayer.

41. James Strong, "A Concise Dictionary of the Words in the Hebrew Bible," in *Strong's Exhaustive Concordance of the Bible, with Key-Word Comparison of Selected Words and Phrases in the King James Version with Five Leading Translations* (Nashville: Abingdon Press, 1980 [1894]), 30, 78, 123 (separately paginated).

a contrite heart exists; and the milder sense of "being sorry" is certainly a possible reading. Nevertheless, verse 51:8 clearly implies that God is the one who has crushed (*dâkâh* — broken) the psalmist's bones. In light of this, it is a liturgical curiosity that the text of 51:17 can also be read more personally as "My sacrifice, O God, is a broken spirit," a reading that offers a very different view of faith. It is one thing to hear the psalmist offer God a contrite heart and hope it will be accepted;[42] it is another thing entirely to make such an offering *normative* for religious experience, as later Christians do by repeating this more personal image in their liturgical prayers. The notion of thanksgiving is thus displaced by the broken and contrite spirit, which becomes the more acceptable sacrifice in Reformed liturgies.[43]

Though Reformed liturgies speak of a "sacrifice of praise and thanksgiving," such language remains embedded in a eucharistic theology that, in actual praxis, offers only passing reference to praise and thanksgiving. Rather than emphasize the resurrection of Christ, these liturgies dwell on the death of Christ and his once-for-all sacrifice on the cross. Moreover, the imagery of Paul — "present your bodies as a living sacrifice, holy and acceptable to God, which is your spiritual worship" (Rom. 12:1) — reinforces a sacrificial understanding of the eucharist. The value of self-giving is not in question here, for much good has come from such acts. Nevertheless, self-giving in the context of dominarchy is a questionable "sacrifice" based on the inherent inequities of the dominarchal system. The suggestion that one's inner disposition be dependent on contriteness is rendered suspect when associated with the imagery of brokenness. Such imagery speaks of power-over as domination; it does not suggest companionship. In contrast, self-giving in the context of communal well-being assumes that the relational self gives to others out of an awareness of self-transcendence because it is filled with the fullness of God. A eucharist grounded in praise and thanksgiving is surely reflective of Christianity's best moments. Nevertheless, the rejoicing of glad and grateful hearts beating to the life-giving rhythms of compassionate love is ultimately our goal.

The Reformers' Use of Sacrifice

The reformers had broken through a critical dimension of liturgical entrenchment: they had restored the table to the imagery of the sacrament and the cup to the laity, and although they retained the image of sacrifice

42. Rabbi Margaret Moers Wenig suggests that contrition can be viewed in an unoppressive way, as being humble before God or in having one's arrogance or hardheartedness broken, rather than the will of a person being destroyed. Judaism, she notes, uses contrition in a mild way.

43. Richard Baxter's Savoy Liturgy of 1661 (in Thompson, *Liturgies*, 375–405).

as proclamation, they overturned the Roman notion that Christ's sacrifice was being repeated by the priest's actions. While we may regret that they were unable to free this rite from its sacrificial history, and very likely contributed to its penitential nature, we must still appreciate the sense of intimacy and community their celebrations conveyed. That in itself must have been an exhilarating experience in a world besieged by death and demons. Holy Communion had great meaning for those who participated in it, for it gave focus to their lives and assurances to their hearts in ways few other events could. They gathered to commune with their gracious God and be fed. Most of all they rejoiced and gave thanks. Nevertheless, those who come to be fed today have a right to wonder why this meal no longer satisfies every Christian.

Martin Luther

Liturgical reform was not Luther's original intention. His primary concern was to counter the sacrificial implication of the Roman mass — God was an angry God who demanded appeasement — with the image of a loving and gracious God whose Son sacrificed himself once and for all to save us. He relied on Matthew's institutional narrative, which emphasized the forgiveness of sins and retained the Peace of the Lord, since he considered it "a public absolution of the sins of the communicant, truly the Gospel voice announcing remission of sins." He also continued the singing of the Agnus Dei, a chant that associated the breaking of the bread with Jesus' suffering and death and the "Lamb for sinners slain" of John's Apocalypse.[44]

To prevent the eucharist from being taken too lightly, especially by those who were known for their past transgressions, Luther required all communicants to undergo questioning once a year related to the manner of their life. However, in some cases no questioning was needed. Ever the pastor, Luther was clear that those who "feared" that they were not *pure enough* or not *worthy enough* were the very ones who should come, for the sacrament is "to purify you and help you." The sacrament was thus a "medicine for the soul" that strengthened and refreshed those who received it. If the ones wishing to commune had changed their sinful ways and believed that the sacrament would give them all that they needed, Luther counted them as worthy indeed. Even so, he admonished those about to partake to remember the boundless love of Christ that comes to

---

44. Thompson, *Liturgies*, 112; Josef A. Jungmann, *The Mass of the Roman Rite: Its Origins and Development (Missarum Sollemnia)*, vol. 2, trans. Francis A. Brunner (New York: Benziger Brothers, 1955), 486; James F. White, *Introduction to Christian Worship*, rev. ed. (Nashville: Abingdon Press, 1990), 234.

them because Christ redeemed them (by his atoning blood) "from God's wrath, sin, death, and hell."[45]

Ulrich Zwingli

Unlike Luther, Zwingli stressed that the mass was a memorial of the sacrifice. The mass stood as a pledge of the redemption shown in Christ and an act of thanksgiving. Whereas Luther had dispensed with the consecrating prayer entirely, Zwingli substituted several of his own. In his liturgy of the Word of 1525, the names of those who had died during the week were solemnly recalled as a "warning" to others that they should "prepare" themselves for death. Likewise, the confession of sins was placed late in the liturgy of the Word so the Word preached would serve as a reminder of the misery of those who had died as well as an assurance of forgiveness. These influences seem unsettling until we realize the ever-present fears of the black death that stalked Zurich during this period, along with the belief that illness and death were either God's intended will or divine punishment. Zwingli himself fell ill to the plague in 1519.[46]

Zwingli excluded from the supper all who "defile the body of Christ with intolerable stains and blemishes." In addition, Paul's words from 1 Corinthians 11:17–29 were read to warn those who might seek to communicate in an "unworthy" manner. When the eucharist was observed four times a year — Easter, Pentecost, autumn, and Christmas — people communicated in stillness, following the words of institution: "No words of delivery were spoken, no music sung or played; but the silence prevailed."[47] Since there was no singing, the Agnus Dei was spoken, but only by the clergy. Zwingli's most positive reform was to make the community gathered at a congregational table central to the rite. A negative contribution of some note was his insistence that "the elements of bread and wine were reminders, not vehicles, of grace" that neither mediated the divine life nor remitted sins.[48] Today, Zwingli's emphasis on the commemoration of Christ's passion, combined with his lack of understanding for the nature and power of symbols, continues to have a chilling effect on many Reformed liturgies.

John Calvin

Calvin's renunciation of the Roman rite was more severe. He based his liturgical policy on the "custom of the ancient church" and used Paul's words of institution as a "warrant" of the sacrament. His most consequential practice, however, was the imposition of a quarterly period of

45. Thompson, *Liturgies*, 133.
46. W. P. Stephens, *Zwingli: An Introduction to His Thought* (Oxford: Clarendon Press, 1992), 17.
47. Thompson, *Liturgies*, 143, 145.
48. Ibid., 143.

preparation that intensified the introspective nature of late medieval piety. Indeed, Calvin's tenacious devotion to self-examination may well have been the primary force that kept alive the medieval emphasis on "human unworthiness before a just and angry God."[49] The service began by drawing the worshiper's attention to God's glory and human frailty: "Our help is in the name of the Lord." Then in keeping with Calvin's views on self-examination, proper worship turned to a general confession of sin, stressing human wretchedness before the goodness and mercy of God. Calvin's intention for the service was clear: "it ought to lead us straight to Christ."[50] He thus stressed simplicity and a decorum fitting to the reverence of the sacred mysteries. The joyful dimension of Calvin's liturgies was evident in the singing of the psalms as an instrument of praise.

In Calvin's own words, "one of the principal points in the reception of the sacrament — yea, the whole matter — is to meditate upon the passion of Christ." Thus one took the body of Jesus remembering that he had been "delivered unto death for you." While Calvin believed the "sum of the Gospel" was contained in the notion that Jesus was the Lamb of God who takes away the sin of the world, it is noteworthy that he did not keep the Agnus Dei in the eucharistic liturgy.[51] Since Calvin argued that the eucharist had no power apart from the Word, the impression was given that forgiveness took place before one came to the table, rather than experiencing forgiveness through the reception of the eucharistic sacrament. The sacraments (baptism and Lord's Supper) thus functioned as a sign and seal of the covenant of grace revealed in the Word rightly preached. Calvin's theology of the sacraments was consistent — the clarity of the gospel rested in the proclamation of the crucifixion.[52]

Although Calvin bequeathed to us a powerful sense of God's majesty and awe-filled presence and suggested a strong eucharistic role for the Holy Spirit, his own terror before the powerful "wrath of God" led him to stress human unworthiness over against divine connection. He liturgically supported and encouraged the view that God chastened the believer in body, mind, and spirit because of the condemnation that human sinfulness deserved. Lastly, in his exhortation to the supper, he "fenced the table" in strong legalistic terms, lest the "holy food" that belonged only to Christ's

49. James F. White, *Protestant Worship: Traditions in Transition* (Louisville: Westminster/John Knox Press, 1989), 66; Calvin, *Institutes*, 20:634–35.

50. Calvin, *Institutes*, 21:1207; Thompson, *Liturgies*, 197.

51. Thompson, *Liturgies*, 213, 208; Bryan D. Spinks, *Freedom or Order? The Eucharistic Liturgy in English Congregationalism 1645–1980*, Pittsburgh Theological Monographs, no. 8 (Allison Park, Pa.: Pickwick Publications, 1984), 10.

52. Calvin, *Institutes*, 20:1289–91; Thompson, *Liturgies*, 195.

"household of faith" be defiled and contaminated.[53] Despite these punitive strains, Calvin's eucharist was viewed as a "spiritual banquet" — an exhortation (to pious worshipers) to "mutual love among themselves." In tasting it they were moved to thanksgiving.

Calvin's Liturgical Stepchildren

Calvin's eucharistic influence can be found in a number of liturgical postscripts that followed his lead. In 1645 "The Westminster Directory for the Publique Worship of God" was published by the English Parliament as a corrective to the Book of Common Prayer after heavy lobbying by Puritans. From the assembly's entry in a "grave and seemly manner" to the climactic moments of eucharistic reception, participants rehearsed their great unworthiness and contemplated the eternal damnation that would be their lot were it not for the grace of God in Jesus Christ. Puritan piety, highly introspective and evocative in nature, presented the Lord's Supper as a "dramatic exhortation" in order to evoke appropriate psychological imagery. However, this "hyper-Calvinist" piety was criticized for its undue attention to the breaking of the bread, which reduced the supper to "little more than an occasion for evoking mental images of the crucifixion."[54]

Although the directory's influence was somewhat short-lived in England because of the restoration of the monarchy in 1660, it continued to influence Free Church worship, particularly through the 1661 Savoy Liturgy of Richard Baxter, an English Presbyterian. While it was never officially used in England because of the political climate of the time, Baxter's work had a significant impact on the worship life of Congregationalist Separatists and English Puritans. In a significant way, Baxter's piety furthered the notion that the human senses could be important instruments for "Christian meditation."[55]

Nevertheless, in the eucharistic sacrament, the faithful receive "a crucified Christ," not the risen Christ, for the imagery of the "Lamb for sinners slain" dominates Baxter's words spoken over bread and cup. The fear of apocalyptic "judgment" and the "feast of endless glory" thus live in dramatic tension in Baxter's liturgy. The same is true of the Provisional Liturgy of 1857 and 1866 of the Mercersburg tradition, which began as a protest movement against the subjectivism of frontier revivals and became a shaping force in the liturgical tradition of the Evangelical and Reformed

---

53. Thompson, *Liturgies*, 206; James Hastings Nichols, *Corporate Worship in the Reformed Tradition* (Philadelphia: Westminster Press, 1968), 46, 47.

54. E. Brooks Holifield, *The Covenant Sealed: The Development of Puritan Sacramental Theology in Old and New England, 1570–1720* (New Haven: Yale University Press, 1974), 53, 55.

55. Thompson, *Liturgies*, 375–405; Spinks, *Freedom or Order?* 53–69; Holifield, *Covenant Sealed*, 134–35.

Church.[56] At the very center of the church's faith and practice, the Lord's Supper stood as a sacrament of *nourishment for eternal life* in which the believer was "mystically united to the full glorified Humanity of Christ."[57]

Only through the infinite merits attained by Christ through his offering of his body once for all, wherein *full satisfaction* has been made for the sins of the world, could Christians hope to be saved. In echoing both Anselm and Calvin, the Mercersburg movement produced a liturgical tradition that has been described as the "finest liturgy of any Reformed Church in the world."[58]

The Feast of the Lamb

In *Trouble with Jesus,* L. Susan Bond offers a "metaphorical Christology of salvage" that manifests a relationship "of compassion for all those who are not present, the invitation to all who are outcast, and radical hospitality to those who are not worthy." For her eucharistic model, she relies on *BEM*'s meal of the coming kingdom as "foretaste of the world as it should be" where all, including the nonbaptized, are welcome. While her primary task is to advance new strategies for preaching that include the concerns of women theologians, she rightly notes the critical relationship between preaching and the sacraments and recognizes the power of ritual to shape imaginations. In acknowledging that her "radical egalitarian and prodigal practices would be unpopular within the broad constituency of the WCC," Bond admits that her model would also "never be ratified by those who have coercive power within ecclesial bodies."[59] Bond speaks eschatologically (of the future) but not apocalyptically, using Luke's wedding feast as the primary model for the eucharistic model she is advocating. Her instincts for re-imaging the eucharist inclusively share many affinities with my own. At the same time, Bond, like other contemporary theologians, appears to underestimate the relationship of eschatological banquets to sacrificial metaphors as well as the persistence of punitive imagery for God.

One of the most powerful images of sacrificial atonement is the "Lamb for sinners slain" who becomes the host of God's messianic wedding banquet at the end of time. Horton Davies likens the messianic banquet to

56. Jack Martin Maxwell, *Worship and Reformed Theology: The Liturgical Lessons of Mercersburg,* Pittsburgh Theological Monograph Series, no. 10 (Pittsburgh: Pickwick Press, 1976), 439–55; George H. Bricker, *A Brief History of the Mercersburg Movement: An Occasional Paper* (Lancaster, Pa.: Lancaster Theological Seminary, 1982), 18, 19.

57. Bricker, *A Brief History,* 18, 19.

58. Cited in Morris D. Slifer, "The Liturgical Tradition of the Reformed Church in the U.S.A.," *Studia Liturgica* 1 (December 1962): 237, 238.

59. L. Susan Bond, *Trouble with Jesus: Women, Christology, and Preaching* (St. Louis: Chalice Press, 1999).

the feast of joy prophesied by Isaiah: "On this mountain the Lord of hosts will make for all peoples a feast of rich food, a feast of well-aged wines, of rich food filled with marrow, of well-aged wines strained clear" (Isa. 25:6–8). While this image offers great hope, its promise is, nevertheless, short-lived, for Davies goes on to image the "feasts of judgment" found in Isaiah 34:1–6 and Jeremiah 46:10.

These feasts, which consume the body and blood of the Lord's enemies, stand in stark contrast to the feast offered to all peoples hailed by First Isaiah. In fact end time feasts of joy are hardly the mark of a punitive god. As Davies notes, "with the exception of Isaiah, there is little sense of God's joyful celebration with the godly at the end of history."[60]

Faced with this incongruity, Davies suggests our true hope lies in the anticipation of Christ's return in victory. At the same time he suggests that Isaiah 66:18 assures us that this feast is for all humankind, ignoring the imagery of Isaiah 66:24: "[those whom God has saved] shall go out and look at the dead bodies of the people who have rebelled against me; for their worm shall not die, their fire shall not be quenched and they shall be an abhorrence to all flesh." Subsequently, Isaiah's fearful imagery of worms and fire will become Mark's imagery for Gehenna, the first scriptural reference to the development of hell in Christian thought. Such is the downside of eschatological hope too easily overlooked by Christian preachers. The image of God the avenger — the one who punishes his disobedient children — lurks in the shadows, threatening to release tears of lamentation.

Isaiah 25:6 is a wonderful image, but the image of a feast for all peoples does not make up the entirety of messianic banquet imagery; the remaining images carry the weight of apocalyptic fears of hell and damnation for those who fail to obey. Moreover, the Apostles' Creed and the Nicene Creed, in professing belief in a Christ who will come again to judge the living and the dead, fail to conjure up Isaiah 25:6.[61] Regardless of Christianity's promotion of a "day of judgment," the stress falls on the image of punishment more than judgment. This distinction is critical. Judgment is a dimension of faithful living that is necessary for communal well-being. Community members must be able to discern good and evil and be accountable to others for harm done. Without such discernment, earthly communion is elusive. That said, judgment must be given a wider berth and removed from the punishment paradigm. Unless we understand that God's judgment is a present encounter that takes place in every moment of existence, not through a future day of reckoning, we will fail to know the

60. Davies, *Bread of Life,* 91, 88.

61. UCC, *Book of Worship* (New York: Office for Church Life and Leadership, 1986), 509–10.

power of Christ-Christa in and through the Spirit present here and now. Judgment has to do with the healing power of God, not God's power to punish. The latter, as we shall see, is a remnant of human imagination that owes much of its staying power to the presence of corporal punishment.[62]

For the eucharist to truly be a feast of God's realm it must enact mercy and justice in our time. Nevertheless, the imagery of future-oriented meals "at the end of history" keeps the eucharist tied to powerful intimations of eternal damnation awaiting the unbeliever. As such, the image of God as punisher is always just beneath the surface, ready to break forth imaginatively for anyone who has lived through experiences of brokenness, degradation, or unresolved terror.

Making the Liturgical Connection

Given my comments earlier about the censoring nature of the performative aspects of liturgy, it is difficult to ignore theological claims that the eucharist is "the liturgical representation of the Atonement," based on the teachings of Jesus and the life-experience of the church.[63] Clearly, discerning how atonement imagery shapes our view of God is a necessity, not a luxury. We also need to know if this imagery effects at-one-ment for everyone or further fragments our relational selves. To address these concerns, we will need to uncover the historical layering that creates the illusion of one unified tapestry, for no "ecumenical declaration of an orthodox position on Christ's work" yet exists.[64] At the same time, images of brokenness and humiliation dominate its eucharistic expression.

Dillistone spoke of the eucharist as the "supreme" opportunity for Christians to identify themselves afresh with Christ's saving death and resurrection. Hence he described the eucharist as manifesting the "whole *quality*" of the life of the Christian community."

> It is a <u>self-denial</u> leading to self-affirmation, it is a <u>self-immolation</u> leading to self-fulfilment, it is a <u>corporate expression of humiliation</u> leading to a corporate experience of enrichment. But all of this only

62. Jeanette Anderson Good, *Shame, Images of God, and the Cycle of Violence in Adults Who Experienced Childhood Corporal Punishment* (Lanham, Md.: University Press of America, 1999).

63. Robert S. Paul, *The Atonement and the Sacraments: The Relation of the Atonement to the Sacraments of Baptism and the Lord's Super* (New York: Abingdon Press, 1960), 267; A. G. Hebert, introduction to Gustaf Aulén, *Christus Victor: An Historical Study of the Three Main Types of the Idea of Atonement* (New York: Macmillan, 1951), viii.

64. Jeffery Hopper, *Understanding Modern Theology II: Reinterpreting Christian Faith for Changing Worlds* (Philadelphia: Fortress Press, 1987), 14.

> finds its origin and secret of continuity in the actual self-oblation of the Christ to death and in His glorification in the resurrection.[65]

Robert Browne, a formidable figure in Congregational history, saw the eucharist similarly: "The Supper, 'by the breaking and eating of bread and drinking the Cup,' seals to us the fact that 'we are happily redeemed by the breaking of the body and shedding of the blood of Christ Jesus.' "[66] Likewise, P. T. Forsyth viewed the eucharist as the center of the church's common life because the church's life is centered in Christ's atonement. Forsyth's imagery is quite graphic:

> The bread was broken. It *must* be broken. The loaf cannot be eaten whole. So it was a spiritual necessity, a necessity in God, that Christ should die. . . . Just as truly as food must be destroyed before it can be of use to us, so *He* had to be destroyed before *He* could savingly serve us. *We must be broken ere we deeply bless.*[67]

United Church of Christ theologian Gabriel Fackre builds on the work of Forsyth and describes the Last Supper as a taste of the heavenly banquet:

> It is as *sacrifice* that the future comes into our midst in the sacrament. . . . And we see the sacrifice for what it is, the bleeding body of Christ and the broken heart of God taking the consequences of our sin and communicating to us the forgiveness of sin in the bread and wine.[68]

Given this brief sampling, the influence of *belief,* in the form of atonement imagery, on the form of the eucharist as *prayer* is clear. To argue that contemporary praxis may be better served by understanding the nature of the eucharist prior to this influence is not to tie us to the past irrevocably, as though a past moment in time must be definitive. Rather, I seek to broaden the base of current praxis and offer contemporary Christians a eucharistic theology that is reflective of the ongoing work of the Spirit. As Sallie McFague has argued, a theology truer to the cosmic needs of our time must be willing to "think differently, to think in metaphors and models that support a unified, interdependent understanding of God-world and human-world relationships."[69] Since much of Christianity's theological and liturgical life remains tied to a view of the God-world relationship

---

65. F. W. Dillistone, *The Christian Understanding of Atonement* (Philadelphia: Westminster Press, 1968), 19, 143, 144, 146; underlining added.

66. Cited in Paul, *The Atonement and the Sacraments,* 360.

67. P. T. Forsyth, *The Church and the Sacraments* (London: Independent Press, 1955), 239; underlining added.

68. Gabriel Fackre, *The Christian Story: A Narrative Interpretation of Basic Christian Doctrine* (Grand Rapids, Mich.: William B. Eerdmans, 1978), 193; underlining added.

69. Sallie McFague, *Models of God: Theology for an Ecological, Nuclear Age* (Philadelphia: Fortress Press, 1987), 27.

in which the divine is distinct from humanity and possesses no need of human cooperation, her point is well taken.

Clearly, the eucharist has multiple meanings and multiple contexts. Jesus did not "institute" one meal tradition. Hence there is more than one way to make eucharist and more than one way to understand "traditional" meanings. It is not the case that sacrifice is the only meaningful image for making eucharist; nor is it the case that the Passover meal is the only true image of the joyful feast Jesus celebrated. But it is the case that eschatological banquet imagery is intimately tied to sacrificial imagery, as the "feast of the Lamb" reveals, and that for much of the tradition eschatology has been wedded to apocalyptic imagery. Fear of punishment has often been the subtext of Christian joy, which is why many believers approach Holy Communion with caution. Liturgical reforms of the twentieth century gave birth to a variety of positive liturgical innovations, including use of the lectionary, greater participation of the laity, and increased use of the arts. Still, eucharistic praxis has been slow to change. Burdened by its deep ties to medieval understandings of Jesus' death, the eucharist remains wedded to the imagery of substitutionary (sacrificial) atonement.

Numerous Christians lead faithful lives while participating in traditional celebrations and consider themselves blessed. At the same time, countless others experience *the union of atonement and eucharist* as a deterrent to faith and well-being. In part their experience can be attributed to a sense of powerlessness before an all-powerful God as well as the oppressive images of shame, humiliation, and guilt. For these believers, our ability to interrupt the suffering of others is compromised by unconscious fears of a punitive God, even as we offer conscious allegiance to a gracious one. If we agree that eucharist begins with the gathered assembly, as liturgical theologian Alexander Schmemann suggests, then the lived experience of those gathered has everything to do with the nature of the rite enacted.[70] Making eucharist is a communal activity that is intimately tied to those who commune and their reasons for communing. Small wonder then that those who find themselves unable to perform acts of thanksgiving congruent with their experiences of divine grace feel bereft, even as those around them give thanks in "traditional" ways.

Difficult questions remain: How is it that fear shaped medieval atonement theories? How does our suffering relate to Jesus' suffering? And to what extent is God's forgiveness beholden to the cross? As we search for answers, one thing will become clear: those who argue against a view of atonement as a blood sacrifice for our sins rest their arguments on the

70. Alexander Schmemann, *The Eucharist: Sacrament of the Kingdom*, trans. Paul Kachur (Crestwood, N.Y.: St. Vladimir's Seminary Press, 1988), 15.

premise that God's love is clearly shown in the life and resurrection of Jesus. Not his death. While traditional views have never denied the importance of Jesus' life-work, they have surely compromised the power of his ministry for the sake of sanctifying — not condemning — the violent death he endured. The images of brokenness, guilt, shame, humiliation, and destruction that theologically frame Christ's redemptive work are stunning contradictions to the fruit of the Spirit that sustains and renews our communal lives. Dare we suggest these contradictions are not of God's choosing?

If this so-called sacrifice is really a meal, "a sharing of food in thanksgiving," why not say so once and for all? How different might the plight of those who suffer be if we truly celebrated this event for what it is — a feast of life for the body of Christ-Christa in the Spirit of the Risen One, which is always the Holy Spirit of God?[71] Jesus calls us into community and offers nourishment to those who gather in his love. By keeping this relational imagery before us the eucharist may well become a *sacrament of community* that overturns sacramental sacrifice. Augustine admonished his community to "be what you see [the body of Christ] and receive what you are." In opening ourselves to God's "eucharistic force field of love,"[72] we open ourselves to new possibilities. Within this blessed field of dreams our imaginations thrive through the power of the Holy Spirit, as we experience Jesus' saving grace and become Christ-Christa *now.*

---

71. Karl Barth, *Church Dogmatics,* vol. 4, *The Doctrine of Reconciliation,* pt. 3.1, "The Holy Spirit and the Sending of the Christian Community," ed. G. W. Bromiley and T. F. Torrance (Edinburgh: T. & T. Clark, 1961), 681.

72. John C. Haughey, "The Eucharist and Intentional Communities," and Thomas Richstatter, "Alternative Futures for the Eucharist," in *Alternative Futures for Worship,* vol. 3, *The Eucharist,* ed. Bernard J. Lee (Collegeville, Minn.: Liturgical Press, 1987), 63, 127.

FIVE

Deliver Us from Fear

> And these things shall come to pass in the day of judgment of those who have fallen away from faith in God and have committed sin: cataracts of fire shall be let loose; . . . and the waters shall be changed and transformed into coals of fire, and all that is in it [the earth?] shall burn and the sea shall become fire; under the heaven there shall be a fierce fire that shall not be put out and it flows for the judgment of wrath. —The Apocalypse of Peter[1]

> Now I insist on this, since it is the central pillar of the Catholic faith. From the presence to the disciples of the risen victim, the crucified one risen *as crucified,* the lamb triumphant *as slaughtered,* everything else flows. Without that insight, nothing unfolds, no clear perception of God, of grace, of eternal life, about what we must do, how we must live. —*James Alison*[2]

The image of God's messianic banquet has lightened the mood of many eucharistic celebrations. Yet beneath the surface of this eschatological hope ambivalence abounds. Jesus' table-fellowship included sinners and outcasts, but the same cannot be said for the church that gathers in his name. How can this be? This chapter explores why apocalyptic imagery has played such a large role in shaping our perception of God and by implication the eucharist. The punishing god who reigns in many Christian imaginations has a long and undistinguished history, which needs to be sketched in greater detail. By tracing apocalyptic influences on the nature of God, we begin to glimpse why the eucharist assumed the mantle of atonement.

We are accustomed to praying, "Deliver us from evil." Yet when it comes to understanding God, a new petition may prove more effective: "Deliver

---

1. Section 5, The Apocalypse of Peter, in *Apocalyptic Literature: A Reader,* ed. Mitchell G. Reddish (Peabody, Mass.: Hendrickson Publishers, 1995), 248.

2. James Alison, *Raising Abel: The Recovery of the Eschatological Imagination* (New York: Crossroad Herder, 1996), 30.

us from fear." To re-image the eucharist, we must first re-image God and the notion of suffering love.

The Suffering Love of God

Most orthodox Christians believe the "good news" of the gospel and the heart of Christianity is the saving work of God reconciling the world to Godself in Christ: "For God so loved the world that he gave his only Son, so that everyone who believes in him may not perish but have eternal life" (John 3:16). Here, God's capacity to suffer out of love for the world is proclaimed. Yet echoes of apocalypse lie hidden in John's promise of eternal life. The death of God's beloved son reveals God's gracious love toward humankind, even as it subtly counters the fear of eternal punishment. Likewise, God's love is interpreted as a suffering love, since it demonstrates an act of self-giving, also known as a self-emptying. When they deny themselves and take up their cross, Christians model their lives accordingly. This is imperial Christianity's core message.

Critics of such love think otherwise. In proclaiming a crucified and risen Savior, their emphasis falls not on Jesus the crucified but on Jesus the risen. Without denying the manner of Jesus' death, they experience God's saving love through the power of Christ's resurrection. They also believe that by interpreting Jesus' death as a sacrifice, the church allowed the eucharist to become a sacrament of sacrifice for individual salvation rather than a sacrament of communion for the well-being of all. As the eucharist became more restrictive, so too did God's love.

Medieval Shifts

Subtle and profound influences led to transformations in the church's eucharistic liturgy and the establishing of rules for who could approach Christ's table. Consider the changes they wrought. Once the imagery of sacred food displaced Paul's imagery of the gathered community, the power of Christ's risen presence in communal life was seriously compromised. As the experience of Easter became less accessible to memory, and its celebration shifted to Sunday (rather than falling on a weekday near Passover), the bread and the cup — the body and blood — began to dominate the meal's symbolism. Over time, the cup was withheld from the laity for fear participants might accidentally spill the sacred blood of Jesus. The bread became "the host," a wafer placed by the priest in the communicants' mouth so that the body of Christ would not fall to the floor and potentially be eaten by vermin. In the thirteenth century, adoration of the host, a form of spiritual communion, replaced eating in the practice of many believers. Consequently, theologians such as Thomas Aquinas "saw the priest in the mass as receiving for the people."[3]

The shroud of mystery surrounding the rite was also affected by the use of Latin in the West. Most clergy could read and write, but many laypeople in the Middle Ages lacked access to education. In the East, the congregation heard and understood the words spoken by the priest. However, after the fourth century, the iconostasis, a screen erected between the people and the altar that was intended to encourage a sense of "holy terror,"[4] reinforced not only a sense of the holy but a sense of the unworthiness of ordinary laypersons. Further changes brought on by the reforms of the emperor Charlemagne in the ninth century included the removal of the altar from the congregation to the rear wall of the chancel, a move that required the priest to turn his back to the congregation during the mass proper. Both acts ensured that the Western rite would be more accessible visually than audibly and encouraged the adoration of the host when the priest elevated it in the air during the fraction (breaking) and consecration. The Eastern rite provided mostly auditory cues. As religious leaders sought to explain how and when the elements of bread and wine became the body and blood of Christ, the imagery of community faded while the imagery of consecration grew.

After the fall of Rome, the invasion of German "barbarians" (as the church called them) further complicated sacramental understandings. Under Germanic influence, the nature of symbols deteriorated so that the host became not a symbol but the thing itself — the body of Jesus. As a result, heated controversy concerning the nature of Christ's presence broke out in the West in the eighth and ninth centuries between those who believed Jesus' body was actually present on the altar in the form of the host and those who argued for a greater symbolic awareness. "Faced with growing devotion to the bread and the wine themselves, exactly because the crumbs and drops masked (thinly) the substance of Christ, theologians struggled to retain a firm emphasis on Christ's body as one, because one church and one humanity are saved in it."[5]

In sum, once the focus shifted from the community as a symbol of the body of Christ to the body of Christ present in the eucharistic host, the experience of a shared meal (which was literally dropped from the rite in the second century) was buried under the weight of sacrificial imagery. In other words, the "sacrifice of Christ" turned the table on the inclusivity of Jesus' table-fellowship as the post-Constantinian church became

---

3. Caroline Walker Bynum, *Holy Feast and Holy Fast: The Religious Significance of Food to Medieval Women* (Berkeley: University of California Press, 1987), 45.

4. Gregory Dix, *The Shape of the Liturgy* (Westminster: Dacre Press, 1945), 480–85.

5. Bynum, *Holy Feast,* 51.

entrenched in matters of doctrine and domination. In effect, the words of Jesus and the elements of bread and wine were endowed by the church — under the authority of the empire — with a saving power that only the priest could access directly. In this way sacrificial imagery ensures that only the saved may commune. But what is it that people need saving from? The answer lies in the development of apocalyptic thinking and the imaginative construction of hell.

The Wolf in Disguise

Apocalyptic imagery is like the wolf in sheep's clothing. It looks harmless enough because it surrounds itself with the language of hope and a future where God is victorious over evil. Nevertheless, as the Apocalypse of Peter pronounces, apocalyptic is steeped in fear and grounded in the destruction of those who have fallen away from faith in God. Texts that bear the title "Apocalypse," meaning that which is unveiled or revealed, are not necessarily apocalyptic in content. "Apocalypse" describes "a genre of revelatory literature" in which a story is used to show how a particular revelation is mediated by an otherworldly being to a human recipient.[6] So, for instance, in the Revelation to John, "one like the Son of man" tells him to "write what you have seen, what is, and what is to take place after this" (Rev. 1:13, 19). Apocalyptic eschatology, which has to do with a particular teaching about the approaching end of history, appears to be related to Jewish apocalypses, though questions of origin remain. Regardless, apocalyptic imagery is associated with a divinely determined sense of history and the triple-act drama of crisis, judgment, and vindication. Thus an earthly crisis occasions God's judgment and results in the vindication of God's chosen people. While individual historical apocalypses may present variations on this theme, and differ as to the kind of history they are interested in, the only temporal feature common to all is "the expectation of a future judgment in which the wicked are punished and the good rewarded."[7] Apocalyptic eschatology is thus tied to the image of a great battle between the forces of good and the forces of evil.

Many scholars of the Christian Scriptures argue that apocalyptic eschatology emerged as a continuation of the prophetic eschatology found in the Hebrew Scriptures, which is a this-worldly eschatology. The transformation to an otherworldly view of the future is usually hastened by community crisis and national disintegration. Others argue that severe

6. Bernard McGinn, "Early Apocalypticism: The Ongoing Debate," in *The Apocalypse in English Renaissance Thought and Literature: Patterns, Antecedents, and Repercussions*, ed. C. A. Patrides and Joseph Wittreich (Ithaca, N.Y.: Cornell University Press, 1984), 4.

7. Ibid., 10, 33, n. 46.

national crises or traumas are insufficient by themselves to account for these movements since not all crises produce apocalyptic outpourings or movements in opposition to the ruling powers.[8] However, the notion of crisis can be associated with psychic factors, such as a "loss of world" as well as the "erosion" of cultural and psychic structures that individuals have relied on as foundational to their very being. Knowing that "happy people do not write apocalypses,"[9] it is not hard to imagine that everyday lived experiences of *extreme fear* lie behind the imaginative acts of apocalyptic visions. In accepting an apocalyptic view of the world, Christian believers found themselves in need of a savior who could comfort their increasing sense of powerlessness before God and the forces of hell arrayed against them.

Apocalyptic End Times

Christian theology uses the word "eschatology" to refer to "the doctrine of last things." In the context of devotional and liturgical life, eschatological events — framed as future events, either immanent or distant — conjure up images of death and resurrection, the end of the world, the hell of eternal damnation, and the eternal life of heaven. Such is the imagery of apocalyptic symbolism, which still captures the imaginations of those who turn to scripture with a literal mindset. Far from being a minor player, eschatology has been characteristic of Christian thinking.

Ernst Käsemann once described apocalyptic as "the mother of all Christian theology."[10] While this assertion seems simplistic, scholars have long wrestled with the presence of apocalyptic imagery in the New Testament. Theodore Jennings has argued that contemporary theology draws many of its central insights regarding the future transformation of historical conditions from apocalyptic eschatology. Still, he relegates such images as a final resurrection, the last judgment, and the return of Christ to the "gothic nursery of the human imagination." In Jennings's view, only the "ignorant and gullible fringe factions of pentecostal and millenarian" sects are subject to such thinking.[11] I disagree. The last judgment and the notion of Jesus' second coming have been formative in shaping not only the way we think about God but also how we think about ourselves and our neighbors.

---

8. Ibid., 14–17.

9. Paula Fredriksen, *From Jesus to Christ: The Origins of the New Testament Images of Jesus* (New Haven: Yale University Press, 1988), 82.

10. Ernst Käsemann, "The Beginnings of Christian Theology," in *Apocalypticism*, ed. Robert W. Funk, *Journal for Theology and the Church*, vol. 6 (New York: Herder & Herder, 1969), 40.

11. Theodore W. Jennings, "Apocalyptic and Contemporary Theology," *Quarterly Review* 4 (fall 1984): 54.

Even if we consider ourselves intellectually mature and too advanced spiritually to take this symbolism seriously, we cannot ignore the depth of its reach. Apocalyptic symbolism is not merely outside us; it is in us.[12] The continued reliance on apocalyptic texts for Christian proclamation, particularly on the first Sunday in Advent, reinforces this imagery as a present phenomenon. Reminders of Jesus' coming again to "judge the living and the dead" are evident in the Nicene Creed, the Apostles' Creed, and the eucharistic proclamation: "Christ has died, Christ is risen, Christ will come again." One can also find it referenced in the secondary scripture of our hymns, even though hymnals published in the 1990s may downplay the more obvious imagery of Christ returning out of the clouds.[13]

Whenever the emphasis on Jesus' return becomes a primary message in Christian proclamation, fear is its subtext. Christian eschatology is not merely about a hope-filled future, no matter what new phrase — realized or ethical — we attach to it. Christian eschatology is rooted in apocalyptic thinking and its roots are ancient. The imagery of punishment that accompanies this thinking cannot be dismissed easily by attempts to speak of Jesus' eschatological statements as merely a call to stand under the necessity of decision *now,* as Rudolph Bultmann suggested by his existential view of eschatology. We must acknowledge eschatology's problematic history even as we try to re-image its capacity to transform an "object of fear into the site of hope."[14] While some have tried to divorce eschatology from the more pejorative term "apocalyptic," its presence in the Christian Scriptures hampers this effort. Eschatological language in the Christian Scriptures "is apocalyptic language; as such it is cosmological, universal, political and mythological."[15]

Jesus and Apocalyptic Thinking

Apocalyptic thinking clearly underwent several stages in the history of its transmission. Israel's early emphasis on a this-worldly prophetic eschatology held no vision of heaven or life after death. Instead Israel put its hopes in the imagery of a land flowing with milk and honey in this life, where the

---

12. Catherine Keller, *Apocalypse Now and Then: A Feminist Guide to the End of the World* (Boston: Beacon Press, 1996), 23.

13. Carl E. Braaten, "The Kingdom of God and Life Everlasting," in *Christian Theology: An Introduction to Its Traditions and Tasks,* ed. Peter C. Hodgson and Robert H. King, 2d ed. (Philadelphia: Fortress Press, 1985), 328–52; Demetrius Dumm, "Why Apocalyptic Gospels in Advent?" *Worship* 63 (November 1989): 487.

14. Keller, *Apocalypse Now and Then,* 6; Jürgen Moltmann, *The Coming of God: Christian Eschatology,* trans. Margaret Kohl (Minneapolis: Fortress Press, 1996), 19ff.

15. Elisabeth Schüssler Fiorenza, "Eschatology of the New Testament," in *The Interpreter's Dictionary of the Bible,* supp. vol. (Nashville: Abingdon Press, 1976), 272.

fruits of the earth would abound, justice and righteousness would triumph, and shalom (peace/wholeness) would reign. The destruction of Solomon's Temple by the Babylonians and the subsequent exile of their Hebrew captives (587 B.C.E.) slowly dislodged this vision from the collective Hebraic imagination. Zoroastrian eschatology, with its sharp delineation of good and evil and its roots in Persia, may well have contributed to this radical shift.[16] It was, after all, the Persian king Cyrus who defeated the Babylonians and allowed exiled Jews to return to Jerusalem to rebuild their sacred Temple.

During the Intertestamental Period (ca. 334 B.C.E. to the birth of Jesus) apocalyptic eschatology flourished in the postexilic writings of Daniel, Ezekiel, and Third Isaiah;[17] yet it is the appearance of apocalyptic language in the teaching and preaching of Jesus that makes apocalyptic eschatology problematic. In the early twentieth century, Albert Schweitzer precipitated a crisis in theological circles with his insistence that eschatology was at the core of Jesus' message.[18] Today, many scholars downplay the apocalyptic elements in Jesus' preaching, preferring to say that although he used the language of his time, some of which was apocalyptic, he did not stress apocalyptic imagery. Crossan argues that Jesus ultimately abandoned John the Baptist's message of repentance in order to fashion his own distinctive message and movement. In particular, Crossan argues that the apocalyptic term "Son of man" should be read as the "human one" since it refers to human beings rather than some angelic figure. Crossan also believes Jesus' audience would have understood this use of the term. He therefore suggests that the Son of man expression was applied to the image of Jesus as the coming judge not because Jesus used it this way, but because the sayings Gospel Q and the Gospel of Mark expanded Jesus' use of the term under the influence of Daniel's vision of "one like the son of man" coming with the clouds of heaven (Dan. 7:13, RSV). Even more striking was Mark's decision to reshape Jesus' generic use of this term in order to support his own view of Jesus as the *suffering* and rising Son of man.[19]

Crossan's attempt to downplay the continued association of apocalyptic imagery with Jesus has significant scholarly support, particularly from the Historical Jesus Seminar that has been active in moving these dis-

---

16. McGinn, "Early Apocalypticism," 13–17.

17. Susan Ackerman, "Isaiah," in *The Women's Bible Commentary,* ed. Carol A. Newsom and Sharon H. Ringe (Louisville: Westminster/John Knox Press, 1992), 166.

18. Albert Schweitzer, *The Quest for the Historical Jesus: A Critical Study of Its Progress from Reimarus to Wrede,* trans. W. Montgomery, preface by F. C. Burkitt (New York: Macmillan, 1961).

19. Crossan, *The Historical Jesus,* 238–59; see also Barnabas Lindars, *Jesus, Son of Man: A Fresh Examination of the Son of Man Sayings in the Gospels in the Light of Recent Research* (Grand Rapids, Mich.: William B. Eerdmans, 1983), 114; Burton Mack, *A Myth of Innocence: Mark and Christian Origins* (Philadelphia: Fortress Press, 1988, 1991), 276–81.

cussions beyond the academy into wider public discourse. On the other hand, there are those who find the historical methodology of E. P. Sanders more plausible.[20] Regardless, Sanders's work lends support to Crossan's effort. Even as he attempts to argue that Jesus' message entailed a "Jewish restoration eschatology" that looked toward an imminent end to the current order, there is, in Sanders's view, a striking scarcity of material attributable to Jesus that concerns the preaching of repentance in expectation of the coming judgment. Moreover, Jesus promised the kingdom to the wicked—in sharp distinction to the worldview of his day, which spoke of their destruction.[21] While one could infer that Jesus omitted John's emphasis on judgment and repentance because he came to disbelieve in them, Sanders suggests that Jesus "continued to believe in a judgment (though he did not teach about it)."[22]

The Gospel of Mark ties Jesus' apocalyptic teachings with the suffering servant of Isaiah 52:13–53:12. However, this imagery also bears the footprints of apocalyptic. Of all the servant songs,[23] Isaiah 52–53 is the one most cherished by Christian atonement theorists because of its compelling imagery: "he was wounded for our transgressions, crushed for our iniquities; upon him was the punishment that made us whole, and by his bruises we are healed" (53:5). It is worth noting, however, that Reformed Judaism never uses this text liturgically. In fact, where you would expect it to follow Isaiah 49 in Reformed Judaism's lectionary, it is always omitted.[24]

The imagery of corporal punishment and the Hebraic word for bruises permeates much of Isaiah's prophetic writings, particularly the first oracle (1:5–6). In chilling fashion, within the context of Yahweh threatening his rebellious children with punishment, we find the imagery of bleeding wounds and bruises related directly to divine beatings. While the apocalyptic associations within Isaiah (66:15–16) differ from the apocalyptic eschatology developed more fully in the Revelation of John and medieval Christianity, the notion of a punitive God who redeems his obedient children but destroys the rebellious is clearly part of God's "plan" (Isa. 1:19–20). In contrast, the servant of Yahweh describes himself as one who was *not rebellious* (Isa. 50:5) yet was wounded for our transgressions. The structure of Isaiah as a whole is heavily influenced by the later chapters of "Trito-Isaiah," which contain clear references to God's

---

20. Paula Fredriksen, "Who Do You Say That I Am?" *Books and Religion* 19, no. 1 (spring 1992): 17–18, 27–28.

21. E. P. Sanders, *Jesus and Judaism* (Philadelphia: Fortress Press, 1985), 322, 326, 335.

22. Ibid., 322, 119.

23. Ackerman, "Isaiah," 165.

24. Conversation with Rabbi Wenig, March 5, 1993.

coming retribution.[25] Here, too, Sanders is instructive. Earlier arguments that claimed Jesus identified himself with the suffering servant of Isaiah have been discredited. Likewise, attempts to justify Jesus' death as an act of atonement no longer rest on "safe historical ground."[26]

Scholars also believe Matthew's parable of the last judgment (25:31–46) lacks authenticity as a saying of Jesus and very likely is a product of the early church. At the same time, this parable, with its threat to separate the sheep and the goats, offers a critical perspective on Christian ethics. The likelihood that the church placed this parabolic imagery on the lips of Jesus,[27] however, need not diminish the parable's mandate for enacting social justice. Indeed the threat of eternal punishment (25:46) for those who fail this test of compassion makes the early church's tendency toward apocalyptic eschatology all the more striking.

Historical associations with a punitive image of God make it difficult to reduce apocalyptic eschatology, particularly the form we find in the Apocalypse of John, to a motivational technique for justice-seekers, as some scholars suggest.[28] Despite the efforts of the apostle Paul to build a "pluralistic and egalitarian community," and despite Mark's desire for "social reform [and] open borders," the apocalyptic solution forged by Mark (and present in Paul) ultimately sacrificed the constructive elements of Jesus' ministry to a theology of divine vindictiveness under the guise of suffering love.[29] Jesus may have been influenced by apocalyptic imagery, but he did not advocate the destruction of the wicked, nor punishment for those who have "spurned the Son of God, profaned the blood of the covenant by which they were sanctified and outraged the Spirit of grace" (Heb. 10:29). How is it then that it became "a fearful thing to fall into the hands of the living God" (Heb. 10:31)?

The Letter to the Hebrews

The Letter to the Hebrews offers a unique window into early Christianity's use of apocalyptic imagery. It also sheds light on the use of sacrificial imagery in relation to Jesus' death. While uncertainties exist, one likely date for this letter is 67 or 68 C.E., a time when the Temple was still standing and Jerusalem was still the cultic center of Jewish ritual life.

25. Kathryn Pfisterer Darr, *Isaiah's Vision and the Family of God* (Louisville: Westminster/John Knox Press, 1994).

26. Sanders, *Jesus and Judaism*, 333.

27. Ibid., 111.

28. Elizabeth Schüssler Fiorenza, *The Book of Revelation: Justice and Judgment* (Philadelphia: Fortress Press, 1985).

29. Mack, *A Myth of Innocence*, 331.

Despite doubts about the location of the community being addressed, most scholars agree that these were mostly second-generation Christians who had begun to waver in their faith. Tensions existed between Romans and Jews as mounting evidence pointed toward a bloody clash.

Christians also found themselves in tension with those who remained true to their Jewish ritual heritage. For those Christians who were losing hope in Jesus' return, lingering questions as to Jesus' true identity made it difficult to meet with other believers (Heb. 10:25). Was Jesus the Son of God, a mere human, or the highest of angels? Is he now the high-priestly mediator of a new covenant whose sacrifice brings forgiveness of sins and renders Temple sacrifice a remnant of history? Or have Christians endured public abuse, persecution, and the plundering of possessions (Heb. 10:32–34) for an impostor whose coming is false prophecy of the cruelest kind? These are some of the concerns the author addresses as he coaches his audience to hold fast to the faith, which is the assurance of things hoped for, the conviction of things not seen (Heb. 11:1). As they await the day of Christ's return, however, the inner world of these Christians suffers from public humiliation and fear. Their confidence lags as their faith is besieged by doubt. But there is more at work here than the forces of religious persecution.

As historian Philip Greven notes in *Spare the Child,*[30] the imagery of punishment in Hebrews 12:5–11 has emerged as a critical voice in the Christian Scriptures for the harsh discipline of children. By drawing on his own personal memories of pain and suffering at the hands of his father, the anonymous author of Hebrews likens the actions of earthly fathers to the caring activity of God:

> And have you forgotten the exhortation which addresses you as sons? — "My son, do not regard lightly the discipline of the Lord, nor lose courage when you are punished by him. *For the Lord disciplines him whom he loves, and chastises every son whom he receives.*" It is for discipline that you have to endure. God is treating you as sons; for what son is there whom his father does not discipline? If you are left without discipline, in which all have participated, then you are illegitimate children and not sons. Besides this, we have had earthly fathers to discipline us and we respected them. Shall we not much more be subject to the Father of spirits and live? *For they disciplined us for a short time at their pleasure, but he disciplines us for our good, that we may share his holiness.* For the moment all discipline seems painful

---

30. Philip Greven, *Spare the Child: The Religious Roots of Punishment and the Psychological Impact of Physical Abuse* (New York: Alfred A. Knopf, 1991; New York: Vintage Books, 1992), 52–53.

rather than pleasant; later it yields the peaceful fruit of righteousness to those who have been trained by it. (RSV, emphasis added)

Most commentators seem to overlook this passage and dwell upon the preceding athletic imagery of running "the race that is set before us." In so doing, they imply that Jesus gives divine sanction to the activity of chastisement even though no such evidence exists. Barnabas Lindars, who encourages us to read Hebrews with imagination and sensitivity, argues that the double description of Jesus as "the pioneer and perfecter of our faith" captures the "essential theology of Hebrews" in such a way that all other aspects of the letter are subordinate to the author's desire to show that his readers too can reach salvation if they cling to faith in Jesus. Yet in setting the way of Jesus before them, the author appears to associate the physical chastisement that his readers seem to know all too well with the chastisement that the human Jesus receives in "offering his will to God even in death." Lindars thus concludes, Jesus " 'learned obedience through what he suffered' and so can save 'all who obey him' (verse 9). The readers too need to learn obedience through their sufferings and temptations."[31]

Frederick Danker tries to be inclusive by imagining the anonymous author as a female. However, the images of a father disciplining his son and the notion that illegitimacy is related to being "left without discipline" make this approach seem misguided.[32] Greven notes, poignantly, that while we can never know for certain if his earthly parents subjected Jesus to the pain of the rod, we must surely wonder how the *scourging* of Jesus could become "the model for Christian parents to follow with their children in the centuries to come."[33] Such an extreme view may seem out of place to the majority of Christians who have never physically disciplined their children; but as we will soon see, there is more truth than fiction to Greven's observation. Nevertheless, given Jesus' inclusive imagination and his questionable ties to apocalyptic thinking, it appears unlikely that Jesus was ever subjected to the rod in his formative years.

The Letter to the Hebrews is not an apocalypse in the manner of John's Revelation. Nevertheless, it "conveys apocalyptic thought" and presupposes an audience that is apocalyptically aware. Because the promise of entering God's rest is still open in Christ, the author exhorts his readers not to ignore the foundation laid for them in the teaching about Christ they

31. Barnabas Lindars, *The Theology of the Letter to the Hebrews* (New York: Cambridge University Press, 1991), 136–37, 62 (1 Pet. 4:13).

32. Frederick W. Danker, *Invitation to the New Testament Epistles IV: A Commentary on Hebrews, James, I Peter, 1 and 2 and 3 John and Jude* (New York: Images Books, Doubleday, 1980), 18, 81–82.

33. Greven, *Spare the Child*, 50.

have received: "instruction about baptisms, laying on of hands, resurrection of the dead, and eternal judgment" (Heb. 6:2). Greven's main concern is the presence of abuse and apocalyptic eschatology in Hebrews. However, if we take his insights further we find a third phenomenon: sacrificial/substitutionary atonement. As John McRay observes, "The Letter does not argue or explain the classical view [of atonement]; it *presupposes it and proceeds to set its picture of the high priestly work of Christ against this apocalyptic background. . . .*" The Letter to the Hebrews may also have served as "a *crucial bridge* between the fading apocalypticism of the Maccabean era and the peculiar form of Jewish Christianity which developed after the destruction of the Temple in 70 A.D."[34]

The arguments of Hebrews presuppose a worldview that values the Aaronic priesthood as a mediator of divine rule and the Temple cult as the sole means of atonement for sin. In this context, the author focuses on the uniqueness of Jesus' sacrifice and the present greatness of Christ. The letter also looks to the city of God, symbolic of God's kingdom, which is to come on earth when Christ returns. In this Hebrews bears similarities to John's Apocalypse, whose eschatological orientation and lived experience of persecution make John's apocalyptic perspective a critical factor in the continuing presence of this eschatological phenomenon.[35]

The Revelation to John

The Revelation to John, received on the island of Patmos most likely around 96 C.E., is full of vibrant symbolism that would have been easily accessible to those who received it and were immersed in its context—the threat posed by the religious and political force of Roman rule.[36] The revelatory vision at the center of the book comes to John on a Sunday, when he is "in the Spirit" and hears a loud voice behind him like a trumpet (Rev. 1:10). Turning to see whose voice it is, he sees "one like the Son of Man" in whose presence John "fell at his feet as though dead" (Rev. 1:13, 17). The voice instructs him to write what he sees and what will take place and send it to seven churches in Asia Minor.

Greven tags what John sees and what he writes as the most violent and punitive book in the Bible. Nevertheless, many Christians champion this

34. John McRay, "Atonement and Apocalyptic in the Book of Hebrews," *Restoration Quarterly: Studies in Christian Scholarship* 23, no. 1 (1980): 2, 4, 8; emphasis added.

35. A. N. Chester, "Hebrews: The Final Sacrifice," in *Sacrifice and Redemption: Durham Essays in Theology*, ed. S. W. Sykes (Cambridge: Cambridge University Press, 1991), 58–59; Ray Stedman, *Hebrews*, New Testament Series InterVarsity Press, available at *www.pbc.org/dp/Stedman/hebrews2/heb2intro.html.*

36. L. Michael White, "Understanding the Book of Revelation," in *Frontline: Apocalypse!* available at *www.pbs.ord/wgbh/pages/frontline/shows/apocalypse/revelation/white.html.*

book as a definitive mediator of God's saving Word. Liberation theologians have even looked to John's vision to counter oppression. Elisabeth Schüssler Fiorenza argues that John uses rhetorical devices to motivate his readers' emotions — to make the right decision here and now, by exhorting believers to live in obedience to God in this life, resist Roman oppression, and be saved in the next. She also recognizes that the oppressive nature of John's language could, if not properly translated outside of this "rhetorical situation," perpetuate prejudice and injustice toward women.[37]

Her tendency to disregard the lived experience of John as a source for the violence and misogyny she identifies, however, is puzzling. While noting that John's Revelation is a visionary, ecstatic experience similar to prophecy, Schüssler Fiorenza argues that the symbolic language of Revelation speaks more about institutions and political-religious collectives than about individuals. Yet how can one argue that John used hate-filled language to *mobilize his readers' emotions* and never question the emotional resources of the seer? In John's Revelation, the election of Christians through the death of Christ brings about a new kingdom on earth in the eschatological future, a future promised to all who are written in the Lamb's book of life. Those not listed, however, can only await their destruction in "the lake of fire" (Rev. 20:15).

John's Revelation speaks of the threefold worthiness of the Lamb's sacrificial death (Rev. 5:9–10), much like the christological perspective of Hebrews. With similar associations to the blood of salvation, Jesus is hailed as the one whom God raised from the dead, "the great shepherd of the sheep, by the blood of the eternal covenant" (Heb. 13:20). Two separate communities thus share a common vision. Though one appeals to the eternal priest who intercedes on our behalf and the other to the Lamb slain for our salvation, both place great emphasis on the value of sacrifice while revealing the pervasiveness of apocalyptic imagery. Once again, reliance on sacrificial imagery addresses the believer's need for a hopeful future to counter the subtext of apocalyptic fears.

Those who find meaning in this imagery often live worthy lives dedicated to justice and communal well-being. Nevertheless, when sacrificial imagery and apocalyptic rhetoric are joined, domination and the punitive use of power are never far away. While John's Revelation originally addressed Roman imperialism, Augustine, in the context of an imperial church that needed to secure its hold on the faithful, accommodated John's vision to the needs of the very empire it once critiqued. In Au-

---

37. Schüssler Fiorenza, *The Book of Revelation*, 7, 192, 199; Keller, *Apocalypse Now and Then*, 22.

gustine's reading, apocalyptic themes become literal manifestations of the church's authority and subsume the use of apocalyptic imagery for sustaining aspirations of justice. In Augustine's hands, Catherine Keller argues, "Revelation is skillfully de-revolutionized."[38]

Apocalyptic Imagery and the Eucharist

My critique of apocalyptic and sacrificial imagery relates directly to the role each has played in the creation of a *de-revolutionized eucharist.* Recall Besert's concern for the eucharist to once again become the "seed of revolution that awakens the mind to what is possible, to what is not yet achieved." Instead of awakening many Christians to their own capacity for compassion, Holy Communion in Reformed churches often becomes an exercise in soul-searching, weighted heavily toward penitential imagery (often unconscious, but nevertheless potent). When the imagery of eternal punishment and forgiveness of sins encounters this self-reflective moment, communicants are encouraged to dwell on their personal salvation, often at the expense of radical world openness. Can mindlessness be far behind? Reflecting on one's unworthiness in this context surely reinforces a negative and limiting self-image that undermines one's potential for fullness of being.

In speaking of the role of pilgrimage in Christian devotional life during the Middle Ages, Margaret Miles reminds us that "fear of hell was cultivated — vividly described and visually depicted — in the daily communications of their societies, sermons and paintings."[39] In the work of Albrecht Dürer, the most famous artist of Reformation Germany, the Apocalypse loomed large indeed. In this context, both Calvin and Luther appropriated the sacrifice-of-praise motif (Heb. 13:15) to substantiate their view that the eucharist proclaimed (rather than repeated) Christ's once-for-all sacrifice on the cross (Heb. 10:10).

Neither Hebrews nor John's Apocalypse deals directly with the eucharist as ritual. However, each contains eucharistic allusions that, when amplified, reinforce the nature of sacrifice as a primary eucharistic metaphor with an apocalyptic subtext. With Hebrews as a foundation, the eucharist becomes the "meal of Melchizedek" where the high priest makes a "perpetual offering" by his "once-for-all" sacrifice on our behalf. Here Jesus the high priest offers his own body and blood as the Lamb of God, the same

---

38. Keller, *Apocalypse Now and Then*, 99, 97–103.

39. Margaret Miles, *Practicing Christianity: Critical Perspectives for an Embodied Christianity* (New York: Crossroad/Continuum, 1988), 47.

Lamb enthroned in Revelation.[40] In the worldview of apocalyptic politics, victim and priest seem forever one.

Earlier, in the context of Isaiah's feast for all people (Isa. 25:6–8), I questioned the use of eschatological-banquet imagery when the subtext of Isaiah's feast is clearly aligned with the destruction of God's rebellious children (Isa. 66:24). A similar moment of dissonance occurs in the context of the "marriage supper of the lamb." As Catherine Keller acknowledges, three feasts merge into one within the "literary structure" of chapter 19:

- The great whore of Babylon will be burned and devoured (Rev. 17:16; 19:3).
- The faithful who have endured to the end are invited to the "marriage supper of the lamb" (Rev. 19:9).
- And the feast of vultures precedes the devil's binding for a thousand years. An angel invites the birds to gather for the "great supper of God," to eat the flesh of kings, captains, and the mighty, "the flesh of horses and their riders — flesh of all, both free and slave, both small and great" (Rev. 19:17–18).

Form and content go together, and in this case the evidence is striking. The invitation to the marriage supper of the Lamb is encircled by the sacrifice of "the great whore" and the image of vultures "gorged" with the flesh of those whom the "Word of God," the "King of Kings and Lord of Lords," has slain with the armies of heaven.

These apocalyptic images come with stunning speed, "blending," as Keller suggests, "in a bitter imagistic aftertaste." The irony of ironies follows when Jesus, who rehearsed the eschatological banquet by eating with outcasts and whores, presides over the final victory of God, which requires the great whore's destruction. Hence Keller concludes, "There is no veiling the way this vision of justice boils down to the burning and devouring of a woman's body."[41] The misogyny at the heart of the Apocalypse has now claimed the "Last Supper" as the true victim. Jesus presides over the gruesome "supper of God," which connotes, as Keller rightly observes, "The Lord's Supper." Truly the marriage feast of the Lamb has made this an eschatological feast unworthy of the name. Sacrificial imagery is sanctioned in John's Revelation, but the cost seems steep. Liturgically, the eucharist

40. Robert J. Daly, *Christian Sacrifice: The Judaeo-Christian Background before Origen* (Washington, D.C.: Catholic University of America Press, 1978), 262–63; Ronald Williamson, "The Eucharist and the Epistle to the Hebrews," *New Testament Studies* 21 (January 1975): 300–312; Scott Hahn, "The Eucharist as the Meal of Melchizedek," available at *www.ewtn.com/faith/teachings/euchc4.htm.*

41. Keller, *Apocalypse Now and Then,* 76.

has traveled far from the inclusiveness of Jesus. Yet it travels even further thanks to the apocalyptic preferences of the influential *Didache*.

The *Didache*

Functioning as a community rule in Syria, most likely in the first century C.E.,[42] the *Didache* offered guidelines for discipline as well as for rituals and prayers. Three sections prove critical, however, for the evolution of eucharistic practice. Chapter 14 advises the community to come together on every Lord's Day (Sunday) to break bread "and give thanks, first confessing your sins so that your sacrifice may be pure." This reference to Malachi's pure sacrifice (Mal. 1:11) shares associations with Hebrews and the Revelation to John, all of which reinforce the second coming of Jesus. The term *Maranatha* (Come, Lord!) in *Didache* 10:6 belongs most likely at the opening of the eucharistic liturgy proper: "It is either an acclamation of the presence of the Lord who has been in the assembly through the service of the word and who will continue to be there in the eucharist, or else . . . a prayer for the eucharistic presence of Christ as at least a partial anticipation of the parousia."[43] More striking is the rule that those invited to come to the table are "the holy," for *only* those who were baptized in Jesus' name are permitted to eat or drink — lest what is sacred be given "to dogs." Significantly, those who use the *Didache* as a guide to their eucharist are encouraged to exclude those with whom Jesus ate and drank as a matter of course. Exclusion thus appears as the functioning pattern for the community's communal meal. But is this its only message? It appears so, until we bring chapters 9 and 10 to the foreground:

> CHAPTER 9
>
> Now concerning the Thanksgiving meal [eucharist], give thanks in this manner. . . .
>
> But let no one eat or drink of your Thanksgiving, unless they have been baptized in the Name of the Lord; for concerning this the Lord said, "Do not give what is holy to dogs."
>
> CHAPTER 10
>
> After the meal, give thanks in this manner. . . .
>
> Let Your grace come,
And let this world pass away.
Hosanna to the God of David!

42. Bradshaw, *Search*, 84–86.
43. Wainwright, *Eucharist and Eschatology*, 70.

May all who are holy, come;
Let those who are not, repent.
Maranatha. Amen.[44]

When chapter 10 of the *Didache* is placed before chapter 9 and assumed to be the original text, a fascinating shift emerges. The lack of ritualization for the bread and cup in *Didache* 10 suggests it was composed before chapter 9 and represents an earlier understanding of the meal. In addition, chapter 10 allows the unholy to come to the meal if they first repent. In *Didache* 9, which was written later but placed earlier in the document to give it more authority, we find a number of interesting additions: Jesus is called the Child/Servant but also "the Christ," and the meal is called a eucharist. Lastly, while both 9 and 10 have eschatological imagery, the language of chapter 9 clearly shows a more developed sense of exclusion, since only the baptized may eat and drink.[45]

Crossan argues that the dual existence of *Didache* 10 and the pre-Pauline tradition in 1 Corinthians 10–11 undercuts the notion of a Last Supper "with its passion symbolism institutionalized and commanded to repetition by Jesus himself on the eve of his death." He also shows the importance of the meal as the primary eucharistic reality.[46] As with the Letter to the Hebrews and John's "marriage supper of the lamb," apocalyptic imagery has been tied to the eucharist through the use of sacrificial imagery (*Didache* 14). Consequently, community restrictions as to who may receive Christ's saving body and blood continue to tighten.

Come Again?

When carried forth in the writings of Augustine, with his developed notion of original sin, apocalyptic imagery clearly becomes a formidable force in the shaping of Christian identity. As many of the early liturgies attest, the *parousia* was vitally present in second-century Christianity. Despite its delay, it continued to have a strong hold on the minds of believers, even though Augustine argued against systematizing the time of Christ's return. In fact, Augustine bequeathed to the medieval world a pessimistic view of the future, as individual souls made their pilgrimage through the earthly city waiting for Jesus' return. Further evidence of the *parousia*'s influence can be seen in the evolution of Christian art, where sobering

44. *Didache*, trans. Ivan Lewis, 1998; available at *www.earlychristianwritings.com/didache.html.*
45. John W. Riggs, "From Gracious Table to Sacramental Elements: The Tradition-History of *Didache* 9 and 10," *Second Century* 4 (summer 1984): 83–101.
46. Crossan, *The Historical Jesus*, 361–65.

images replaced resurrection imagery. Catacomb images of Jonah and the whale and images of the raising of Lazarus, along with meal imagery and many allusions to the feeding miracles, gave way to depictions of the Last Judgment. This image was so widespread in medieval ecclesiastical art that it was often found over the chancel arch or on the west wall of churches as a vivid reminder of the judgment to come. Its presence also reminded believers of the final options of heaven or hell that awaited believers and nonbelievers alike.[47]

Perceiving God

James Alison, whose quote begins the chapter, seeks the recovery of an eschatological imagination for contemporary Christians. At the same time he laudably presents a living and loving God who is "pruned of violence" and bears no responsibility for Jesus' death. I share his vision of divine vitality; yet I cannot support his methodology, as it relies on the apocalyptic imagery of a "forgiven victim" and a slaughtered yet triumphant lamb. Alison suggests that the vitality of God can best be perceived through one choice: we must fix our minds on the things that are above — the imagery of a risen victim and a slaughtered lamb — and actively create "the wedding banquet of the lamb in the midst of this world, in God's creative vivaciousness, utterly incapable of frustration." Alison concludes his book with a summary taken directly from Hebrews 12:18–24, which suggests that the blood of Jesus speaks more strongly than the blood of Abel. Because of this, he would have us "make of our lives the joyous preparation of the feast of the innocent victim."[48] Tellingly this text is sandwiched between two problematic images of God: the image of one who punishes the believer as a father punishes his son (12:3–11) and the clearly apocalyptic image of consuming fire (12:29). Seen in this light, can there be any doubt that human representations have the power to radically limit our experience of God's incomprehensible mystery? After all, hell is hardly the place to look for a compassionate deity.

Divine Punishment and the Creation of Hell

Within the tribal era of Israelite history, the theological basis of punishment was related to the covenant between YHWH and his chosen people.

47. Wainwright, *Eucharist and Eschatology,* 42–43; Marjorie Reeves, "The Development of Apocalyptic Thought: Medieval Attitudes," in *The Apocalypse in English Renaissance Thought and Literature: Patterns, Antecedents, and Repercussions,* ed. C. A. Patrides and Joseph Wittreich (Ithaca, N.Y.: Cornell University Press, 1984), 40–72.

48. Alison, *Raising Abel,* 195–97.

While divine revelation was understood to be their inspiration, Israel's laws often reflected the standards of neighboring communities. Scholars also speculate that punishment, as a method of response to injury, began as vengeance. In setting a limit to vengeance, the law prescribed penalties that were deemed reasonable.

The prophets spoke of the divine intention to purify and not destroy. However, a significant theological shift pictured YHWH "himself" taking responsibility for vengeance (Deut. 32:35).[49] Under the influence of prophetic orations, the Hebrew people thus came to believe that YHWH had the power to punish the tribe or nation and to punish children for the iniquity of their parents, to the third and fourth generation (Exod. 34:7; Num. 14:18). The precise means whereby God came to be understood as one who punishes may be traced to the concept of the mighty king that played a central role in the Israelite doctrine of God, particularly the notion that God was an all-powerful judge who enacted retributive justice.[50]

For our purposes the postexilic notion that banishment to hell was the severest chastisement God could impose proves noteworthy, for in preexilic Israel "hell" was nonexistent. Israelites believed in Sheol, a shadowy underworld existence — imaged as a pit or bog — that awaited all who died and carried no threat of punishment.[51] Before the Exile, Israel believed that the requiting of wrongs or the vindication of the innocent took place in this life or not at all. With the rise of Jewish apocalyptic literature after the Exile, however, the notion that life after death existed began to take hold. At the same time, Hebraic thought began to show affinities with the Zoroastrian (Persian) belief that supported a universal divine judgment after death in which the soul would either be rewarded in heaven or punished in hell.[52] From this point onward, the image of hell took hold of Christian imaginations, with the exception of Paul. While Paul looks at judgment (in 1 Cor. 3–4 and in other places) as more individual and relative, his primary teaching is that "God for Christ's sake will judge all Christians to be righteous and grant them salvation, in contrast to the unbelieving world."[53]

---

49. Abraham J. Heschel, *The Prophets: An Introduction* (New York: Harper & Row, 1962), 187.

50. J. Arthur Hoyles, *Punishment in the Bible* (London: Epworth Press, 1986), 3–14, 27.

51. Martha Himmelfarb, *Tours of Hell: An Apocalyptic Form in Jewish and Christian Literature* (Philadelphia: University of Pennsylvania Press, 1983), 107.

52. Hoyles, *Punishment*, 42–44; Colleen McDannell and Bernhard Lang, *Heaven: A History* (New Haven: Yale University Press, 1988), 12.

53. F. F. Bruce, *Philippians* (San Francisco: Harper & Row, 1983), 105; David W. Kuck, *Judgment and Community Conflict: Paul's Use of Apocalyptic Judgment Language in 1 Corinthians 3:5–4:5*, Supplements to Novum Testamentum, no. 66 (Leiden: E. J. Brill, 1992), 239.

Tours of Hell

The genre of Christian apocalypse, also known as "tours of hell," came into being in the mid–second century, even though textual evidence existed as early as the third century B.C.E. in the Book of Watchers (chapters 1–36 of 1 Enoch). The earliest datable tour is the Apocalypse of Peter and the latest is Dante's *Divine Comedy* (fourteenth century). Sharing a common theme, they nevertheless were products of their times.[54] Scholars once believed the prehistory of the Apocalypse of Peter rested in the classical Greek descents into Hades and the Greek mysteries. However, notions of judgment tied to a "final apocalyptic act of God" are not part of Greco-Roman traditions. Where it was used, judgment language in relation to the afterlife functioned as moral exhortation and consolation concerning death, not unlike today. Some individuals were also known to use this imagery "for the control of the uneducated."[55]

In the Middle Ages, the Apocalypse of Paul proved to be the most influential tour, having been translated from Greek into five languages. Curiously, it devoted ten chapters to describing the punishing torments of hell,[56] and of these, the most prominent were postexilic measure-for-measure punishments such as an eye for an eye. A second group relates to the "punishments inflicted by the geography of hell." While Sheol was perceived to be damp and dank, and the Greek Hades was known for its mud and mire, the initial "hell" of Hebrew thought was known as Gehinnom (Gk. *Gehenna,* named after the Hinnom Valley in Jerusalem) and was associated with a vast fire. Martha Himmelfarb traces the transition from fire as punishment on earth to the fire of Gehinnom by exploring the imagery of Isaiah 66:24, which speaks of the dead bodies of those who have rebelled against YHWH being consumed by worms that never die and unquenchable fires.

By the beginning of the Common Era this earthly scene of worms and fire is understood by the Gospel of Mark to be a central image of hell (Mark 9:47–48). Apart from Paul's writings, the "concept of a fiery hell" appears firmly established in the Christian Scriptures, while fiery punishment becomes a common image for the destruction of the wicked in apocalyptic literature. Sheol, which was once the abode of righteous and wicked alike, has been imaginatively superseded by hell, a place of fiery punishment where only the wicked reside. Regrettably, the lived experience of

54. Claudia Rattazzi Papka, "The Limits of Apocalypse: Eschatology, Epistemology, and Textuality in the *Commedia* and *Piers Plowman*," in *Last Things: Death and the Apocalypse in the Middle Ages,* ed. Caroline Walker Bynum and Paul Freedman (Philadelphia: University of Pennsylvania Press, 2000), 233–56.

55. Kuck, *Judgment,* 148–49.

56. Himmelfarb, *Tours,* 16–29, 67.

fear reinforced by bodily pain may well have contributed to humanity's collective failure to track this imaginal process.

By the time of Luther, the fear and despair attached to hell were profound. "Constantly the damned will be judged, constantly, they will suffer pain, and constantly they will be a fiery oven, that is, they will be tortured within by supreme distress and tribulation."[57] Understood to be a consuming fire (Heb. 12:29), God was greatly to be feared, as were the fires of hell, which manifested the eternal wrath of God and the vindication of God's justice. This fear also had physical repercussions. Throughout Luther's life, he was ruled by "a bewildering array of aggressive disorders" that led him at times to act "in ways destructive to himself and to others."[58] Moreover, there is little question that a measure of this turmoil can be laid at the feet of apocalyptic eschatology: "ill health and apocalyptic fears played a large role in [Luther's] bouts of melancholy," for Luther, in his later years, firmly believed he was "living on the eve of the Last Judgment."

Jürgen Moltmann argues that Luther understands hell not so much as a place as a state of being estranged from God, because of God's anger and rejection of sin. Yet if hell is not a place for Luther, it surely is an image that has deep roots in his imagination, as does the image of devil: "He was never so fierce and full of rage as he is now. I feel him well. But when I remember myself, and take hold on the Gospel, and meet him here with, then I overcome him and confute all his arguments; yet for a time I often fail."[59]

Regarding Calvin, Alister McGrath describes him as a "somewhat cold and detached individual [and] . . . an unhappy man" who lacked Luther's "wit, humor, and warmth." He also was known to launch into "abusive personal attacks on those with whom he disagreed, rather than dealing primarily with their ideas."[60] While Calvin understood hell as representing a profound alienation from the fellowship of God, there could be no doubt that hell had geographical associations both for him and for his generation. To experience the tortures of hell, he wrote, is to be "eternally and unceasingly besieged by [God]."[61]

---

57. Ewald M. Plass, ed., *What Luther Says: An Anthology*, vol. 1 (St. Louis: Concordia, 1959), 627.

58. Roger Johnson, "Psychohistory as Religious Narrative," in *Psychohistory and Religion: The Case of Young Man Luther*, ed. Roger A. Johnson (Philadelphia: Fortress Press, 1977), 138–39.

59. Martin Luther, *Luther's Works*, vol. 54, *Table Talk*, ed. and trans. Theodore G. Tappert (Philadelphia: Fortress Press, 1967), 626; Moltmann, *The Coming of God*, 252; Mark U. Edwards Jr., *Luther's Last Battles: Politics and Polemics, 1531–46* (Ithaca, N.Y.: Cornell University Press, 1983), 15–16.

60. Alister E. McGrath, *A Life of John Calvin: A Study in the Shaping of Western Culture* (Oxford: Basil Blackwell, 1990), 17.

61. John Calvin, *Institutes of the Christian Religion*, Library of Christian Classics, ed. John R.

Studies have shown that anxieties related to physical illness and death were constant psychic companions for those living in preindustrial societies, and Luther and Calvin were no exception. The pain each experienced as a result of their numerous ailments no doubt had a profound effect on their bodies as well as their minds.[62] Indeed, those of us living in industrial societies where innovations in technology are the rule, and easy access to a physician is assumed, can barely comprehend the deep anxiety produced by such illnesses as well as the fear of death they generated. We may come close to understanding when we recall the "nuclear nightmares" that accompanied the dreams of many children during the Cold War as well as the deep anxiety that follows terrorist acts. But such fear is still beyond the grasp of many. Without a doubt the fears underlying the imagery of hell and damnation in the writings of the reformers were cultivated by physical ailments, the "tours of hell," the focus on the individual as sinner, as well as sermons and paintings that latched on to the imagery of the Last Judgment with a vengeance. As in earlier times, hell could hardly have been an occasional concern.

While some would argue that the "hell, fire, and brimstone" sermons of Jonathan Edwards and other preachers of the Great Awakening no longer hold sway in many mainstream churches, such assertions ignore the power of these images to remain embedded in the Christian psyche, as well as the fears that are continually generated through personal and societal experiences of violence. For many biblical literalists these fears continue to shape their lives and liturgies. Amos Wilder blamed the great revivals of the nineteenth century for a "basic insensitivity and inhibition with respect to the aesthetic order and the impulse to celebration." He writes, "The history of the revivals meant no less than a trauma in the American psyche, in Middle America, one whose effects still go on for better and worse both in our culture and in our religiosity. The awakenings and the revivals . . . blew the minds of our populace as only an overwhelming experience of the sacred can do." The emotions expressed in these revivals were subsequently channeled into "individualist," "anti-intellectual," and "anti-aesthetic" sensibilities.[63]

The notion of hell we have come to fear once existed as the realm of Hel, the goddess of death, in the Germanic languages. Like Sheol, hell was not a place to be feared and Hel was not an evil goddess. However, when Christian theologians began to renovate it, the symbolic power of hell

---

McNeil, trans. Ford Lewis Battles (Philadelphia: Westminster, 1960), 21:1007–8; McGrath, *A Life of John Calvin*, 15.

62. Crossan, *The Historical Jesus*, 4; Edwards, *Last Battles*, 6–19; George, *Reformers*, 246.

63. Amos Niven Wilder, *Theopoetic: Theology and the Religious Imagination* (Philadelphia: Fortress Press, 1976) 50–51.

was re-imaged, in the words of Uta Ranke-Heinemann, to serve "the holy purpose of cradle-to-grave intimidation."[64] The Christian image of hell, however, has always been a human construction — based on the embodied experience of fear. Influenced by the literary gifts of Isaiah, Mark, John of Patmos, and the genre of tours, hell became the dominating image of imperial Christianity. In authorizing penitential practices as a remedy for eternal punishment, the church effectively reinforced *hell on earth.*

---

64. Uta Ranke-Heinemann, *Putting Away Childish Things: The Virgin Birth, The Empty Tomb, and Other Fairy Tales You Don't Need to Believe to Have a Living Faith*, trans. Peter Heinegg (San Francisco: HarperSanFrancisco, 1992), 228.

SIX

What Price Forgiveness?

> One of the first faculties to be subjected to the discipline of penance is the imagination. So powerful is this faculty, and so subtle its work, that with these beguiling fancies, it can, before the soul knows what is happening, substitute one set of motives for another.
>
> —*Dom Hubert van Zeller*[1]

> Properly speaking, our redemption in Jesus Christ is found neither in the cross, nor in his blood, nor in his death. Instead, we are redeemed by Jesus' attitude of love, surrender, and forgiveness. But it was not only his death that was loving, surrendering, and forgiving. It was his whole life.
>
> —*Leonardo Boff*[2]

As Boff suggests, a defining mark of Jesus' earthly ministry is his capacity to forgive. This begs the question: Is Jesus' suffering the only way to secure divine forgiveness? Those who seek a picture of grace other than Jesus on the cross seek to witness to the forgiving grace of God already in their midst. Finding human tragedy, not divine necessity, at work in Jesus' death, they imagine a world where the price of forgiveness for each of us becomes truthfulness within ourselves and truthfulness before God and neighbor. It is equally true, however, that a defining mark of Christianity is its willingness to cloak God's forgiveness in the mystery of Jesus' death and perpetuate itself through fear. To see this at work we need to appreciate imperial Christianity's capacity for dominating nonbelievers and believers alike. In their desire "to secure the political unity and religious power of the empire,"[3] Christian emperors advocated for christological doctrines that solidified their authority by appropriating the authority of Jesus. In

1. Dom Hubert van Zeller, *Spirit of Penance, Path to God: How Acts of Penance Will Make Your Life Holier and Your Days Happier* (Manchester, N.H.: Sophia Institute Press, 1998), 12.

2. Cited in Darby Kathleen Ray, *Deceiving the Devil: Atonement, Abuse, and Ransom* (Cleveland: Pilgrim Press, 1998), 92.

3. Elisabeth Schüssler Fiorenza, *Jesus: Miriam's Child, Sophia's Prophet* (New York: Continuum, 1994), 23.

doing so, they manipulated the power of ritual to serve their dominarchal purposes. This chapter explores this trend by looking at the power of fear (persecution), the power of guilt (atonement), and the power of shame (penance). Although each of these areas deserves fuller treatment than I can give them here, I intend to identify patterns and connections that narrow social and personal horizons of meaning. In each instance fear became an embodied reality that eroded imaginal possibilities and perpetuated suffering, both within and without Christian communities.

The Power of Fear

By the time the Gospels offered their unique liturgical remembrances of Jesus' last evening with his disciples (John's involved foot-washing), an anti-Jewish bias had made its presence known. Whereas John's Gospel had faulted the Jewish leaders, later Christians (among them Tertullian, Augustine, and Martin Luther) laid responsibility for Jesus' death with the Jews generally. In order to "salvage" the God of the Hebrew Bible from those who wanted to disconnect Christian faith from its past, as well as salvage the writings of Paul, Christian leaders perpetuated an "anti-Judaic myth"[4] that contributed to centuries of Jewish persecution, well before the Holocaust of the twentieth century. The continuing presence of this myth, despite enormous strides in Jewish-Christian relations, leads James Carroll to argue passionately that the church's ability to take a firm stand against religious oppression remains impossible without ending its "fixation on the death of Jesus as the universal salvific act."[5]

While Christianity has kept alive memories of its own persecution, it has been less forthcoming about its persecution of others. The evidence, hidden well into the twentieth century, reaches into antiquity. For Socrates and other pagan philosophers, the Greek term *diamones* represented sustaining spiritual energies. With the ascendancy of Christianity to a position of dominance, these *diamones* evolved into the *demons* of Christianity's collective imagination. As historians have noted, "It was conventional wisdom among the leadership of the church that fear constituted a most essential element in the mix of motives that could bring an audience round."[6] Christianity's persecution of pagans involved the destruction of non-Christian writings in public bonfires, threats of amputation for anyone

4. Gerald S. Sloyan, *The Crucifixion of Jesus: History, Myth, Faith* (Minneapolis: Fortress Press, 1995), 84.

5. James Carroll, *Constantine's Sword: The Church and the Jews, a History* (Boston: Houghton Mifflin, 2001), 583.

6. Ramsay MacMullen, *Christianity and Paganism in the Fourth to Eighth Centuries* (New Haven: Yale University Press, 1997), chapter 1; Elaine Pagels, *The Origin of Satan* (New York: Vintage Books, 1995), 120.

daring to copy banned material, suppression of facts in recorded history so as to favor Christian versions of the truth, as well as clear evidence of church leaders inciting mob violence against those they deemed to be wrong. In addition to the destruction of sacred images in homes and temples, torture and crucifixion were key methods of eradicating nonbelievers. Those who were active in the eradication of nonconformity included "zealots, monks, bishops, and civil officialdom."[7] For pagan and Jew alike, the consequences of Christianity's fearfulness have been severe. At the same time, the church's teaching on atonement merits mixed reviews.

The Power of Guilt

Traditionalists argue that by overstepping God-given boundaries, humankind came to know fear, shame, and death as God's presence was overwhelmed by the appearance of God's absence. That is until God proved his love by sending Jesus to die for us: "For if while we were *enemies,* we were reconciled to God through the death of his Son, much more surely, having been reconciled, will we be saved by his life" (Rom. 5:10; emphasis added). Paul confesses that the sign of God's love — the death of Christ — is the antidote to God's wrath! Yet how strange is this? With one critical shift of imagery the violence perpetrated on Jesus becomes romanticized into *suffering love* — a love that suffers on our behalf. Incredibly, the violence that leads to the death of Jesus becomes less important than his death and the benefits it brings, notably forgiveness of sins. In contrast to Paul, H. D. McDonald declares that the price of forgiveness is punishment, not love, for "only punishment" can remove guilt and without atonement there is no forgiveness.[8]

In elevating punishment and guilt, atonement imagery put legalism before love. Indeed the terms "sacrifice," "ransom," "satisfaction," "substitution," and "representative," are all tied to the belief that humankind transgressed the laws of God (thou shalt not...) and was found guilty of disobedience in Eden. Yet earlier interpretations were more positive. Through the first four hundred years of Christian interpretation, Genesis 2–3 was regarded as a story about human freedom. Christians sought to free themselves from the bonds of pagan tradition and custom as well as the persecution that accompanied their refusal to honor Roman gods.[9]

7. MacMullen, *Christianity and Paganism,* 11.

8. H. D. McDonald, *Forgiveness and Atonement* (Grand Rapids, Mich.: Baker Book House, 1984), 96, 121.

9. Elaine Pagels, *Adam, Eve, and the Serpent* (New York: Vintage Books, 1989), xxv.

In the fourth century, however, after Constantine's conversion, Christians experienced a vastly different worldview. Clergy, who once lived under threat of death, now received financial donations, tax exemptions, and enormous prestige. Writing after this seismic shift, Augustine, who at one time had espoused a positive view of human freedom, advanced his personal interpretation of Genesis 2–3, arguing that the events depicted therein were the source of original sin and human corruption. Although his views were controversial, they triumphed over Pelagius's view that death was not divine punishment for sin. In the aftermath of 381, when heresy became a crime against the state, Augustine's influence also led to a "theory of suppression" that justified the "imposition of church authority — by force, if necessary — as essential for human salvation."[10]

Augustine's views triumphed not because they were popular but because they offered a "psychologically simple and compelling" explanation of why human beings suffer. In Elaine Pagels view, Augustine "addresses the deep human longing to be free of pain" and assures the sufferer that "pain is unnatural, [and] death an enemy."[11] At the same time, Augustine reinforced the notion that sin and suffering are causally related by suggesting that blame lies not with the one suffering but with Adam and Eve. In confronting the helplessness human beings experienced in the face of inexplicable pain, Augustine served up a large dose of guilt that many willingly swallowed. In doing so, the foundational guilt that feeds atonement theories was theologically authenticated. More importantly, it was liturgically rehearsed and thus reinforced by the necessity of undergoing the cleansing waters of baptism.

As atonement imagery flourished, Western Christianity used it to elevate God's power (over guilty humanity) and sacrifice human agency. Of necessity, the omnipotence of God requires that human powerlessness be accepted *without question.* Only a sovereign God can save us from sin. To see this theology fleshed out, we consider the three conceptions of atonement described by Gustaf Aulén in his 1931 study, *Christus Victor:*

- the *Christus Victor* or "classic" idea promoted by the Greek fathers of the East
- the satisfaction theory of Anselm (1033–1109) in the West
- and the moral influence theory of Abelard (1079–1142)[12]

---

10. Ibid., 125; Gary Wills, *Saint Augustine* (New York: Penguin Putnam, 1999), 101–2.

11. Pagels, *Adam, Eve,* 147.

12. Gustaf Aulén, *Christus Victor: An Historical Study of the Three Main Types of the Idea of the Atonement,* trans. A. G. Hebert (New York: Macmillan, 1951), chap. 1.

From Paul to the Puritans, apocalyptic imagery reduced the work of Christ to the suffering love revealed by his death. Why? I suspect the possibility of hell got too close for comfort.

Paul's Legacy

Paul's vision of Christianity was centered on atonement and the significance of Christ's death. He neither associated this death with punishment nor stressed the need to appease an angry God. The impression remains, however, that the nonbeliever is left to the mercy of God's wrath in Paul's theology, and that the notion of wrath, however much we try to downplay its power, reinforced the understanding that God's justice involved punishment.[13] Christ's death thus benefits the believer because the believer can relate his or her own life to Christ's suffering on the cross. Suffering, according to Paul, is not the goal of the believer's life or a sign of sin or of God's absence; suffering is a sure sign of being in Christ and of belonging to God (2 Cor. 1:3–7). At the same time, death is viewed as "inconsequential," for the believer has already died with Christ and thus will surely rise with Christ.[14] Through baptism the believer is assured of eternal life, for in Christ, there is a new creation (2 Cor. 5:17).

If the purpose of Christ's death is the *benefit* of living with Christ, whether one is living or dead when he comes (Rom. 14:8–9), redemption for nonbelievers who live apart from Christ remains nonexistent. As Paul repeatedly argued, "apart from Christ, everyone will be destroyed."[15] Indeed, Paul wept over the destruction that awaited those who, in his words, "live as *enemies of the cross* of Christ" (Phil. 3:18; emphasis added). In addition, Paul's theology had an apocalyptic edge. Paul is confident that God is waging a war in Christ and "in the end Christ will hand over the kingdom to God the Father, *after* he has destroyed every ruler and every authority and power (I Cor 15:24)."[16] The benefit Christ offers, then, is not only the freedom to resist sin but the assurance that resurrection, rather than destruction, awaits the true believer. There is more than a little irony, though, in Paul's decision to identify God's love with a declaration of war. One has to wonder how much of Paul's lived experiences of suffering influenced his "reception" of the view that God's love was expressed in the imagery of a suffering Christ who died for our sins. We know

13. Anthony J. Tambasco, A *Theology of Atonement and Paul's Vision of Christianity*, Zacchaeus Studies: New Testament (Collegeville, Minn.: Liturgical Press, 1991), 13, 32.

14. J. Paul Sampley, *Walking between the Times: Paul's Moral Reasoning* (Minneapolis: Fortress, 1991), 32, 80.

15. E. P. Sanders, *Jesus and Judaism* (Philadelphia: Fortress Press, 1985), 473.

16. J. Louis Martyn, *Theological Issues in the Letters of Paul* (Nashville: Abingdon Press, 1997), 156; emphasis added.

Paul was no stranger to suffering, as his litany to the Corinthians suggests (2 Cor. 11:24–25). He also experienced pain from the thorn given to him in the flesh, which he describes as "a messenger of Satan to torment me" (2 Cor. 12:7). We also know that in an earlier incarnation, Paul excelled at persecution.

Based on his own revelatory experience (1 Cor. 15:3; Gal. 1:11–12), Paul discounted the political dimensions of Jesus' death under Roman rule by teaching that Christ's death was salvific and that individual suffering is a sign of the believer's being in Christ. As one scholar noted, Paul's apocalyptic theology encouraged him to see in Christ's death "God's liberating invasion of the territory of tyranny."[17] Given the principalities and powers of his day, we should not be surprised by Paul's references to cosmological warfare. Nor should we be surprised that the language of divine invasion becomes an important metaphor for those who will systematize Paul's diverse thought. When coupled with belief in God's omnipotence, those who believe God is on their side easily distort the language of invasion.

Christus Victor, Anselm's Satisfaction Theory, and Abelard's Response

The period between the second and sixth centuries of the Common Era saw the imagery of struggle between God and evil take center stage, particularly following the daily encounters with hostile powers and tyrannical leaders endured by the fledgling church. The "fathers" of the early church looked to Paul's imagery of redemption and victory as well as the Gospel imagery that spoke of the Son of man who had come to give his life as a "ransom for many" (Matt. 20:28). As time passed, the notion of ransom was joined with the motif of deceiving the devil as a way of explaining God's active engagement in the defeat of evil. The forces that sought to separate humanity from God were understood to be death, the power of sin, and the law — the principalities and powers of institutions and government as well as the work of Satan, who eventually came to personify evil in its entirety.[18] According to Aulén's "classic" idea, God triumphantly defeats these forces by way of Jesus' resurrection from the dead. Early Christians also accepted the imagery of Jesus as God's bait luring the devil onto a hook. Thus the cross, which initially appeared to symbolize Satan's power, became the means of God's triumph.

Aulén finds the roots of his "classic" idea in the Christian Scriptures, but

17. Ibid., 154.

18. Darby Kathleen Ray, *Deceiving the Devil: Atonement, Abuse, and Ransom* (Cleveland: Pilgrim Press, 1998), chap. 7.

his primary proponent is Irenaeus, a profound Christian thinker of the second century. According to Irenaeus, God so *baffles* the devil by becoming human that the devil is fooled into thinking Jesus is merely human and thus subject to death. The devil is deceived when through Jesus' death and resurrection humankind is released — ransomed — from the devil's control.[19] The flaw in this imagery, though, is the role that Satan plays in the personification of evil. The image of Satan, who once functioned merely as an adversary, encourages the human inclination to demonize those who are different. Moreover, any benefit to Christian self-identity and self-preservation always comes at the expense of those who are seen as enemies of God. The image of the enemy as the evil one allows those who espouse such views to turn away from their own flaws and limitations and justify their own righteousness. As we have seen, Jews, pagans, and dissident Christians have all been subject to this fear-driven process, despite Jesus' call to love one's enemies. When we deceive ourselves by denying our own capacity for evil, self-deception leads to the imposition of suffering in the absence of justice. As Edward Ingebretsen observes in his study of religious terror as memory, "Evil is rarely allowed to remain abstract in any society. God might be faceless; the demonic, never."[20]

Irenaeus's reliance on the image of "ransom" was so offensive to Anselm that it motivated him to rework the atonement imagery of his predecessors. Thus (based in part on the feudal system of his time), Anselm argued that an infinite satisfaction (penance) was due God because man (*sic*) had insulted God's honor by permitting himself to be overcome by the devil. By their own actions human beings became subject to divine punishment, which only the God who became human could overturn. In order to be restored to the blessedness — eternal life — for which it was created, humankind must experience forgiveness, "the remission of sins," which only Christ, the sinless God-man, can bring about through his obedience through suffering.[21] Anselm argued that with the death of Christ, the mercy of God had satisfied the justice of God, which permitted nothing but punishment to be returned for sin.

Abelard's critique of Anselm, on the other hand, centered on the impossibility of the idea of satisfaction because of the greater sins committed against Christ. For Abelard, Christ is the "great Teacher and Example," one who awakens a meritorious love within persons because he graciously suffered on our behalf and bore the penalty/punishment of our sin. Unlike

---

19. Ibid., 34, 122.

20. Edward J. Ingebretsen, *Maps of Heaven, Maps of Hell: Religious Terror as Memory from the Puritans to Stephen King* (Armonk, N.Y.: M. E. Sharpe, 1996), xxvii.

21. Anselm, *Cur Deus Homo? Why God Became Man*, Christian Classics Series I, trans. Edward S. Prout (London: Religious Tract Society, n.d.), 61, 64, 104–5.

Anselm's appeal to our acceptance of the *objective fact* of Christ's death, Abelard's emphasis on forgiveness relied on the internal effects of love (the *subjective experience* of the individual) and the view expressed in Luke 7:47: "Much is forgiven to them that love much."[22] Those who find this theory wanting insist that our salvation lies in the fact of Jesus' death, not in the possibility that the human heart will be moved by the example of Jesus' sacrifice. Given the dogmatic influence of various emperors on the church's teaching, it should not surprise us that the power of salvation in the realm of atonement always rests with God, the King.

The divine necessity so crucial to Anselm's theory of forgiveness is reminiscent of scripture — "in him we have redemption through his blood, the forgiveness of our trespasses" (Eph. 1:7), and "without the shedding of blood there is no forgiveness of sins" (Heb. 9:22). In Abelard's theory the primary grace is union with Christ. While these nuances might seem inconsequential to the average believer, they are not. The images that accompany these ruminations are never far removed from our daily lives. Day after day clergywomen and men dust them off and pass them on though sermons, pastoral care, confirmation classes, and, lest we forget, the sacraments.

Until we understand the consequences of these views we will never appreciate the extent to which our lives remain at the mercy of Christianity's medieval captivity. Anselm's theology, with minor alterations, influenced both Roman Catholic and orthodox Protestant thinking, while liberal theologians of the nineteenth and twentieth centuries looked to Abelard. Even so, Anselm's greatest influence has come through the impact of art and liturgy — specifically, the role Handel's *Messiah* has played. Its stunning rendition of the "redemptive power of Christ's suffering," shaped by Handel's use of the Psalms, the imagery of the suffering servant in Isaiah, and its celebration of the Messiah's triumphant victory over Satan and the powers of evil remain unparalleled.[23] Whether we consciously know it or not, these images live within each of us. We dream about them, sing about them, and rehearse them in our liturgies, even though this imagery no longer fits our view of the world.

Anselm's theory was tied to a set of assumptions that are alien to many of us — the place of suffering and the inclusion of families in the penalties any individual received as a result of losing a legal battle. Since nations and tribes were represented by their leaders and shared their just rewards or

---

22. Aulén, *Christus Victor,* 96.

23. F. W. Dillistone, *The Christian Understanding of Atonement* (Philadelphia: Westminster Press, 1968), 426; Jaroslav Pelikan, *The Melody of Theology: A Philosophical Dictionary* (Cambridge, Mass.: Harvard University Press, 1988), 13; Paul Tillich, *Systematic Theology,* vol. 2 (Chicago: University of Chicago Press, 1957), 173.

punishments, Anselm could argue that Christ could represent humankind and make satisfaction for all, a pre-Enlightenment view that few Westerners hold today. Likewise, suffering was viewed as "deserved punishment from God [for God was believed to be on the side of the innocent] and an expression of God's compassion because of its effects upon our eternal destiny."[24]

The differences among these three theories are real. Yet their power lies in their ability to reinforce the image of sacrifice:

- For Aulén, the sacrifice is made by God to God.
- For Anselm, the sacrifice is made by the humanity of the God-man, Jesus, to God.
- For Abelard, the sacrifice is an example of how we ought to live and love.

When combined with the eucharistic proclamation and enactment of sacrifice, atonement becomes a formidable interpreter of God's relationship with humankind, as Luther and Calvin witnessed.

Luther's Witness

Luther's view of atonement grew out of his specific critique of the practice of indulgences (paying one's way out of doing penance) and his belief that forgiveness was "the gift of God, not the result of human merit."[25] Using strong and almost shocking imagery to convey his understanding of the work of Christ as God's victory, Luther lent credence to the notion of penal substitution: Christ upon the cross bore in his body "my sin, the law, death, the devil and hell," and only Christ "killeth my sin [and] destroyeth my death in his body."[26]

Ironically, Luther's journey to the doctrine of justification by grace through faith alone grew out of his own life's anguish. When his early attempts to satisfy God through prayer, fasting, good works, and vigils left him no inner peace, he admitted that he hated the God "who punished sinners." His hatred of God emerged out of his own self-loathing and despair and his obsessive fear that he would suffer God's punishment because he failed to confess certain sins. In turning his rage from self to God, Luther often viewed God more as a destroyer than a deliverer. Under the weight

24. Jeffery Hopper, *Understanding Modern Theology II: Reinterpreting Christian Faith for Changing Worlds* (Philadelphia: Fortress Press, 1987), 22.

25. Timothy George, *Theology of the Reformers* (Nashville: Broadman Press, 1988), 63.

26. Robert S. Paul, *The Atonement and the Sacraments: The Relation of the Atonement to the Sacraments of Baptism and the Lord's Supper* (New York: Abingdon Press, 1960), 94–97; Dillistone, *Christian Understanding*, 104.

of despair, Luther found solace in the counsel of Johann von Staupitz, his confessor and superior in the Augustinian order, who instructed him to meditate on the wounds of Christ.[27] This led him to profess that only the shedding of Christ's blood could restore human beings to God's grace. Luther readily admitted, however, that the appeal of this message lies in the pervasive human fear of hell as well as God's wrath and judgment. Luther understood that the forgiveness of God had been earned for us by the sacrifice of Christ, an act in which Christ took the punishment and wrath of God that had been destined for humankind. Moreover, this act, which cost Jesus his life, was a clear sign of God's graciousness. Luther held that without believing in the forgiveness of sins, one could not be a genuine Christian, nor have access to eternal life. He also believed that when one was given Christ through the act of eating and drinking the body and blood of Christ, the forgiveness of sins was also "given."[28]

Calvin's Legacy

Calvin was convinced that without the knowledge of the substitution of the Son of God we would be "anxious throughout life" because the vengeance of God "still hung over us."[29] Calvin also presented a harsher picture of penal substitution. As the advocate of sinners, Christ, in Calvin's words, "suffered the punishment that, from God's righteous judgment, threatened all sinners, . . . [and] as intercessor he has appeased God's wrath, . . . [for] we are taught by scripture to perceive that apart from Christ, God is, so to speak, hostile to us, and his hand is armed for our destruction."[30] His views, however, were tempered by three significant teachings: on the love of God, the role of obedience, and his belief that we partake of the benefits of Christ's death and share in his sacrifice. Jesus appeases God on our account, but he does this, according to Calvin, as a sacrifice, for he is priest for us.[31] Indeed, Calvin points to the words of John the Baptist in John 1:29—"Behold, the Lamb of God, who takes away the sin of the world!"—as being the "sum of the gospel."[32]

Calvin took to heart the notion of sacrifice in the Hebrew Scriptures and the notion expressed in Hebrews 9:22 that "without the shedding of

---

27. George, *Reformers,* 63–65.

28. Ewald M. Plass, ed., *What Luther Says: An Anthology,* vol. 1 (St. Louis: Concordia, 1959), 519, 808.

29. John Calvin, *Institutes of the Christian Religion,* ed. John T. McNeill, trans. Ford Lewis Battles, Library of Christian Classics (Philadelphia: Westminster Press, 1960), 20:505, 510.

30. H. D. McDonald, *The Atonement of the Death of Christ: In Faith, Revelation, and History* (Grand Rapids, Mich.: Baker Book House, 1985), 188.

31. Calvin, *Institutes,* 20:365–66, 427; Paul, *Atonement and the Sacraments,* 105–7.

32. Calvin, *Institutes,* 20:504–5.

blood there is no forgiveness of sins." He also relied on the imagery of the suffering servant who, in Isaiah 53, was "bruised for our iniquities," and in 1 Peter 2:24 "bore our sins in his body on the cross, so that . . . by his wounds you have been healed." For Calvin, the sole purpose of Christ's incarnation was our redemption, which God accomplished alone without our participation, through the obedient life and sacrificial death of Jesus.

Calvin and Luther both labeled the sufferings we experience as evil and refused to counsel stoic indifference in the face of suffering. Together they held to the graciousness and mercy of a loving God who promised never to forsake us. At the same time, neither was able to shake the belief that God could punish. Despite their eloquent testimony to the graciousness of God, there remained a serious strain of retribution in both men. Each believed that atonement was limited to the elect, while the rest faced damnation.[33]

Puritans and Beyond

Calvin's thoughts on the atoning work of Christ underwent significant revision in the writings of John Owen and Jonathan Edwards. Owen was known as a systematizer of English Congregationalism and a leading Calvinist theologian of the seventeenth century, while Edwards is remembered as the primary impetus behind the eighteenth century's Great Awakening in New England. Together, Owen and Edwards outdid Calvin in their attention to the penal aspect of the atonement and the sufferings of Christ.[34] Despite variations on a theme, the penal theory of atonement captivated human imaginations (particularly evangelical ones) through the hymns of Isaac Watts and the eucharistic hymns of John and Charles Wesley.[35] In the nineteenth century, however, its power appeared to wane as McLeod Campbell in Britain and Horace Bushnell in America offered impressive critiques of Calvinism and penal substitution by advancing their own revisions of Abelard's moral theory. Legalistic metaphors now gave way to metaphors of personal and familial relationships (stressing God as a loving father rather than judge), but the notion that Christ had died for our sins through an act of sacrificial and suffering love remained unquestioned. In the twentieth century the legalism of the Anselmian model received new life through the profound thinking and prolific writing of Karl Barth. In speaking of Christ's atoning work, Barth proposed that "[Christ] has therefore suffered for all men what they had to suffer: their end as evildoers; their overthrow as the enemies of God."[36] While the death of Christ

33. George, *Reformers*, 77, 210–11, 233, 246.
34. Paul, *Atonement and the Sacraments*, 120, 128.
35. Paul, *Atonement and the Sacraments*, 135.
36. Cited in McDonald, *The Atonement*, 308.

functions as a consoling image for those who gravitate toward Anselm's model, his imagery often undermines consolation. In effect, these theories reinforce a notion of God as the divine punisher who allowed Jesus to take our place — to suffer the punishment we deserved.

Finding Meaning in the Cross

Suffering for another may lead to victory in the minds of some, but for those who most often do the suffering — the poor and disenfranchised, the outcast and the different — the consolations of self-sacrifice ring hollow. In the 1990s Joanne Carlson Brown and Rebecca Parker addressed the increasing incidences of domestic violence and sexual abuse by arguing that "Christianity is an abusive theology that glorifies suffering" and acculturates women "to accept abuse."[37] When Jesus' suffering is understood to be a reflection of God's suffering love for us, suffering is wrongly accepted as the way of love in the world.

Despite objections raised by orthodox Christians, many received Brown and Parker's arguments as a breath of fresh air since suffering often has been misunderstood as the "necessary road to glory" for Jesus and his followers.[38] Brown and Parker sought to overturn the necessity of the crucifixion by separating it from the hands of God; at the same time, they tried to free the resurrection from the weight of the cross and release its life-giving power. What shines through the cross, they argued, is the light of resurrection, not the suffering love of God. They thus challenged Jürgen Moltmann, among others, who argued, "There is no suffering which in this history of God is not God's suffering; no death which has not been God's death in the history on Golgotha."[39]

Brown and Parker's naming of Christianity's God as a "divine child abuser" seriously alienated those who find salvation by way of the cross. At the same time, they drew rigid lines of defense by arguing that "no one was saved by the death of Jesus" and that "suffering is never redemptive, and suffering cannot be redeemed."[40] The bold notion that suffering is never redemptive stands on its own, and I concur with their argument: though the "labor pains" of living may lead to growth and new life, suffering that involves a disruption of our sense of self and safety does not. Nevertheless,

37. Joanne Carlson Brown and Rebecca Parker, "For God So Loved the World?" in *Christianity, Patriarchy, and Abuse: A Feminist Critique,* ed. Joanne Carlson Brown and Carole R. Bohn (New York: Pilgrim Press, 1989), 1–30.

38. Eduard Schweizer, *The Good News according to Luke,* trans. David E. Green (Atlanta: John Knox Press, 1984), 157; *Daughters of Sarah* 18 (summer 1992): 24–40.

39. Jürgen Moltmann, *The Crucified God: The Cross of Christ as the Foundation and Criticism of Christian Theology,* trans. R. A. Wilson and John Bowden (New York: Harper & Row, 1974), 246.

40. Brown and Parker, "For God So Loved?" 27.

I take issue with the notion that suffering cannot be redeemed. Truly God takes our pain and tears, even death itself, and fashions new life out of them. Such is the power of resurrection love.

Likewise, to argue "no one was saved by the death of Jesus" is misleading. Brown and Parker argued that traditional teaching undermine the experiences of women and men who suffer abuse. This critique is valid. Yet it is equally true that those who believed themselves saved by the death of Jesus — Paul, Luther, and Calvin, to name but a few — were indeed "saved." To the extent that they believed Jesus' death had saving power, they experienced the freedom to be in Christ and know God's love. Christ on the cross was and is a saving image for many Christians, though clearly not all. Moreover, the glorification of suffering is but one path through the imperial maze of atonement in which many of us find ourselves wandering aimlessly.

Women's Understandings of the Cross

Womanist theologian Delores Williams enters this argument via a particular historical structure of domination: the issue of surrogacy (coerced and voluntary) and its unique impact on black women before and after the American Civil War. In her view, Jesus is the "ultimate surrogate figure standing in the place of someone else: sinful humankind."[41] Arguing by way of the language and sociopolitical thought of the black woman's world, Williams understands the cross as "an image of defilement, a gross manifestation of collective human sin." Jesus, in Williams's view, did not conquer sin by being obedient onto death, but *in life* he resisted the temptations of sin (Matt. 4:1–11).[42]

Williams finds "nothing of God in the blood of the cross." Why? Because just as God did not intend the death of Jesus as a surrogate, God did not intend for black women to function in surrogacy roles — to experience *the rape* of their bodies as they were forced to perform sexual pleasures in the place of white women under systemic slavery. Nevertheless, she urges black Christian women to neither forget the cross nor glorify it. "To do so is to make their exploitation sacred. To do so is to glorify sin."[43] In the name of the kingdom, Williams argues, Jesus called people to live in hope, encouraged by the abundant life that springs forth when justice shapes our

41. Delores Williams, "Black Women's Surrogacy Experience and the Christian Notion of Redemption," in *After Patriarchy: Feminist Transformations of the World Religions,* ed. Paula M. Cooey, William R. Eakin, and Jay B. McDaniel (Maryknoll, N.Y.: Orbis Books, 1991), 9, 12.

42. Ibid., 12.

43. Ibid., 12, 13.

relations with one another and truth-telling defies the principalities and powers that foster racism, sexism, and classism.

In Alice Walker's imaginative world, the secret of joy is *resistance*.[44] Likewise, Wendy Farley urges us to receive the cross as a symbol of resistance, a resurrection of "the power of divine compassion to endure, to be deathless." The cross, having been freed from the theologies of penalty and substitution, becomes, in her view, the manifestation of divine presence resisting the assaults of sin and suffering. For all time and in every season of life, divine love thrives on perennial incarnations rather than one redemptive moment in time.[45] Similarly, Rita Nakashima Brock seeks to reinterpret Christianity and turn patriarchy "inside out" because she believes Trinitarian formulations of atonement highlight the child's total dependence on the will of the father and perpetuate child abuse. Whether Jesus is understood to take the punishment that humanity deserved because of sin, or suffers the consequences of evil brought into the world through humanity's freedom, the effect is the same, she argues: the innocent Son is sacrificed by the divine Father in order to save humanity.[46]

Brock, like Williams and Farley, clarifies contradictions within sacrificial love that atonement theorists ignore. In societies heavily structured by class, issues of social worth inevitably become issues of personal worth. When a person knows that he or she is not respected by society at large, issues of freedom and self-respect often come into conflict with one another. Self-denial signals a lack of respect, not only for oneself but for others, and a desire to limit the other's freedom, particularly in dominarchal societies where authoritarianism means that power is defined as power over another.[47] Self-sacrifice and self-denial are virtues consistently touted as a worthy goal; yet rarely are they practiced with equanimity. Indeed self-effacing servanthood appears to speak more to "pathology or oppression than love," especially when it replaces "the robust desire for the other's good."[48] Self-denial thus lends itself to the growth of mindlessness and imaginative constraint.

Responding to these challenges, Darby Kathleen Ray presents us with a "novel possibility" for atonement that she hopes will bridge the concerns of feminist and Latin American theologians. What is unique in Ray's ap-

---

44. Alice Walker, *Possessing the Secret of Joy* (New York: Harcourt Brace Jovanovich, 1992), 279.

45. Wendy Farley, *Tragic Vision and Divine Compassion: A Contemporary Theodicy* (Louisville: Westminster/John Knox Press, 1990), 114, 118, 132.

46. Rita Nakashima Brock, *Journeys by Heart: A Christology of Erotic Power* (New York: Crossroad, 1988), xvi, 50, 54.

47. Richard Sennett and Jonathan Cobb, *The Hidden Injuries of Class* (New York: Vintage Books, Random House, 1973), 119–50; Farley, *Tragic Vision*, 86.

48. Farley, *Tragic Vision*, 77.

proach is her reworking of the "classic" model associated with early church fathers. Because this model is less a theory than a set of images and themes drawn together, Ray attempts a contemporary reading using the imagery of the devil to represent the sum total of evil, which is the abuse of power. To call Jesus the Christ is to see in his cross "the actual and symbolic meeting point of good and evil, of justice and injustice."[49] Ray also finds redemption as a past event done for us by another to be inadequate, suggesting, along with Farley, that the possibility of redemption lies in the everyday enactment of compassion.[50]

In stressing the patristic emphasis on "deceiving the devil," Ray appeals to a symbolic and mythic reading. Her attempt to reframe this model for a contemporary audience shows genuine integrity. She knows the dangers of devil imagery and is not naive about its historical consequences. Nevertheless, in choosing this model as a means of keeping atonement central to Christian identity and community, Ray makes only a passing reference to the role of symbols in theology and liturgy. More telling for my own work is the absence of any critique of punitive God-imagery in her arguments. Ray acknowledges the historic references to the role of punishment in the satisfaction and substitution models and rightly critiques the fear-based theology of a "big brother" God who is all-seeing. Nonetheless, she is less explicit when it comes to addressing how social realities in a dominarchal culture perpetuate the belief that punishment is a legitimate prerogative of the divine will. Ray speculates that the patristic model, once so popular with early Christians, "fell out of favor" when "Christianity gained acceptability and power."[51] My own view differs. The parallel development of the sacrament of penance and its evolution under the Celtic penitential system could have easily contributed to the abandonment of the patristic model. Baptized Christians, burdened by severe and lengthy penitential sanctions and the fear of eternal damnation, began to look elsewhere for the certainty of personal salvation.

The Power of Shame

Despite numerous references to the healing benefits of penance and the bishop's role as a physician of the soul, apocalyptic thinking signals a fear-constrained imagination. Apocalyptic imagery reinforced the church's use of punishment to remedy sin, applied restrictions to the social boundaries of Holy Communion, and disassociated the experience of God's forgiveness

49. Ray, *Deceiving,* 144.
50. Ibid., 143.
51. Ibid., 159n.39.

from Jesus' ministry. In so doing, penance and its punishments secured the need for theories of satisfaction and substitution to guarantee forgiveness to a beleaguered penitent. While many fault atonement theories for perpetuating suffering, I suggest that the practice of penance, more so than the image of Calvary, allowed the imagery of suffering love to dominate imagination.

Christianity's embrace of penitential practices was due in no small measure to the church's fear that the devil was winning the hearts of baptized believers. Nevertheless, by using their authority to instill fear, church leaders compounded the very problem they sought to erase. By imposing punishment to fight sin, church leaders perpetuated suffering in the name of the Christ, whose suffering they deemed the world's saving grace. Invariably the interwoven symbols of apocalypse, penance, sacrifice, and eucharist point to issues of power, not communion.

The transformation of Jesus' welcome table into the image of a sacrificial altar, and ultimately a sign of exclusion through excommunication, was carried forward by three related ideas: satisfaction, penance, and punishment. Satisfaction entered the vocabulary of Christian theology in the second century as a result of Tertullian's response to the complex issues regarding the lax treatment of sinners and the imposition of insufficient penance. Though he admitted that satisfaction could be made by confession of sin, Tertullian also said that meritorious works of fasting, bodily mortification, and penitential prayers could have the same effect. For the general harmony of the community to be restored, the sinner must offer due reparation publicly. As a consequence, the practice of penance shaped Christian imagination through humiliation and self-abasement. Known as "second baptism," penance was driven by apocalyptic fears from its inception. At the same time, public penance was a "ritual of power" that "went hand in hand" with the emergence of the power of bishops.[52]

After Tertullian's appeal to right order, interior actions of being sorry, grieving, and expressing regret tilted toward outward expressions that became vivid reminders of the punitive nature of God. To those who were hesitant to participate in the act of *exomologesis* — to confess their sins and do penance — Tertullian touted its healing potential: "picture the magnitude of its punishments, so as not to hesitate about adopting the remedy.... When you realize that after the first remedy of the Lord's baptism there still remains a second aid against hell, why despair of your

52. José Ramos-Regidor, "'Reconciliation' in the Primitive Church and Its Lessons for Theology and Pastoral Practice Today," in *Sacramental Reconciliation*, ed. Edward Schillebeeckx, *Concilium* 61: *Dogma* (New York: Herder and Herder, 1971), 76–88; Maykede Jong, "Transformations of Penance," in *Rituals of Power: From Late Antiquity to the Early Middle Ages*, ed. Frans Theuws and Janet L. Nelson (Leiden: E. J. Brill, 2000), 189.

salvation, why delay to enter upon a course which you know will be your healing?"[53]

The punishment spawned by penance used "social and religious exclusion as its chief sanction."[54] While baptism gave the believer a sense of social identity — a sense of safety and selfhood — as a member of the body of Christ, the eucharist kept the social body of the believer intact since only the baptized could receive the sacramental body and blood of Jesus. However, after publicly confessing to being a sinner, the believer entered into the Order of Penitents and was immediately excluded from receiving the eucharist.[55] Unrepentant wrongdoers were subjected to the curse of anathema and shunned socially. They were identified not only by their absence from worship but by having their name read from a registry of excommunicates one Sunday a month — as persons who could contaminate the community by their very presence. Failure to abide by these penalties meant that the person would be designated as a "bystander" (they could worship but not commune). They were also denied the eucharist until death approached.[56] Small wonder, then, that excommunication was known to hasten sickness and death.

In addition to the major sins of idolatry, adultery, incest, and bloodshed, questioning orthodox doctrine clearly made one a prime candidate for public penance.[57] Eventually those branded by the heretic's curse would also suffer the penalty of death. As they attempted to consolidate power in the presence of "heretical" factions, the clergy claimed that their authority to bind and loose sins was given by Christ to the church as recorded in Matthew 16:19 and John 20:22–23. Despite verbal assurances that it was being enacted for the believer's salvation, penance manifested itself as cruelty in the name of love (mindlessness, indeed), growing more rigid during the third and fourth centuries when doctrinal arguments became more forceful. As penance continued to be avoided because of its severity, it came to be part of one's immediate preparation for death. Unintentionally, penance thus undermined the three-year process of baptismal preparation known as the Order of Catechumens.

---

53. Cited in Paul F. Palmer, ed., *Sacraments and Forgiveness: History and Doctrinal Development of Penance, Extreme Unction, and Indulgences*, Sources of Christian Theology, vol. 2 (Westminster, Md.: Newman Press, 1959), 26–27.

54. Elisabeth Vodola, *Excommunication in the Middle Ages* (Berkeley: University of California Press, 1986), 191.

55. Palmer, *Sacraments and Forgiveness*, 73–74; John T. McNeill and Helena M. Gamer, *Medieval Handbooks of Penance: A Translation of the Principal Libri Poenitentiales and Selections from Related Documents*, Records of Western Civilization Series (New York: Columbia University Press, 1938, 1990), 7–8.

56. Vodola, *Excommunication*, 49–50.

57. McNeill and Gamer, *Medieval Handbooks*, 18–19.

Penance was often extolled as a means of reconciliation. However, the power-over nature of this rite, exercised by bishop and priest, betrayed the trust of the common folk, who looked to penance as a genuine aid to salvation. For one thing, serious sinners were not treated alike. At the same time, clergy and religious were officially excluded from participating in public penance.[58] By the seventh century, what was once public and unrepeatable was gradually transformed (though not entirely suppressed) into a private and repeatable act, under the influence of Irish monasticism — and here, the practice became even more humiliating.

The Rise of the Penitentials

Apart from the option to live "an ascetic life at home," wayward clergy could enter the monastic life and come under the "yoke of perpetual lamentation."[59] Monasteries thus offered the option of private confessions and graded penance. After the collapse of public penance, the abbots of Celtic monasteries, who had jurisdiction over their monks and the surrounding communities, drew up manuals known as the Penitentials to oversee matters of discipline. However, in light of the harshness of monastic justice, tariff payments — which led to the sale of indulgences — were used to aid those who wished to avoid these practices. Celtic practice also influenced the practice of penance on the European continent, where, in many cases, priests would lead illiterate penitents in a recitation of their sins.

Despite humane intentions, church leaders and abbots used their clerical power to correct moral defects they alone had the social and religious power to judge. In effect they abused their power through harsh penalties. As penitents found their emotional resources under attack, the actions of their confessors bordered on the institutionalization of evil. As Nel Noddings suggests, evil is characterized "by the presence or infliction of pain, separation, and helplessness.... [Thus] having a sense of evil as that which induces pain, separation, and helplessness allows us to focus on what we can do to avoid evil, or if we cannot avoid it, how we might reduce its effects."[60] Because they often relied on pain, separation, and helplessness to shape the character of individual Christians, the Penitentials allowed evil to thrive in the context of shame and fear. When shame arises from the realization that we have violated basic experiences of relationality, it

58. Paul Anciaux, *The Sacrament of Penance* (New York: Sheed and Ward, 1962), 57, 59, 76; Ramos-Regidor, "Reconciliation," 81.

59. McNeill and Gamer, *Medieval Handbooks*, 14; Jong, "Transformations of Penance," 207.

60. Nel Noddings, *Women and Evil* (Berkeley: University of California Press, 1989), 116, 121.

is not an unhealthy response. However, shame that arises from a self that has been denied its psychic integrity poisons rather than heals.

As Judith Jordan argues, shame is a "felt sense of unworthiness to be in connection, a deep sense of unlovability, with the ongoing awareness of how much one wants to connect with others. . . . [T]here is [also] a loss of empathic possibility, others are not experienced as empathic, and the capacity for self-empathy is lost. One feels unworthy of love."[61] The shame and humiliation of penance ultimately contradict the receiving dimensions of empathy and compassion. More so, shame undermines the very ministry Jesus modeled. In his earthly ministry Jesus freely offered God's love by way of forgiveness and inclusion. Repeatedly he undermined the honor-and-shame system of his day and extended the realm of divine grace to those who were sinners and outcasts. While many members of the clergy sought to extend mercy and compassion to their flock, severe acts of penance were questionable at best. The detailed prescriptions of the Penitentials were intended to effect an "inward moral change, the setting up of a process of character reconstruction which involves the correction of special personal defects and the reintegration of personality."[62] In actuality, the Penitentials effected a disintegration of the self that diminished the believers' ability to trust their relationship with God and their own God-given uniqueness. Over time, the Penitentials evolved into the existing form of private confession now practiced by Roman Catholicism.

Baptism to Penance to Atonement to Eucharist

The impact of penance on eucharistic piety is hardly negligible. When Anselm refashioned Tertullian's use of satisfaction to amplify the salvific nature of Christ's death, the interdependent nature of belief and prayer once again became apparent. Anselm's theory revealed a significant shift in the liturgical and sacramental life of Christianity at a time when "Christ's presence on the altar" in the form of the host was becoming a major theological concern. Formerly baptism had been the main signifier that a believer was in Christ and therefore "saved" by Christ's atoning work on the cross. However, Anselm's writings suggest that the eucharist was "emotionally" displacing baptism as the vehicle for accessing Christ's saving grace. The "Eucharistic experience of consuming the crucified and risen body of Christ and absorbing each day more of that celestial body in

61. Judith V. Jordan, "Relational Development: Therapeutic Implications of Empathy and Shame," Stone Center Work in Progress, no. 39 (Wellesley, Mass.: Stone Center, 1989), 6; John Bradshaw, *Healing the Shame That Binds You* (Deerfield Beach, Fla.: Health Communications, 1988), 13.

62. McNeill and Gamer, *Medieval Handbooks*, 46.

a process of devout consumption and imitation of Christ which is to be completed only when He Himself comes in glory" became the method by which medieval believers appropriated the "benefits of Christ's work."[63]

Thus the imagery of dying and rising with Christ gave way to the image of believers feeding on him in their hearts through faith. Ironically, in the context of penance, Christianity's emphasis on Jesus' atoning work appears to have offered limited psychic capacity for ensuring salvation on a day-to-day basis. Consequently, the stronger liturgical presence provided by the *repeatable* eucharist came to be seen as more powerful than the *unrepeatable* rite of baptism. In this context, Luther's use of the sacrament to offer the forgiveness of sins to the unworthy would surely have been salvific. Nevertheless, the tendency for crucifixion imagery to dominate this sacrament, as it did with Calvin's "stepchildren," ultimately proved too great a burden because it reinforced the believer's sense of unworthiness.

Humility vs. Humiliation

John Donne once described humiliation as the "beginning of sanctification." In so doing, he passed on without reservation a false assumption: the sting of shame leads to the holiness of God.[64] Surely the time has come for Christianity to disengage from this dogma and admit that shame-based messages often lead to psychic disintegration. Humility and humiliation may share the same Latin root — *humilis* — but they produce a vastly different flower. Humiliation has to do with degradation, shame, disgrace, and religious mortification. Humility, although it can refer to an act of submission or self-abasement, also means to be humble. When we trace this word back to its root, we find the word *humus*, meaning ground or earth, and once again we are reminded of our humble beginnings; in Genesis 2:7, *ha-'adam* (the earth creature) comes from *ha-'adamâ* (the earth).[65]

In heavily penitential liturgies, the Ash Wednesday mantra — "Remember that you are dust, and to dust you shall return"[66] — adds to the sense of human nothingness before the wholly otherness of God. However, if we replaced the image of "dust" with the image of earthiness, we might better understand our humble beginnings as central to our divine relationality and interconnectedness with all of creation. If, as creatures of

63. George Huntson Williams, *Anselm: Communion and Atonement* (Saint Louis: Concordia Publishing House, 1960), 50, 51.

64. *The American Heritage Dictionary of the English Language*, 1979 ed., s.v. "humiliation."

65. Charlton T. Lewis, *An Elementary Latin Dictionary* (Oxford: Oxford University Press, 1891, 1987), 372; *The American Heritage Dictionary of the English Language*, s.v. "humility," "humiliation"; Phyllis Trible, *God and the Rhetoric of Sexuality* (Philadelphia: Fortress Press, 1978), 78.

66. *From Ashes to Fire: Services of Worship for the Seasons of Lent and Easter with Introduction and Commentary*, Supplemental Worship Resources 8 (Nashville: Abingdon Press, 1979), 47.

the earth, we lived with a sense of deep humility, we could experience self-transcendence — the awareness of our deep relationality — and lean with grace into well-being.

We could also live with a sense of awe, rather than pride, for the presence of awe reflects our self-knowledge of the divinity within all creation. When we live with *humiliation,* we experience shame and degradation and become overwhelmed by our disconnection — excommunication, if you will — from communion and community. In humiliation, there is little room for awe to take root, but room enough for fear. Yet misplaced fear, as I have tried to say before, defies the relational self's search for meaning — leaving it subject to despair and stranded at the gates of its own earthly hell.

To be overcome by fear is to lose heart, whereas to hope in God is to gain courage, to have one's heart strengthened. It is thus not possible to love and fear God at the same time and expect to experience well-being. In Hebrew the words for fear and awe both imply an attitude of trembling. One can thus read *awe* where others have translated "tremble" to imply the presence of fear.[67] While I was raised with the notion that "the fear of God is the beginning of wisdom" (Ps. 111:10), Abraham Heschel assures us that awe precedes faith, and the awe of God is the beginning of wisdom. While fear constricts our engagement with the world, awe calls us forth into a world of wide horizons. "Awe enables us to perceive in the world intimations of the divine, to sense in small things the beginning of infinite significance, to sense the ultimate in the common and the simple; to feel in the rush of the passing the stillness of the eternal."[68] In this sense awe opens us to the mystery of life. Imagination and awe become cocreators in the realm of God.

With due respect to John Donne, *self-transcendence* is the true beginning of sanctification, for sanctification arises from immersing ourselves in the loveliness of God's entire creation. Sanctification, in my view, implies more than personal holiness. It points to our commitment to embrace the divinity of all life, including our own. The more we grow in sanctification, the more we can become icons of God's grace and live in communion with all of creation. Psychic integrity is thus essential to sanctification and self-transcendence. When we trust in our original loveliness and love accordingly, divine grace sanctifies us for the work of compassion, which is always and everywhere the encouragement of justice, communion, and well-being for all.

---

67. Abraham J. Heschel, *Between God and Man: An Interpretation of Judaism,* ed. Fritz A. Rothschild (New York: The Free Press/Macmillan, 1959), 50–54.

68. Ibid., 52.

SEVEN

The Embodied Soul

> Apocalyptic is not a fit vehicle for conveying the truth about forgiveness.
> —*Leon Morris*[1]

> I find in my soul a strange Experience. I meet with very breaking and killing Things, which are the Chastisements of the holy God upon me, for my manifold Miscarriages. . . . I fly away from even my very self into Him, and I take part with Him against myself: and it pleases me, that He is pleased, tho' I myself am dreadfully torn to Peeces in what is done unto me.
> —*Cotton Mather*[2]

The rigors of asceticism and strong penitential practices have diminished dramatically, but they have not disappeared from Christian practice. Many believers, willingly and unwillingly, still present their bodies as a living sacrifice to God in search of forgiving grace. Although canon law and custom attempted to limit extreme practices, they inflicted considerable harm on the believer's mental and physical health and left many people struggling with a deep sense of despair and unworthiness. Evidence of self-flagellation, scourging with a rod, sustained periods of bread and water (years as well as weeks), solitary confinement, extended vigils, and forced pilgrimages all conjure up the torturer who displaces the "spiritual father."

Of equal concern is the torture of the imagination (the embodied soul) that has suffered the ritual loss of identity in the context of terror. In Chile, as we noted earlier, the eucharist failed to inspire early resistance to the military. Instead, in the coup's aftermath, the regime benefited from ecclesiastical impotence. The experience of eucharist undermined courage, as the body of Christ and the body politic sanctioned repression in place of resurrection. "The food of life became the food of death, poison to the imagination and the political will."[3] We may choose to overlook the experience of an overzealous penitent, the fate of a woman religious, and the

1. Leon Morris, *Apocalyptic* (Grand Rapids, Mich.: William B. Eerdmans, 1972), 85.
2. Cited in Philip Greven, *The Protestant Temperament: Patterns of Child-Rearing, Religious Experience, and the Self in Early America* (New York: Alfred A. Knopf, 1977), 79.
3. Glenn Miller, e-mail correspondence, September 9, 2001.

arduous lives of early monks. Nevertheless, their lives allow us to glimpse the debilitating effects of religious fear that diminish communal life.

Whatever the origins of fear may be, each unexamined manifestation contributes to the erosion of well-being and the erosion of hope. Instead of witnessing to the hope within us, we live the fear we cannot shake. The magnificent contributions of a few — Julian of Norwich, Catherine of Siena, and others — do not counteract the potential for harm that religious excesses unleash. Because the imagination is an embodied gift of the spirit, and the infinite locus of soul, it matters how we treat our bodyspirits. It matters too what kind of embodied presence we bring to our eucharistic assemblies. As we approach a re-imaged eucharist, I bring apocalyptic fears into conversation with contemporary research on the effects of corporal punishment, the wisdom of the body, and the role that emotion plays in shaping our thoughts. I also address the role fear plays in narrowing the horizons of meaning by which we construct our inner worlds. Fear profoundly affects an individual's imagination through changes in the physiology of one's body as well as its particular effect on one's developing representations of god.

Apocalyptic thinking is not a choice; it is a consequence. It emerges in the context of cultural and personal chaos amid any number of social traumas, including war, famine, economic deprivation, and injustice. Accordingly, the suffering of the body (physically or mentally) becomes the subtext of fear that dominates the apocalyptic thinker. The believer loses hope in the possibility of change and comes to demonize a perceived enemy as evil. The dangers to community and communion are obvious. In a relational world there can be no enemies in the life of faith, as Jesus taught us.

Imaging God

Developmental research suggests that a child's capacity to symbolize — to make associations of meaning — begins well before the second year of life.[4] Likewise, Ana-Maria Rizzuto suggests that our *initial* representations of self and God are intimately tied to our childhood experiences with authority figures (those with power over us) and become well established before we as children participate in formalized religious education. Shaped through imagination by our wishes, defenses, and fears, our god-representations are intimately tied to our well-being as they affect the development of self. To ensure the development of mature religious belief, our representations

4. Jessica Benjamin, *The Bonds of Love: Psychoanalysis, Feminism and the Problem of Domination* (New York: Pantheon Books, 1988), 29.

must be amenable to change even as we change in the process of human becoming. Flexibility and elasticity are therefore critical keys to keeping our imaginations free enough to encounter the One whose mystery births us all.[5]

While God remains God, full of majesty and hidden within unfathomable mystery (as Calvin eloquently reminds us), the god who lives within us imaginatively — through our mental *representations* — can be a formidable presence. Our ability to create and project our constructions of god from our early experiences, and "the deep sentiments both of love and dread that are attached to them, frequently constitute a powerful bedrock of conviction on which later, more adult, forms of faith may be grounded."[6] As we grow into mature adulthood seeking the fullness of life we equate with well-being, the elasticity (the capacity for change) of our god-representations is continually put to the test. Wherever we go we carry them with us, especially when we are not aware of their influence; whether repressed or revised, they are never completely destroyed. If we permit them to solidify under the weight of fear, the constructions of god we give allegiance to may well leave us entombed. Every one of our mental representations shapes our lives for good or ill. They persecute us and make us anxious or they sustain and console us. They can also allow our fears to be projected onto others with horrifying results. Clearly our self-representations and god-representations are major actors in the drama of life.

Rizzuto's studies also suggest that those who have been abused as children may find themselves living with a restrictive view of God, one that is capricious, judgmental, and often punitive, and a restrictive view of their own ability to relate to others. This becomes all the more tragic when abused individuals find corroboration of their childhood experiences in biblical and doctrinal representations of god that stir their deep memories of abuse.[7] To protect themselves, such individuals may choose to disavow belief in God in order to resist the "experiential terror of a *sadistic invader* who violates the protected nucleus of bearable self-experience."[8] Individuals who have been deeply wounded by loved ones instilling fear rather than love survive any way they can. Such survival, however, is not without cost; for the territory of the inner self always remains vulnerable to the *all-seeing eye* of God and can easily become a solitary prison rather

5. Ana-Maria Rizzuto, *The Birth of the Living God: A Psychoanalytic Study* (Chicago: University of Chicago Press, 1979), 46, 52, 78.

6. Jim Fowler and Sam Keen, *Life Maps: Conversations on the Journey of Faith,* ed. Jerome Berryman (Waco, Tex.: Word Books, 1978; Minneapolis: Winston Press, 1978), 48.

7. Annie Imbens and Ineke Jonker, *Christianity and Incest,* trans. Patricia McKay (Minneapolis: Fortress Press, 1992), 189–208.

8. Rizzuto, *Living God,* 134.

than a place of secure selfhood. Tragically, thousands of young people who have been abused at home increase their risk of physical violence and sexual abuse by running away only to fall victim to juvenile pornography and street prostitution. To a child who has been taught that God is all-powerful and always aware of their inner thoughts, inner safety thus remains an elusive quest.[9] Situations such as these remind us that inner *conquest,* even by one's god, has deep and abiding consequences. Without interventions of grace by authority figures who know a more gracious god and enact this knowing consistently, abused children may become bound by fears they dare not speak well into adulthood, for fear of invoking the wrath of the deity they dare not abandon.

Tillich once observed, "The human mind is not only, as Calvin has said, a permanent factory of idols, it is also a permanent factory of fears — the first in order to escape God, the second in order to escape anxiety; and there is a relation between the two."[10] Whenever the desire to flee from God orders our lives, it may well be the product of psychic suffering experienced when our imaginations were captured by fear or colonized by violence. God, in this guise, is never the welcomed savior but the enemy within: the one who demands the destruction of the relational self in order to maintain the privileged position of dominance through fear. Psychic suffering occurs when our imagination becomes so damaged by fear that hopelessness rules, for it is then that the possibilities of God become subject to the *im*-possibilities of our personal deities.

If we believe that God is with us and for us, fear may render us powerless temporarily but not ultimately. When we believe that God is with us and against us at the same time, however, the results can be devastating. Without the cornerstone of psychic integrity — the image of oneself as loved by God and thus infinitely worthy of divine love — life can become hopeless and relationship fruitless. When this happens, fear and suffering are joined and life is imperiled. Fear is, of course, part and parcel of the human condition. But there exists a dimension of fear arising from Christianity's misguided embrace of a punitive god-image that can no longer be dismissed as inconsequential. Death, hell, and the devil have long been allies in the anxious imagination of Christianity. Nevertheless, we must undermine their power and free ourselves from their poisonous fear. Alongside the good news of Emmanuel — "Fear not, for I am with

9. Anne Marie Hunter, "Numbering the Hairs of Our Heads: Male Social Control and the All-Seeing Male God," *Journal of Feminist Studies in Religion* 8 (fall 1992): 7–26; "The Commercial Sexual Exploitation of Children in the U.S., Canada, and Mexico," undertaken by the Center for the Study of Youth Policy at the University of Pennsylvania School of Social Work, September 2001. The U.S. and Mexican studies are available on the World Wide Web at *caster.ssw.upenn.edu/~restes/CSEC.htm.*

10. Paul Tillich, *The Courage to Be* (New Haven: Yale University Press, 1952), 39, 59.

you" — Constantinian Christianity deftly placed the apocalyptic lie: "Forgiveness requires punishment." As long as we persist in allowing this belief to go unchallenged, perfect love will fail to cast out fear (1 John 4:18). The price we pay for such denial is thus the continuation of alienation and the dissolution of hope. Whenever the meaning of love becomes eroded by fear, love truly "suffers." In contrast, divine love calls human love to expand itself — to broaden its horizons and to greaten itself by grace.

The Feeling-Thinking Body

Consider what we know about the body's inherent wisdom. The mind and the body are one. Our minds are thus embodied. Our experiences influence our biology, and our biology influences our future experiences. Our biology is not our destiny, but it is one piece of a very large puzzle that contributes to the development of human consciousness. Our physiological system — our bodily processes — carries on everyday with very little help from our consciousness, as does the biological machinery underlying emotion.[11]

We have come to call the processes that organize the activity of our brains "mind"; yet the mind is fundamentally a humanly constructed concept for understanding the activity of thought — reason, judgment, and memory. Our mind is ultimately the product of molecular interaction on a grand scale.[12] The building blocks of the mind depend on the free flow of information between our external sensory receptors and our internal ones. Touch, vision, taste, smell, and hearing make up our five major senses while intuition — our ability to perceive and to be aware — functions as a sort of sixth sense. It is at this level that imagination — our ability to experience *the more* of life — comes into play. There is more to knowing than what we know in any given moment, and much of our knowing capacity resides in the unconscious dimensions of our brain, where countless memories and symbolic connections reside. "We only know what is *on* our mind, rarely what is *in* our mind."[13] Imagination depends on the integrity of our physical bodies (internally and externally), as I said earlier, as well as the integrity (the receptivity) of the molecular connections and neural interactions that contribute to our emotional, spiritual, sexual, and social well-being. Thus the mental images and representations formed by our brains are as much creations of the sensory and motor activity of

11. Antonio Damasio, *The Feeling of What Happens: Body and Emotion in the Making of Consciousness* (New York: Harcourt, Brace & Company, 1999), 43–47.

12. Sherwin B. Nuland, *The Wisdom of the Body* (New York: Alfred Knopf, 1997), 349.

13. Robert Ornstein, *The Evolution of Consciousness: The Origins of the Way We Think* (New York: Simon & Schuster, 1991), 5.

the brain "as they are products of the external reality that prompts their creation."[14]

The influence emotions have on our capacity to socialize well is dependent upon the basic evolutionary structure of the brain. One way of summarizing this activity is that we feel with our old mammalian brain and think with the new mammalian brain.[15] A critical dimension of this evolutionary process is that the limbic system, which represents the older, more deeply embedded aspect of the brain, generates and regulates the emotion of fear. When fear is generated as either real or irrational, it needs to be processed by the prefrontal lobe and put in perspective so that other parts of the body know how to respond. Emotional cues thus undergird our capacity to discriminate intelligently in the context of social situations. If we "do not develop the ability to use inner images and ideas to deal with our emotions," we are restricted to acting out our feelings rather than processing them. Consequently, "all thought and endeavor... grow out of the ability to create symbols and to forge connections among them."[16]

The emotions that gain the tightest hold on our memories are those that are most intense — such as fear and excitement and passion. This means that the molecular bits and pieces that represent the symbolic image-memories stored in the neocortex can, in the context of trauma, create "burned-in" images whose neural pathways may reproduce permanent behavioral memories, depending on the intensity as well as the duration and context of the original trauma. As Antonio Damasio's research has shown, "Emotions are inseparable from the idea of reward and punishment, of pleasure and pain, or approach or withdrawal, of personal advantage and disadvantage. Inevitably, emotions are inseparable from the idea of good or evil."[17]

As a result of centuries of dualistic thinking, we have lived as though our mind cannot trust our bodies to speak truthfully. Even today, numerous theologians function as though bodily experience has no bearing on theological reflection. Experience, however, is a major indicator of how effectively our neocortex, our thinking brain, will function.[18] Human experience — what happens to our embodied souls — is essential to the formation of our god-representations. Moreover, our capacity to dis-place the image of a punitive god with that of a loving and encouraging God who

14. Damasio, *Feeling*, 320.

15. Barry S. Philipp, *The Fear Factor: The Core of a Desperate Society* (Wimberley, Tex.: I Corinthians XIII Publishers, 1998), 55.

16. Stanley I. Greenspan with Beryl Lieff Benderly, *The Growth of the Mind and the Endangered Origins of Intelligence* (Reading, Mass.: Addison-Wesley, 1997), 86.

17. Damasio, *Feeling*, 55.

18. Nuland, *Wisdom*, 351.

seeks the world's and our well-being depends not on the fragmentation or humiliation of our bodyspirits, but on the integration of our bodyminds.

The Apocalyptic Impulse and Corporal Punishment

The Christian obsession with saving souls from hell lives on today in the lives of believers whose life-experience has narrowed the horizons of their own imagination. Philip Greven thus connects the continuing presence of the apocalyptic impulse with the alarming incidence of corporal punishment in the lives of Protestant Christians. The wide-ranging consequences associated with corporal punishment include anxiety and fear, anger and hate, melancholy and depression, obsessive and rigid personality structures, ambivalence and insecurity, disassociation from one's feelings and relationship to the world (including the formation of multiple personalities), sadomasochism, paranoia, domestic violence, aggression and delinquency, authoritarianism, and, lastly, in Greven's view, *the apocalyptic impulse*.[19]

By documenting the biblical roots of discipline — exemplified in the nonbiblical aphorism, "Spare the rod and spoil the child" — he reminds us how easily nonbiblical material can be given biblical warrant. "Ironically," this aphorism comes from a "satirical poem written by Samuel Butler between 1663 and 1678," which had nothing to do with parenting.[20] Despite the absence of these particular lines in scripture, there are more than enough biblical references to the rod being used as a chastening measure to see how the connection could be made. Neither Paul nor Jesus, in Greven's view, advocated the punishment of children, though many Christians have followed this path with a vengeance. Some have even cited Jesus' teachings as proof of its propriety, even though in the Gospel accounts he never speaks of the rod. Although it is difficult to prove that Paul advocated this type of discipline, we know he had knowledge of such practices (1 Cor. 4:21) and clearly understood himself and his authority in terms of the "fatherhood" common to his day.[21]

Greven relies on the work of Alice Miller, who argues that "Children who have been beaten, humiliated, and abused, and who find no witness to come to their aid often . . . have no knowledge of their true feelings,

19. Philip Greven, *Spare the Child: The Religious Roots of Punishment and the Psychological Impact of Physical Abuse* (New York: Alfred A. Knopf, 1991; New York: Vintage Books, 1992), 121–212.

20. In Robert R. Gillogly, "Spanking Hurts Everybody," *Theology Today* 37, no. 4 (January 1981): 416–17.

21. Elisabeth Schüssler Fiorenza, *In Memory of Her: A Feminist Theological Reconstruction of Christian Origins* (New York: Crossroad, 1983) 234; Robert Banks, *Paul's Idea of Community: The Early House Churches in Their Historical Setting* (Grand Rapids, Mich.: William B. Eerdmans, 1980), 56.

fear them like the plague, and are therefore incapable of recognizing vital connections."[22] Miller's findings are reinforced by the research of Murray Straus in *Beating the Devil out of Them,* a study of corporal punishment in U.S. families. In distinction to physical abuse, Straus and his colleagues define socially accepted and legal corporal punishment as "the use of physical force with the intention of causing a child to experience pain, but not injury, for the purpose of correction or control of the child's behavior."[23] Their findings make a strong case for the elimination of corporal punishment as a way to reduce the stress and trauma of parent-child relationships, incidents of delinquency, depression, suicide, and domestic violence.

Similarly, in *Ghosts from the Nursery,* Robin Karr-Morse and Meredith Wiley demonstrate how violent behavior is very likely the consequence of multiple factors, including abuse and neglect of children that occur before the child is two.[24] Of their many findings, the most troubling is the role that emotions play in the development of cognition. Early trauma, emotional as well as physical punishment or neglect, can actually alter the child's developing brain and leave the child "without the ability to connect, to trust, and ultimately to experience empathy." As a consequence the individual is unable to respond to another's pain.[25] We now know that the body and brain store memories of abuse, even though the victims are left with no conscious memory of early assaults. These lingering unconscious effects shape an individual's sense of self as well as his or her representations of God, as evidenced by the personal diaries of our Puritan forbears.

The Self under Siege

Greven's research on the Protestant temperament in early America reveals three pieties tied to the history of substitutionary atonement: evangelical, moderate, and genteel. Despite the differences in their child-rearing practices, evangelicals, moderates, and genteels shared a dualistic notion of heaven and hell and the view that salvation meant the reward of eternal life through the merits of Christ's sacrifice. Unlike evangelicals in Reformation times, evangelicals such as Jonathan Edwards, Cotton Mather, and

22. Alice Miller, *Breaking Down the Wall of Silence: The Liberating Experience of Facing Painful Truth,* trans. Simon Worrall (New York: Dutton, 1991), 153.

23. Murray A. Straus, with Denise A. Donnelly, *Beating the Devil out of Them: Corporal Punishment in American Families* (New York: Lexington Books, 1994), 4.

24. Robin Karr-Morse and Meredith S. Wiley, *Ghosts from the Nursery: Tracing the Roots of Violence* (New York: Atlantic Monthly Press, 1997), 3–15.

25. Ibid., 198.

John Wesley were raised by repressive, authoritarian parents who, viewing their children as innocent but dangerous, sought to instill love and fear toward parents and God while allowing obedient submission as the only acceptable response. Fearing that the souls of their children would be damned for eternity, evangelicals railed against disobedience while breaking the child's will through the infliction of corporal punishment, often before conscious memory began.

Susanna Wesley's recollection of disciplining her children at the age of one and earlier is truly stunning, for she taught them to "fear the rod and to cry softly, by which means they escaped abundance of correction which they might otherwise have had." No wonder then that evangelicals like John Wesley would later urge parents to "break their [children's] wills that you may save their souls."[26] Small wonder too that these children, now filled with guilt and shame, sought refuge in the act of being *born again* as children of God to avoid the fires of hell. Denying their own self-needs, they sought to suppress their wills and make themselves as nothing, so Christ could be all in all. As Jonathan Edwards professed, "a truly Christian love . . . is a humble broken-hearted love." Ironically, these same individuals, intent on issues of purity and control, used the political sphere to liberate their own inner feelings of anger and hostility, by moving from waging war on themselves to waging war on others.[27]

Today we know that not all who have been abused abuse others, but those who do abuse others most certainly have learned from their intimate experiences of fear to respond to the world in a violent manner. Because these are the memories that lie deep within their embodied and entombed souls, they do unto others what was once done unto them. To the extent that evangelicals were nurtured by harsh Calvinistic views of God's wrath and caprice, physical and emotional suffering was an ever-present reality, often mediated by loving parents in the name of divine grace. At the same time, hostility toward others flowed from the hostility they experienced toward their own conflicted selves.

In contrast to the evangelicals, moderates such as Horace Bushnell and Abigail Adams gave considerable attention to the process of growth and development of the child from infancy to adulthood. Believing in a God of love and order, they emphasized "love and duty," not love and fear. They also advocated a regulated self-love and sought to bend (conform) the child's will rather than break it. Children raised in such an atmosphere generally experienced an inner sense of freedom and self-worth, unlike

---

26. Greven, *Protestant Temperament*, 35, 36.
27. Ibid., 80, 353.

their evangelical counterparts, yet they often were haunted by the fear that their actions might not prove worthy of God's love and grace.[28]

The desire to be obedient to their parents' will, and therefore God's will, manifested itself in later life when moderates found their own consciences provided stiff inner boundaries similar to the outer limits and controls once applied by their parents under the guise of loving "dutifulness." The point is not so much that the child was given loving boundaries in which to grow and mature, but rather the fact that many of these "boundaries" inevitably limited the ability of children to *freely choose* in a manner different from the will of their parents and likewise the will of their god.[29]

Genteels experienced the greatest measure of inner security (often benefiting from the security provided by the external benefits of wealth and leisure). They were distinguished from the other types by the theme of "love and reverence," since fear was "inconceivable" and duty "taken for granted." Not surprisingly, Greven notes that genteel children demonstrated more self-worth, self-love, self-confidence, and inner security than their contemporaries. Because their self-will had not been broken in infancy, these children did not suffer the inner conflicts so tied to the evangelical lifestyle. Nevertheless, the piety of genteels did not aid their ability to discern the suffering they imposed on others through the institutional system of slavery. Confident that they would be among those rewarded with eternal life by a benevolent deity, they treated their slaves just as evangelicals treated their children, by seeking an early conquest of their sense of self and self-will.[30]

All of this is not to say that the pieties described here failed to address the needs of others or even the great concerns of social injustice. The history of Christianity has surely demonstrated that individuals bound by fears and failures of conscience have still managed to be motivated by self-sacrificial love to reach out and care for others. Greven's research does, however, raise a significant cautionary note regarding the relationship of religious motivation and physical abuse, particularly among those who have suffered physical and emotional abuse from infancy. Within Christianity there is ample documentation of a counter history of abuse in which fear and hatred, not love and compassion, motivated "Christian" hearts. Most disconcerting of all is the influence of apocalyptic imagery on the child-rearing practices of devout Christians who firmly believed that the mercy of God required punishment in this life before one could hope to receive the reward of eternal life.

28. Ibid., 151–52, 173, 220.
29. Ibid., 186–90, 193.
30. Ibid., 266–77, 298, 323.

The Rod Not Spared

Apocalyptic eschatology survives and thrives in part because of the continued use of corporal punishment as a vehicle of control and the presence of fear in human imagination. In a world ordered by the fear of hell, obedience matters — even when it means, as in Cotton Mather's experience, one is "dreadfully torn to Peeces" by one's god.

Augustine justified the discipline enacted by fathers whose duty it was to command peace in their homes so that peace would ensue in the civil community as well. With regard to the role of fear as a controlling factor in the raising of children, he writes: "That is why we have tutors and schoolmasters with their ferules and straps and canes, and why, in the training of a child we love, we use the authority of Holy Writ to beat his sides."[31]

Likewise, Luther considered it an unfatherly act to spare the rod, because the child might go its "own wanton way." While Luther tempered his remarks on punishment to insist that parents not "vent their furious temper" on their children, he was clear about the implications of a father's failure to train his children well, for "the child will be required from the parent at death and on Judgment Day in a very strict reckoning."[32] While partially aware of the consequences of corporal punishment — "even if they do not strike or slay with the hand, they nonetheless wish that their parents were dead" — Luther believed this was rooted in the child's unwillingness to learn and keep the "Word of God," rather than stemming from the parents' disposition toward their children.[33] Thus the authority of scripture and the "sovereignty" of God once again act to displace God's love by keeping children "in their place." Likewise, as Greven and others ably document, the fear of hell continues even now to visit the chastisements of a "loving god" upon those less able to guard the integrity of their soul.

For his part, Calvin looked to the Letter to the Hebrews for his understanding that God the Father tested his children so that they could learn obedience through suffering, believing that Jesus' "whole life was nothing but a sort of perpetual cross." To submit to God's yoke was to yield one's hand and back to God's rod. Obedience also required one to experience wounds so severe that the believer felt they were "not far distant from the damnation of hell." In hell the wicked are without hope, Calvin believed,

---

31. St. Augustine, *The City of God: An Abridged Version*, trans. Gerald G. Walsh et al., ed. with a foreword by Vernon J. Bourke (New York: Image Books, Doubleday, 1958), 463, 520; see Sirach 30:1, 7–12.

32. Ewald M. Plass, ed., *What Luther Says: An Anthology*, vol. 1 (St. Louis: Concordia, 1959), 140, 141.

33. Ibid., 144.

for they are pressed by the inescapable sovereign power of God and torn asunder by a hostile deity who crushes them by the mere weight of his hand.[34]

The Erosion of Imagination

Despite critiques leveled against it, sacrificial imagery has had a revival of sorts as a new generation of theologians tries to re-present atonement in ways more conducive to a new millennium.[35] In each case, these are well-intentioned efforts by thoughtful theologians who seek to rework traditional concepts while remaining true to biblical and orthodox insights. Their work is directed to traditional believers who wish to understand the self-sacrificial nature of Christian life and Jesus' suffering on the cross in light of God's love. On the other hand, I have endeavored to show that for numerous reasons, these attempts cannot speak to all Christians. When Jesus' suffering is rationalized as a good and the suffering of the disenfranchised and vulnerable is ignored, traditional atonement imagery is ineffective in stemming the tide of unjust suffering, even among the faithful. We need only sample a few of the above-mentioned arguments to see how easily suffering becomes a theological quagmire.

Douglas John Hall places suffering in the context of a creation theology that allows for both integrative suffering (that which brings life and growth toward maturity) and disintegrative suffering (that which brings bondage and death). This distinction is intriguing yet problematic. Life is an achievement, and fullness of being is a mystery to strive for and embrace with thanksgiving. Life also entails an openness and readiness to change. A discerning being, Hall suggests, is one who can distinguish rightly among actions that lead to life and actions that bring death and destruction.[36] Nonetheless, "suffering as becoming" could leave the ones suffering unable to discern the source of their suffering or to interrupt evil. A better option might be to speak of the "labor pains" of life rather than suffering per se. Suffering has to do with pain that leads to disintegration. Labor pains, in contrast, are a necessary process of human becoming. Life requires that we wrestle with four interrelated factors in the process of discerning our way in a complex world of many connections:

---

34. John Calvin, *Institutes of the Christian Religion*, ed. John T. McNeill, trans. Ford Lewis Battles, Library of Christian Classics (Philadelphia: Westminster Press, 1960), 20:702–5, 661, 1007–8.

35. Robert J. Sherman, "Toward a Trinitarian Theology of Atonement," *Scottish Journal of Theology* 52, no. 3 (1999): 346–74.

36. Douglas John Hall, *God and Human Suffering: An Exercise in the Theology of the Cross* (Minneapolis: Augsburg Publishing House, 1986), 49–71.

- the power of *imagination* — our bodyspirits can leap to imaginative expressions of creativity and joy or fall victim to confusion and despair
- *decision making* — our freedom to choose one life-path over another can enhance or undermine well-being
- *embodied (finite) selfhood* — our bodily senses and emotions can be experienced as blessing or limitation
- *relationality* — our relational hearts can lead us to ecstasy or loneliness

Our capacity to lean toward well-being in each of these dimensions is tied to the integrity we spoke of in chapter 3. Where imagination is unconstrained by fear, well-being flourishes, which is why Hall's advocacy of a redemptive and incarnational "conquest from within" fails to persuade.[37] Hall rightly argues against the interpretation of divine power as omnipotence and is careful to distance himself from imperialistic theology and its need to think triumphantly. Still, he holds to the view that the redemptive work of God must be "conformed to the image of God revealed in the crucified one."[38]

Robert Schreiter describes suffering as the "human struggle with and against pain."[39] Suffering, in his view, involves the breakdown of our systems of meaning — our true stories about ourselves — and the struggle to restore our safety and selfhood. Thus suffering, unlike labor pains, involves the disintegration of psychic integrity. Neither noble nor redeeming, he argues, suffering is an "erosion of meaning." Without a "narrative of identity" (that which preserves the record of our encounters with self and others), we cannot survive the "narrative of the lie" that violence presents. To resist the narrative of the lie, Schreiter urges us to resist the breakdown of our personal narratives.

Likewise, in Farley's analysis, loss of identity is rooted in the soul's inability to defy evil — that is to say, the loss of identity entails the loss of that which makes us most human.[40] In attempting to describe a contemporary *orthopathema* — a right way to suffer — Schreiter appears deeply sensitive to the concerns of Brown and Parker that suffering is not redemptive. Nevertheless, he adds a disturbing tone to his argument when he suggests that suffering can be redemptive if it is placed in the context

37. Ibid., 53–62, 105.

38. Ibid., 105, 143.

39. Robert J. Schreiter, *Reconciliation: Mission and Ministry in a Changing Social Order* (Maryknoll, N.Y.: Orbis Books, 1992; Cambridge: Boston Theological Institute, 1992), 33.

40. Wendy Farley, *Tragic Vision and Divine Compassion: A Contemporary Theodicy* (Louisville: Westminster/John Knox Press, 1990), 34; Rebecca S. Chopp, *The Praxis of Suffering: An Interpretation of Liberation and Political Theologies* (Maryknoll, N.Y.: Orbis Books, 1986), 43.

of a larger narrative. Having argued that violence seeks to destroy the narratives that sustain us and substitute narratives of the oppressor, Schreiter looks to the atoning work of Christ for his redeeming narrative. Thus "the abused body of Christ, both beaten and crucified, and then exposed on the cross, becomes the vehicle of reconciliation for those who have had their own bodies abused."[41] Ironically, Schreiter's definition falls short precisely because many women name his redeeming narrative — atonement — as the narrative of the lie!

Let me suggest an alternative view. If we have lost a sense of safety and selfhood and have come to believe that God is either benignly absent or angry enough to punish, then more than the loss of meaning is at stake. Our ability to imagine a different future is also lost. More profoundly, then, suffering is the *erosion of our meaning-making power* — our capacity to imagine and therefore hope. The ability to imagine that God is still with us and for us in the face of evil and under the influence of despair is a necessary indicator of well-being. Whenever the pain of disintegration conquers imagination from within, evil is truly present. On the other hand, when imagination is liberated from the constraints of pain and fear, our liberated bodyspirits help us build communal well-being. The image of God suffering in empathy is, itself, problematic. When the belief that God suffers with us reinforces the belief that suffering is the "Christlike" thing to do (especially when we are hurt by those who love us), we may well accept pain — rather than resist it by discerning the evil that drives it. Then, much too easily, a love that suffers can become a suffering that knows too little love.

Hall and others are right to argue that God is at work in Jesus' confrontation with the principalities and powers of evil and his efforts to expose them to the light of truth. Jesus knew the difference between good and evil and spoke out strongly against the latter with courage and conviction, regardless of the personal cost. Yet two very different dimensions of life are subtly joined in these arguments. The first is the truth that human becoming and human loving require an ongoing commitment to growth and change that is often painful. Pain such as this often requires us to face the untruth we live by and refuse to give it greater power. This pain has nothing to do with denying the self (or breaking the self, as if we were breaking bread). On the contrary, this pain is a product of the experience of mutuality (shared well-being) and the labor (birthing) pains involved with any attempt to experience abundant life.

Some feminists have indeed spoken of "surrendering" a "false" self, but not one of them advocates a disruption of the deep or core self that holds

41. Schreiter, *Reconciliation*, 55.

our true identity — our narratives of safety and selfhood. Moreover, as Brock points out, the "false" selves we adopt are necessary, but limiting, coping mechanisms. They are reflections of a broken heart, a heart that has been wounded in its relations with others (conquered from within, if you will) such that it can barely recall its true identity — its "original grace."[42] To shatter or break a heart that is already broken is an evil act and never an act of God. As Second Isaiah reminds us, "a bruised reed [my servant] will not break" (Isa. 42:3). Only by helping wounded individuals experience the compassionate love of God and come to a lasting awareness of their own capacity to heal through remembrance and forgiveness can true well-being be achieved.

Divine encouragement allows us to move from suffering to hope because God is the only one who can help us resist those who seek to conquer us from within. Divine compassion already knows the "meaning" inherent in suffering, and names it evil. It is the Divine Encourager alone who understands our suffering and seeks to help us face its source, so that we may wisely and courageously wrest power back from the suffering moment and experience healing at whatever level of well-being we can claim. Suffering love, which leads to disintegration, and compassionate love, which creates well-being, part company the moment we expose them to the light. Suffering resists relationality and seeks the destruction of the one suffering by sowing seeds of alienation and isolation. Compassion, in contrast, thrives on the mutuality of right-relation and opens the one suffering to the redeeming narrative of original grace, which honors our original loveliness.[43] Mutuality and well-being return us to the truth of our divine relationality, to grace-in-relation. Without them we are lost to ourselves and lost to God.

The doctrine of atonement persists because many people have found meaning within its walls. At the same time, fearing other choices, these same believers insist on keeping suffering and love firmly cemented. In the presence of fear, atonement imagery presents a vision of hope that encompasses a feast of thanksgiving, the forgiveness of sin, and life eternal. But is this really enough? Those who see the apocalyptic underside of atonement yearn for more. Have we found within Christianity a word of grace? Yes! Have we found communities of well-being that nurture us in the ways of love? Most assuredly! Is the church the ultimate community of well-being in our lives? More and more of us are discovering that this is less and less the case. Instead of building up the community in love,

---

42. Rita Nakashima Brock, *Journeys by Heart: A Christology of Erotic Power* (New York: Crossroad, 1988), 10, 7.

43. Robert C. Neville, *A Theology Primer* (Albany: SUNY Press, 1991), 48.

communal relations in our worshiping congregations often demonstrate the absence of well-being and a profound lack of praise. The combined influence of apocalyptic fear, atonement guilt, and penitential shame has taken its toll on the bodyspirits of clergy and laity alike. In the place of love, fear looms; in the place of well-being, suffering festers. We have learned the lessons of imperial Christianity too well. Distrusting the truths of our own experience, we have allowed our imaginations to erode. As a consequence, our worlds have narrowed, our lives have diminished, and our ability to love has been constrained by fear. This is not to say we have done this willingly or intentionally. No one in his or her right bodymind would say yes to such a life.

Deliver Us from Evil

In its traditional form Christian theodicy seeks the root cause of evil and tries to justify belief in a good and gracious God, and it does all this without compromising two divine attributes: omnipotence and goodness. Augustine argued that "all evil is the result of sin and its punishment,"[44] while Irenaeus spoke of evil as part of the essential imperfection of creation. Evil is the human act of disobedience and "a means by which we 'learn . . . what is the source of [our] deliverance.'"[45] In *The End of Evil,* process theologian Marjorie Suchocki enlarges the root of evil from its traditional notion of freedom of choice and its later association with the limitations of human finitude to allow for a positive view of humanity's finite limitations and our capacity for creativity. Suchocki also proposes a critical distinction between judgment and punishment: God's judgment has to do with transformation *into* the life of God rather than eternal punishment and banishment *from* God.[46] Without digressing into the complexities of process theology, we can benefit from her imaginative shift away from the notion of punishment. Why? Because punishment is not a given in the justice and mercy of God (1 John 4:18)! Whenever punishment is attributed to God's mercy, we enter the slippery slope of deception, for punishment easily becomes one of the theological masks that evil dons under the guise of suffering love. Equally tenuous are appeals to purgation or purification as acts of God. Attributing a literal notion of wrath and punishment to God "deifies

---

44. Marjorie Hewitt Suchocki, *The End of Evil: Process Eschatology in Historical Context* (New York: SUNY Press, 1988) 5, 157n.1.

45. In Carter Heyward, *The Redemption of God: A Theology of Mutual Relation* (Lanham, Md.: University Press of America, 1982), 112–14.

46. Suchocki, *End of Evil,* 37, 113.

the 'myth of punishment,' and conceals the ultimately redemptive power of God."[47]

These assertions are borne out when we understand that traditional theodicies function as a form of social control. Theodicy is ultimately a theory of power that legitimates the way a society is organized. Stated differently, notions of an all-powerful God serve the well-being of the emperor rather than the well-being of the emperor's subjects. Stanley Hauerwas has argued that Christianity developed a regrettable "habit of mind" when it shifted from "a set of convictions about God's work in Jesus Christ" and oriented itself, as a religion of the state, to "provide the ethos necessary to sustain an empire."[48] Likewise, Hall believes attributions of divine omnipotence have more to do with the things that belong to Caesar than the things that belong to God.[49] Theodicies constrained by the notion of divine omnipotence perpetuate a theology of dominance rather than mutuality. Likewise, punishment sanctioned by dominarchal societies obscures the role of violence within the punitive act itself. Sin and evil are interrelated dimensions of human experience that reveal our failure to love well and encourage well-being for all of creation. Because its presence mystifies our ability to counter the extremities of sin and the structural dimensions of oppression, suffering is surely woven into the fabric of evil.

Knowing God and Knowing Good and Evil

By now it should be clear that our capacity to know the difference between good and evil is not a sign of sinful disobedience (Gen. 2:17), but a sign of our movement toward well-being and solidarity with others. Likewise, knowing good and evil is a condition of being human. We must know the difference between good and evil and seek the good, knowing that evil arises from human choices, desires, and policies — even the best intentioned. We live in a relational matrix where grace and sin abound. There too evil has its way with us; but just as we cannot die to sin, we cannot eradicate evil completely. Try as we might! Evil is fastened to our fears, as Carter Heyward wisely observed.[50] Fear, however, is not a free-floating entity that we can easily pluck out whenever we wish. Fear is molecular; it is in our bones and our blood, our muscles and our nerves. Fear hides in the chemistry of our bodies and rides these interactions as it widens its reach. Fear takes hold of the images and symbols by which we grasp

47. Farley, *Tragic Vision*, 118, 123.

48. Stanley Hauerwas, *Naming the Silences: God, Medicine, and the Problem of Suffering* (Grand Rapids, Mich.: William B. Eerdmans, 1990), 43, 44, 55.

49. Hall, *God and Human Suffering*, 155.

50. Heyward, *Redemption of God*, 155.

the truths of our lives and transforms them into the prison cells of our past. Fear narrows the horizons of grace by which we engage the world and turns us away from the gracious face of God. Yet fear need not be the death of us.

Living with evil is not the same as sanctioning its presence or condoning its consequences. Living with evil means that we take our humanity seriously and learn to recognize evil's many faces. It means that we must "struggle to avoid [evil] when possible,... confront it when it cannot be avoided," and "resist its dehumanizing effects when we find ourselves its victims."[51] Feelings of guilt, deserved or undeserved, often play havoc with our souls. One way of being able to deal with the enormous reservoirs of guilt that are capable of claiming anyone of us is to live the best lives we can. If we are to take responsibility for things that we clearly know we have done wrong, we need to confess to God and to the offended party (whenever possible). We also need to live as truthfully as we can, making amends as we go and trusting in God's grace.

The author of the Gnostic and "heretical" Gospel of Philip offered his followers two critical pieces of wisdom in relation to Genesis 2–3. First, a mature believer is so guided by the love of others that he or she brings no grief to another; and, second, the "root of evil" is to be found in each of us. As long as we ignore its presence, evil is in control. When we become aware of its presence, we limit its destructive power. Philip's insights into the "evil within" resonate with my own.[52]

Coping with pain and suffering requires the courage to discern the knowledge of good and evil that comes from daily living and the learning of new life-lessons. Hence, each of us must develop a hermeneutic of suspicion in regard to power and privilege (asking, Who benefits from it and who does not?). We must also sharpen our personal hermeneutic of truth (asking, What are the truths of *my* experience?).[53] In order to be responsible and accountable to one another in an interdependent world, we must be able to respond imaginatively (with empathetic engagement) to the situations that we find ourselves in, both personally and communally. We need to resist — fear — oppression and injustice, abuse and violence, for what they can do to us; we also need to fear the extremities of pain, loneliness, loss, grief, and death, for the ways in which they can shatter our sense of safety and selfhood. But we need not experience these fears

---

51. Darby Kathleen Ray, *Deceiving the Devil: Atonement, Abuse, and Ransom* (Cleveland: Pilgrim Press, 1998), 129.

52. Elaine Pagels, *The Origin of Satan* (New York: Vintage Books, 1995) 173, 174; Anthony Storrs, *The Essential Jung* (Princeton, N.J.: Princeton University Press, 1983), 88.

53. Susan Brooks Thistlethwaite, *Sex, Race, and God: Christian Feminism in Black and White* (New York: Crossroad, 1989), 141.

in isolation from God or one another. The Spirit of Christ-Christa can encourage us to hold fast to God's promises and fear not!

Imagination has to do with personal choice and responsible choice. Without question, our decisions and nondecisions affect the fabric of our society, and our society affects the fabric of our well-being. Knowing the difference between good and evil is a necessary means of survival if one is to resist the violence of domination and the humiliation of subjection to a higher power, especially when that power mis-represents itself as divine. We must, with God's help, break through this deception and name situations of domination, violence, and terror for what they are, incarnations of evil. At the same time, we must be able to trust the divine power of good that manifests itself in the creativity, wisdom, and compassion of relationships grounded in mutuality. Above all, we must take responsibility for our participation in evil, even as we address the evil that others perpetrate on us. We must acknowledge the mystery of evil while refusing to succumb to its mystifying power.[54] When we turn from evil to enact compassionate love, the feast of our lives takes on new meaning, indeed!

---

54. Farley, *Tragic Vision*, 50, 90–94; Nel Noddings, *Women and Evil* (Berkeley: University of California Press, 1989), 210.

EIGHT

Holy Communion Indeed!

> Feasts are events of human communion, where life itself is spirited and thereby somehow hallowed. . . . [A]ll true feasts are ecstatic. Feasts are ultimately trysts with transcendence, since all glad communion is eucharistic. —*John Burkhart*[1]

> When I dare to be powerful — to use my strength in the service of my vision, then it becomes less and less important whether I am afraid. —*Audre Lorde*[2]

Banquets are planned, but *feasts happen.* When we feast . . . the joy of friendship and the Spirit's power call our embodied souls to the dance of life. When fear distorts friendship, however, joy turns to mourning and feasts turn to fasts. Unable to touch the deep communion within us, we fail the generosity of spirit on which glad communions thrive. Such is the power of table-fellowship gone awry. Fear has the power to silence thanksgiving, and it often has. Because we open ourselves to God in the act of prayer, eucharistic praying goes to the core of our being. The God we find there must ultimately be our judge and our redeemer, not our persecutor. Having exposed the human fears that have allowed the fear of God, via the fear of hell, to undermine the well-being God intends, it is time to draw conclusions and present some constructive proposals.

A Covenant Betrayed

Israel held in tension the notion that God was both lover and punisher, forgiving iniquity, transgression, and sin, while also visiting the iniquity of the fathers upon their children, to the third and fourth generations (Exod.

1. John E. Burkhart, *Worship: A Searching Examination of the Liturgical Experience* (Philadelphia: Westminster Press, 1982), 79.
2. Audre Lorde, from a postcard by the Syracuse Cultural Works, Box 6367, Syracuse NY 13217.

34:6). God's forgiveness, however, was never denied. By the time of the epistles and other New Testament writings, Jesus is presented as the mediator of forgiveness, whose death was a necessary act in the redemptive grace of God. Jesus also seems to give credence to this interpretation by saying, according to Matthew, that his blood was "poured out for many for the forgiveness of sins." However, as we noted earlier, Matthew's theological intention is to show that Jesus' life echoes the Mosaic covenant even as it moves beyond it.

The tendency to set loyalty to Christ and his messianic message as the key to salvation is rooted in apocalyptic eschatology and the notion of repentance; in its guise in the Christian Scriptures, it began with the preaching of John the Baptist, who proclaimed a baptism of repentance for the *forgiveness of sins* (Mark 1:4; Luke 3:3). In the end, it enveloped the table-fellowship of Jesus, by way of Jeremiah's proclamation of the new covenant: "I will put my law within them, and I will write it on their hearts . . . for I will forgive their iniquity, and remember their sin no more" (Jer. 31:31–34). The new covenant of Jeremiah and the new covenant referred to by Jesus appear in chapters 8 and 10 of Hebrews. Veering from Jeremiah's covenant in surprising fashion, Hebrews jettisons the notion of direct forgiveness, as the Lord says, "I will be *merciful toward* their iniquities, and I will remember their *sins* no more" (Heb. 8:12; emphasis added). This variation on Jeremiah's covenant makes clear that the old Mosaic covenant is rendered obsolete by the superiority of Jesus' once-for-all sacrifice. Jesus offered forgiveness directly during his ministry. However, within this covenant forgiveness requires the shedding of blood (Heb. 9:22), as was the case when Moses sprinkled blood to mark the establishment of the first covenant.

The memorial of Christ's sacrifice leads to mercy for those who enact it. Thus Jesus becomes an intercessor, reminding God that he has suffered for these people, so that God will remember God's promise and forgive their iniquity. Ironically, Jesus has become "the Lamb of God who takes away the sin of the world" (John 1:29), even though the boundaries of this "world" exclude many whom Jesus welcomed.

"Lamb of God: Have Mercy On Us"

The transformation of Jesus from healer to lamb is apocalyptically driven. Crossan suggests that John the Baptist offered an "inexpensive" and "divinely authorized rite," baptism, for the forgiveness of sins in contrast to the costly restrictive sacrificial system of the Temple. While John's warning about the coming judgment followed past prophetic predictions, he nevertheless provided a way for those who could not meet the legal demands of Jerusalem to prepare themselves for the "catastrophic coming of the kingdom." The Gospel of Mark reworked the tradition about John the Baptist and ignored the political motivations that occasioned John's death at the hand of Herod. The early stratum of evidence dealing with Jesus being baptized by John thus evolves through a variety of texts until the Gospel of John offers only an indirect allusion to Jesus' baptism. By implication, Jesus no longer needs to be baptized for the forgiveness of his own sins because he is the one, ultimately, who takes away the sins of the world![3] Why must Jesus become a mediator for our sins? Because he is the only one powerful enough to keep the molecularly based embodied fear of hell and damnation at bay. Having been *conquered from within* (internalized oppression) by the multifaceted fears that burdened their external and internal worlds of meaning, early Christians turned the cause of their fear into the source of their hope, the twofold hope of the forgiveness of sins and life eternal in a heaven devoid of punishment. In contrast to the tears Paul shed for nonbelievers, however, these Christians no longer wept for those who worked out their own salvation apart from an imperial Christ.

Temple Tables Revisited

Jesus' disciples appeared unable to rise above the terror of Rome's brutal rule, the trauma they experienced upon witnessing Jesus' violent death, and the trauma they experienced upon witnessing the consequences of their own betrayal. The Gospels agree: his disciples didn't get it. Not only that, they were *so fearful* of being associated with this man that they vehemently denied knowing him. Add to this scenario the influx of priests who, according to Luke, "became obedient to the faith." When the disciples' circumstances are brought together with the continuing power of the priests, it becomes clear why his disciples failed to live out Jesus' vision of compassion. The world Jesus welcomed them into, a world of healing love and intimate table-fellowship, collapsed under the burden of his difficult death. At the same time, the Temple priests, whose religious power remained formidable, continued their sacrificial duties. After all, the destruction of the Second Temple (around 70 C.E.) took place at least forty years after Jesus was crucified. Luke also records that "Day by day, as they spent much time together in the temple, they broke bread at home" (Acts 2:46). While a common meal sustained them, it obviously took place in the shadow of Temple-fellowship, where sacrifice remained a ritual necessity.

---

3. John Dominic Crossan, *The Historical Jesus: The Life of a Mediterranean Jewish Peasant* (San Francisco: HarperCollins, 1991), 230–35.

Lastly, all of this took place in the larger context of a "hierocratic-theocratic outlook widespread within first century Judaism." In other words, prior to the Maccabean era and continuing well after the Second Temple's destruction, the influence of the priesthood was pervasive. There existed a "distinctive understanding of the importance of the levitical, but above all Aaronic priesthood." The Aaronic priesthood and its high priest mediated God's rule over the Jewish people, and their influence had considerable political, social, and economic implications. Thus in the view of several commentators, the influence of the priesthood was understood to impinge "upon the whole way of life in Judaism in the first century, not only in Palestine, but also beyond."[4] This, then, is the context in which the writer of Hebrews introduces Jesus as the high priest Melchizedek whose sacrifice made once-for-all becomes more powerful than the ritual forgiveness offered by the priests of his day.

Few would argue that Jesus believed in a forgiving God, nor deny that he challenged his followers to embody God's forgiveness in their own acts of compassion. Jesus' ministry of forgiveness was grounded in a rich understanding of God's willingness to forgive. At the same time, Jesus challenged the view that God alone offered forgiveness. In the wake of his crucifixion, Jesus' view of forgiveness was undone. As a consequence, the Temple tables, which Jesus angrily overturned, turned his open table upside down. Sacrifice, not forgiveness, became the ritualized sign of God's love.

Grace as Forgiveness

Jesus' death was then taken to be a mediating factor that could bring about salvation for those who trusted in its salvific power. Grace was also interpreted as costly, because divine love had paid such a price. Nevertheless, grace is a given, and costly grace nothing less than an oxymoron. In its name, many have endured the "costly" grace of penitential practices, only to find themselves victimized by the very system established to show them the forgiving love of God in Christ. The premise of costly grace is tied to the notion that grace cost God the life of his Son:

> "Ye were bought at a price," and what has cost God much cannot be cheap for us. . . . Costly grace is the Incarnation of God. *Costly grace is the sanctuary of God; it has to be protected from the world, and not thrown to the dogs.* It is therefore the living word, the Word of God, which He speaks as it pleases Him. Costly grace confronts us as a

---

4. A. N. Chester, "Hebrews: The Final Sacrifice," in *Sacrifice and Redemption: Durham Essays in Theology*, ed. S. W. Sykes (Cambridge: Cambridge University Press, 1991), 59.

> gracious call to follow Jesus, it comes as *a word of forgiveness to the broken spirit and the contrite heart.*[5]

The notion that grace not be "thrown to the dogs" evokes the *Didache's* apocalyptic imagery that longed for this world to pass away. In contrast, Jesus argued that no "dogs" (alias sinners) stand outside the table-grace of God (Mark 7:25–28). Unrestrained by an imperial church, God bestows grace freely to those who genuinely repent. Indeed, divine grace is never dispensed or withheld on the basis of human terms, the power of the keys not withstanding. Grace is never a commodity to be protected; it is always a truth to be lived. God forgives us then not because Jesus was crucified but because *forgiveness is the very nature of God.*

Daniel Day Williams suggested that "the first service ... of grace as forgiveness is service to the truth."[6] For this to be true, grace must confront us with the truths of our lives and encourage us to accept them and take responsibility for them. Even when we discover that the "truths" we live by have silently fragmented our embodied souls, we must not allow fear to bury truth with falsehood. The only way we can bear such truth, however, is if divine love holds us in and through the despair of recognition that accompanies the realization that we have denied not only God's place in our lives but the very relationality of life itself. "Grace is the *re*union of life with life, the *re*conciliation of the self with itself."[7] Grace also confronts the truth of injustice and challenges us to *resist* suffering.

Re-imaging Redemption

In the power of God's companioning presence we participate in the work of Christ-Christa, which is the work of justice-making love. Such love is rooted in human connectedness, a power-in-relation that arises from experiencing God in and through each other. In the context of symbolic actions such as the eucharist, it is the very act of eating and drinking together around a common table — not an altar — that expresses this truth most profoundly. The eucharist is "first of all an assembly, ... a community, a network of relations."[8] We gather as embodied, relational selves, and in so gathering we point beyond ourselves to the Creator who calls us forth.

5. Dietrich Bonhoeffer, *The Cost of Discipleship,* trans. R. H. Fuller, rev. ed. (New York: Macmillan, 1959), 37; emphasis added.

6. Daniel Day Williams, *The Spirit and the Forms of Love* (Lanham, Md.: University Press of America, 1981), 178; Marjorie Hewitt Suchocki, *The Fall to Violence: Original Sin in Relational Theology* (New York: Continuum, 1995), 159.

7. Paul Tillich, "You Are Accepted," in *The Shaking of the Foundations* (New York: Charles Scribner's Sons, 1948), 156.

8. John D. Zizioulas, *Being as Communion: Studies in Personhood and the Church* (Crestwood, N.Y.: St. Vladimir's Seminary Press, 1985), 60.

The more we open ourselves to God's sacramental generosity, the more we receive Spirit-energy. Engaging in the practice of forgiving grace, discerning obedience, and healing love is demanding work — labor-intensive living! Even so, if we remain faithful to this good work, the fruit of our labor can awaken us to the depth and breadth of God's enduring grace. As we embody God's love, we come to know our true selves in relation to the fullness within us. As we express our divine communion, we embody that communion more deeply.

To truly understand the communion at the heart of God we must experience our redemption not as a process completed by Jesus' death but as being fulfilled by God's incarnating presence in Jesus and all of creation. Jesus becomes *Christ Jesus* for us — an icon of cosmic generosity and resurrecting love — by the power of the Holy Spirit at work in us. Likewise, the communion of Christ-Christa becomes a symbol of resurrection in and through community not by our efforts alone but by the power of the Spirit's cocreative grace. When we respond to the enlivening and healing power of the Holy Spirit and embrace the life-work of Jesus, we experience redemption and deepen our experience of well-being. When we trust that we are worthy of God's love and can receive others with the confidence that God receives us, we are liberated from the boundaries of fear and open to the power of resurrection. In Christ-Christa we practice resistance in the face of fear, even as we "practice resurrection."[9] In practicing resurrection, we practice forgiveness, knowing that forgiveness births forgiveness. Forgiveness is an imaginal act, for it allows us to love beyond fear for the sake of well-being and "see" the world anew.[10] As God forgives us, we forgive others.

The Emperor Has No Hope

When we imprison God's forgiveness within Jesus' once-for-all death, we imprison our imaginations as well. In Tom Driver's wise words, "Something done for our freedom has been turned into a mold in which we try to hold God fixed. Since God cannot be contained, we encapture only ourselves."[11] Imperial Christianity's "Christ alone saves" theology denies the divine relationality that shapes our creative and redemptive work through the power of the Holy Spirit. Where once the bodyspirit of Jesus welcomed

---

9. Wendell Berry, "Manifesto: The Mad Farmer Liberation Front"; cited in Robert A. Raines, *The Ridgeleaf: An Occasional Paper from Kirkridge,* no. 190 (May 1992), 1.

10. Robin Casarjian, *Forgiveness: A Bold Choice for a Peaceful Heart* (New York: Bantam Books, 1992), 23.

11. Tom F. Driver, *Christ in a Changing World: Toward an Ethical Christology* (New York: Crossroad, 1981), 60.

human beings into the "deep and dazzling darkness" (the incomprehensibility) of divine mystery, our god-representations now masquerade as the living God. Where divine mystery once offered a profound presence — a communion of our bodyspirits with divine Spirit — false gods now offer a profound absence, one that leaves us longing for *a more* we no longer feel worthy of receiving.

There is not now, nor was there ever, a sound basis for fearing (being terrified of) God. *Nothing* separates us from the love of God (Rom. 8:38)! Nevertheless, within the force field of extreme fear our imaginations erode as we experience psychic suffering. As a consequence of this suffering we are left with the illusion that God and we are not at-one. Hope turns to hopelessness as our heart sickens and our downcast bodyspirit dries up our bones (Prov. 13:12; 17:22). On the other hand, whenever we practice resurrection and say yes to life through visible acts of praise and thanksgiving, our imagination is strengthened, our bodyspirit is healed, and our life-purpose becomes clear. When we live in the encouraging power of Christ-Christa, we have no fear of one another, or ourselves. Instead we live in "radical amazement," knowing that we are part of that which moves us from awe to thanksgiving. In the power of God's beneficence, the time has surely come to amend our ways and challenge our imaginations, for the sake of well-being.

True redemption involves committing our lives to the liberating actions of Jesus' life-work, actions shaped by his imaginative feeling and his profound trust in the goodness and mystery of God. To move beyond the illusionary boundaries of Constantinian Christianity, we must make truth-telling the true measure of our faithfulness. For too long we have let stand the lie that God is merciful yet arbitrary, gracious yet vengeful, a healer who punishes for our own good. It is time to put this god to rest. This emperor not only has no clothes but has no hope. In the hearts and minds of too many Christians, God's call to life goes unanswered for want of a gracious God. If we fail to tell the truth of Jesus' *life*, and the forgiving God he embodied, the fear of God may well be the death of us.

Redemption is a gift that values life, even as it encourages us to resist evil. We should re-member the cross as a symbol of discipleship and its ultimate cost, especially for those who give their lives to Jesus' risk-taking, truth-telling ethic.[12] Whatever symbol conveys it best for you and your community, my point is this: God is a God of redemption through *resurrection*, not by way of the crucifixion. Those who would crucify in the

---

12. Rosemary Radford Ruether, "Feminist Perspectives and the Historical Jesus," panel presentation at the American Academy of Religion, November 25, 1991.

name of love are legion; yet we need not follow them to call ourselves Christian.

Praying Our Hope, Embodying Our Prayers

The larger context for re-imaging communion is one of mystery and wonder. Having surveyed the landscape of "eucharistic thanksgiving" and demonstrated how easily penance has fenced the Spirit from our tables and "altared" our bodyspirits, I offer a sampling of eucharistic prayers for the reclaiming of Jesus' table-fellowship (see Appendix B). To name the sacrament of Holy Communion as a sacrament of community in Christ-Christa is to name and reclaim its connectional foundations of grace. We live in a sacramental world where all matter is symbolic and grace is eternal. In Catherine Keller's words, "To claim that God is always and everywhere self-emptying, in essence and not only in one saving event, relieves christology at once of its exclusivism and of its triumphalism."[13] Both of these "isms" are imperial signs, bearing no resemblance to God's sacramental generosity. In contrast, sacramental generosity transforms the world into the "theater" of God's glory eternally.[14] To be redeemed in Christ-Christa is to receive Christ Jesus as the wisdom of God and the power of God (1 Cor. 1:24), without reducing that wisdom or power to any one expression of God's incarnational grace. God *was* in Christ Jesus! Hence we give thanks in sacramental rituals — baptism and Holy Communion — for the way Jesus' embodiment of divine generosity forever changed human life. Can we say more? Yes! We can bear witness to the Divine Companion of yesterday, today, and tomorrow, the living God who *is* present eternally in Christ-Christa — the communal embodiment of divine wisdom and power.

If we can receive Christ Jesus in faith as an icon of God's "cosmic generosity,"[15] then Christ-Christa — as the symbol of God's sacramental communion — can bestow the promise of eternal life *here and now*. Eternal life symbolizes God's embrace of us in every moment of our existence — indeed "it is as real at any time during our lifetime as it is after death."[16] This truth may seem new to some of us, but there is nothing new about

---

13. Catherine Keller, "Scoop Up the Water and the Moon Is in Your Hands: On Feminist Theology and Dynamic Self-Emptying," in *The Emptying God: A Buddhist-Jewish-Christian Conversation*, ed. John B. Cobb Jr. and Christopher Ives (Maryknoll, N.Y.: Orbis Books, 1990), 111.

14. John Calvin, *Institutes of the Christian Religion*, ed. John T. McNeill, trans. Ford Lewis Battles, Library of Christian Classics (Philadelphia: Westminster Press, 1960), 20:52.

15. Keller, "Scoop Up the Water," 111.

16. Melva Costen, "African American Liturgy in Context: Discovery, Recovery, Renewal," presentation at the North American Academy of Liturgy, Washington, D.C., January 4, 1992; Robert C. Neville, *A Theology Primer* (Albany: SUNY Press, 1991), 44.

the enduring life of the Spirit. Many non-Western peoples believe neither life nor one's sense of community ends with the death of physical persons. To paraphrase an African adage, "I am because you are and since we are therefore I am." To be alive is to be in communion, for "life means *communion.*"[17] When we encounter eternal life in the sacrament of Holy Communion, we experience the sacramentality of all creation. Here we discover the depth of the riches and wisdom and knowledge of divinity (Rom. 11:33), for it is in the matrix of life's interconnections that we encounter "a holiness of Self and Other that is irreducible to any one self or any one other."[18] The embodiment of God in the world is precisely the revelation of divine love within human community, supported and affirmed by the grace of God present in all of creation.

A Picture of Grace We Can Live With

The image of Christ's sacrificial death, so clearly pictured in the Letter to the Hebrews, functioned to console many a believer frightened by apocalyptic fears of God's "Last Judgment." Luther understood the necessity of living with the *image* of a good and gracious God. For him, and for those who accepted the principle of "justification by faith" as he expounded it, God's love was at the heart of the cross. This was the "picture of grace" that allowed him to look at sin and death and not be overcome by despair:

> You must turn your thoughts away from [those who abide in sin and are damned] and look at sin only within the *picture of grace. Engrave that picture in yourself* with all your power and keep it before your eyes. The picture of grace is nothing else but that of Christ on the cross and of all his dear saints.[19]

Those of us who see the terrible and gruesome reality of the cross today must understand that Luther saw it too, but the images of death and hell that haunted the medieval world — the images of actual death and the fear of hell that were fed by apocalyptic fears — were more terrifying than we can imagine. The "terror" with which Luther lived was nurtured by personal experience and societal chaos. In the face of these realities, his gift to the world was remarkable. He allowed forgiveness to flow by the

---

17. John D. Zizioulas, *Being as Communion: Studies in Personhood and the Church* (Crestwood, N.Y.: St. Vladimir's Seminary Press, 1985), 16.

18. Catherine Keller, *From a Broken Web: Separation, Sexism, and Self* (Boston: Beacon Press, 1986), 250.

19. Martin Luther, "A Sermon on Preparing to Die," in *Luther's Works*, vol. 42, *Devotional Writings I*, ed. Martin D. Dietrich, trans. Martin H. Bertram (Philadelphia: Fortress Press, 1969), 104; emphasis added.

act of imaginative feeling. In the face of terror he clung to the truth that God was gracious — and as he believed God, so God was.

Living as we do in a vastly different, yet equally dangerous, world, the terror we live with today is no less compelling. Luther's ability to live in the present and not be overcome by a hellish future was contingent on how he understood the past — Christ's death on the cross. Our ability to live in the present and not be overcome by the hells we carry deep within us as well as those we are exposed to in our global lives also rests on the strength of our faith — with one important difference. Luther's *picture of grace* no longer has the power to reveal a gracious God to every Christian.

Thankfully, our world is no longer the one in which Luther lived. Many of us have had the horizons of our imaginations widened and our fears lessened by the worlds of medicine, science, philosophy, theology, and biblical studies — not to mention images of moon-walkers and space stations, pictures of the earth taken from space, and pictures of space sent back to earth. The world is still a dangerous place, as terrorist attacks reveal; yet many Christians have allowed the wonder of new worlds to temper old world fears. In the process they have re-imaged and reaffirmed their faith and their ritual lives. In the midst of these seismic shifts, however, many communities remain burdened by "medieval celebrations."

While I am convinced that a heavy reliance on sacrificial imagery, conjoined with a heavily penitential focus, belabors our "celebrations," I am not suggesting that the eucharist be divested of all sacrificial imagery. As those who find meaning in such language continue to gather together, they will express their beliefs in the manner that sustains them best. Nevertheless, I would urge Christians whose meaning lies elsewhere to consider new possibilities for celebrating Holy Communion, including the possibility of varying their metaphors and images of God to the exclusion of sacrificial body-and-blood imagery.

Redemption, as Luther and Calvin made clear, is a gift of God's grace. I agree. Nevertheless, the "picture of grace" that I would fashion requires no crucifixions to express God's love. To name the sacrament of Holy Communion as the feast of our lives is to reclaim resurrection as the picture of grace for our time. Unlike Luther's picture of grace, ours cannot be wedded to Golgotha's geographical map of terror or the marriage feast of the Lamb. To the contrary, ours must be a picture in motion, more precisely *e-motion,* a moving out of our small isolated selves into relational and embodied well-being. For some this picture may mean embodying the joyful image of the dancing priests of Valyermo;[20] for others it might be the image of liturgical dancers inviting the community to leave their seats

20. The Benedictine monks of St. Andrew's Abbey, Valyermo, California; see *www.valyermo.com.*

and come to the table just as they are and as they are able. Whatever picture of resurrection we choose, it must always arise from the communal body of Christ-Christa gathered in specific communities of faith. Finding the appropriate image of resurrection for our distinctive communion tables need not involve the abandonment of liturgical practices that have meaning for us. Nevertheless, all of us must demonstrate a willingness to ask ourselves what images gather us. For only then will we be free to ask if the meanings we celebrate are true for us.

For those who believe God is calling them to re-image their liturgical lives in the context of Holy Communion, I offer several proposals. In addition to the cosmetic changes of adopting livelier music that truly witnesses to an Easter faith, encouraging less rigidity on the part of those who distribute the elements, and celebrating communion more frequently, I would urge the following. First, I would shift confessional prayers from their heavy emphasis on personal sin to more communal expressions, thereby unburdening the rite of its previous penitential cast. Second, if it is used regularly, I would re-image the apocalyptic affirmation, "Christ has died, Christ is risen, Christ will come again," to the more resurrection-oriented affirmation, "Christ has died, Christ is risen, *Christ is with us now*." Third, I would re-image the words of institution by shifting away from sacrificial inferences and strengthening the imagery of thanksgiving and resurrection.

Confessing Our Sins

In addition to broadening our definitions of sin to include suffering, we need to consider when, where, and to what extent we call for confession. More often than not, parishioners barely sit down on Sunday mornings before they are asked to confess their sins. This model simply reinforces a Reformation stress on human unworthiness in the face of a sovereign God who waits in the wings to mete out punishment. Too often Isaiah's "Woe is me, for I am a man of unclean lips" (Isa. 6:5) becomes the defining pattern for our confessional prayers, as though scripture has shown us there is only one way to speak the truth of who we are. Yet this is not the case.[21] Nor is it the case that we are called to confess outside of the context of grace proclaimed. A more faith-filled confession would come after the reading of scripture or in the midst of the sacrament. To confess for the sake of confessing expresses a posture of fear attempting to avoid

21. Paul Waitman Hoon, *The Integrity of Worship: Ecumenical and Pastoral Studies in Liturgical Theology* (Nashville: Abingdon, 1971), 51, 287; Ruth Duck, "Sin, Grace, and Gender in Free-Church Protestant Worship," in *Women at Worship: Interpretations of North American Diversity*, ed. Marjorie Procter-Smith and Janet R. Walton (Louisville: Westminster/John Knox Press, 1993), 55–69.

the wrath of a punitive god. Yet other options exist. Some communion services place the confessional prior to receiving the bread and cup, basing this on Jesus' words in Matthew 5 on reconciling with our neighbor before bringing our gifts to the altar. In this context, scripture has been proclaimed, hope has been enacted, and each worshiper has been surrounded by compassionate love.

On the one hand, the church has rightly argued that confession is integral to a repenting faith. On the other hand, the church has wrongly emphasized personal unworthiness over social responsibility. Confession, as Carter Heyward reminds us, "is always our first just act."[22] In loving God, we do not merely confess with our lips but reorient our bodyspirits toward justice — toward the undoing of evil and the enactment of good. Our lives thus become embodied witnesses to Christ-Christa faith.

When we are freed from the debilitating power of a punitive God, the fear that so often isolates us from God and alienates us from the world around us loses its hold on imagination. Only then can we engage in the work of mutuality by accepting others even as we know ourselves received by grace. Once we accept God's love, as revealed in Jesus' life-ministry and experienced in our own fields of relations, we gain what Tillich aptly called "the courage to be," the heart and hope needed to live an "in spite of" faith.[23] Embraced by love and confronted with its demands for right-relation and mutuality, we can step into repentance and commit our lives to compassion. When love orders our life, change follows upon change, for we are always discerning how, and if, our actions here and now destroy relation or build well-being. Eliminating a punitive god as our primary representation of God allows us to move beyond the limitations of parental imagery and take in the depth and breadth of God's vast mystery, not all of which will be to our comfort. A domesticated divinity is, after all, no replacement for a punitive one. Nevertheless, a more just understanding of our interdependence and our need for communal confession may allow us to make our personal confession more substantive than it often is on any given Sunday.

Christ-Christas among Us

My use of the affirmation, "Christ is with us now" in the context of Holy Communion has always been warmly and thoughtfully received. People instinctively know the importance of Christ's presence here and now. While

---

22. Carter Heyward, *The Redemption of God: A Theology of Mutual Relation* (Lanham, Md.: University Press of America, 1982), 161.

23. Paul Tillich, *The Courage to Be* (New Haven: Yale University Press, 1952), 4.

I would prefer to widen the Christic image to Christ-Christa, this symbol of resurrection may not fit the current realities of every congregation, in terms of their imaginative openness. Given the paradigm shifts — patterns of thought — that are necessary to receive such changes, all worshipers need to be given the theological and liturgical resources that will allow them to reflect on the paradigms already shaping their individual faith.[24] Educating for imagination is a critical dimension of Christian education for all ages, and it deserves to be integrated into our worshiping lives. Here are my reasons for rethinking imperial paradigms.

Through Word and sacrament Christians come to a more concentrated expression of who they are in the communion of Christ Jesus. In the words of Cyril of Jerusalem, we become "Christs" in baptism through the power of the Holy Spirit: "Being therefore made *partakers of Christ* ["partners of Christ," Heb: 3:14] ye are properly called *Christs, and of you God said, Touch not My Christs* [Psalm 105:15], or anointed. Now ye were made Christs, by receiving the emblem of the Holy Ghost."[25] All symbols present only partial expressions of the reality to which they point. In speaking here of our baptismal anointment, Cyril says something similar, for the Greek term "Christs" is represented as plural, not possessive. Human beings image the fullness of God in the context of their own particularity. It is only in community, Cyril seems to suggest, that we can understand the depths of the mystery to which we point and from which we come. As Christ-Christas we point to the Christic presence (the resurrected One) in our midst, for it is only in the mystery of another's presence that we experience God's transcendent mystery in each of us.

Words of Institution?

In order to be true to the vision of a Divine Companion who calls us to the table, our eucharistic celebrations should nurture a deep relationality. Rarely, however, is this the case. Each doctrinal alteration of the eucharist diminished its re-creative power. Without the meal itself, the table-fellowship of Jesus was reduced from the communal aliveness of his spirit to a remnant of its empowering past. Likewise, each assault on the body of Christ via apocalyptic fear, persecution, and penance limited the capacity of individual believers to offer praise and thanksgiving with enthusiasm. No longer enthused, en-spirited, they no longer knew the fullness of their Creator's communal grace. As a consequence, our communion

24. See Appendix A, below.

25. St. Cyril of Jerusalem, "Mystagogical Catechesis III: On the Holy Chrism," in *St. Cyril of Jerusalem's Lectures on the Christian Sacraments: The Procatechesis and the Five Mystagogical Catecheses*, ed. F. L. Cross (Crestwood, N.Y.: St. Vladimir's Seminary Press, 1986), 63.

celebrations now emphasize the symbolic power of bread and cup to the exclusion of the symbolic power of the community. Likewise our sacramental focus has shifted from a communal rite to an individualistic rite where the individual sinner has to confess his or her sins before being allowed to commune. The present emphasis on bread and cup as the body and blood of Jesus was thus apocalyptically motivated. In the aftermath of Jesus' death, when the meal itself had deteriorated into the ritualized eating and drinking of bread and wine, the risen Christ was transformed into the "eschatological Deliverer"[26] who, having ascended into heaven to sit at the right hand of God, would return to judge the living and the dead.

In the early years of eucharistic practice, after Jesus' death and before the Apostolic Tradition Prayer associated with Hippolytus (215 C.E.) became a model for the Western church, the *Apology of Justin* and the *Didache* were indications of the flexibility that once existed. The presider (the president of the assembly) was encouraged to pray as he, and some suggest she, was able. As prayers became more formal, they tended in the East to present a large sweep of salvation history, from creation to the second coming. The Western church showed a preference for commemorating Jesus' passion and death, and its eucharistic celebrations bear this out. The sparseness of prayer inherited from the Reformation reinforced the tendency to view the words of Jesus as the "moment of consecration." In the light of twentieth-century liturgical renewal, more attention has been given to a recovery of resurrection imagery and the use of the epiclesis — the invocation of the Spirit — affirming the Spirit who gives us life. There is also more emphasis given to the prayer itself as the consecrating act, rather than Jesus' words (in the West) or the epiclesis (in the East). Nevertheless, it is still the case that the Spirit is seldom invoked in Reformed celebrations.

Despite considerable evidence to the contrary, as earlier chapters suggest, many clergy and laity cling to the assumption that the "words of institution" are the words of Jesus. My own anecdotal study of what is said in Reformed liturgies reveals a salt-and-pepper approach, at best. Matthew (for the forgiveness of sins) and Paul (we proclaim the Lord's death, until he comes) appear to be the versions most often relied on; yet even they receive their fair share of emendations as celebrants using an extemporaneous approach shift their chosen imagery midway through the process. Presiders often lean on the words of institution heavily — repeating them for bread and cup — as though without them, there would be nothing to

26. Paula Fredriksen, *From Jesus to Christ: The Origins of the New Testament Images of Jesus* (New Haven: Yale University Press, 1988), 61.

say. At the other end of the spectrum, presiders can be found who appear so uncomfortable with sacrificial imagery that they jettison any significant connection to the historical Jesus. The meal thus becomes a collection of images strung together in such a way that those communing are hard pressed to know the meaning of what they are about to receive. Given the diverse denominational journeys many contemporary Christians have taken, it is not unusual to have former Catholics, Baptists, Methodists, Presbyterians, and Lutherans (and the list could go on) passing the elements to one another in the same pew. If we were to ask each of them what they were doing, their answers would vary considerably. Consistency from celebrants would help remedy some of the current confusion. At the same time, clarity of purpose on the part of those who preside, as to their own words and actions in light of the fullness of our received heritage, would go a long way to restoring this sacrament to its rightful place at the center of our communal lives.

My own prayers, which are included in Appendix B, seek to honor a Trinitarian view of salvation history, giving equal attention to the creative activity of God, the redemptive work of Jesus in his life and ministry, and the life-giving/resurrection power of the Holy Spirit. In each instance, I have chosen to re-image the Reformed tradition's use of the institutional narratives by removing them from before the prayer and in some cases by removing them from the prayer itself. I have taken these steps to be consistent with my intention of eliminating apocalyptically motivated associations from the sacrament. The re-imaging of the use of these words as a "warrant" for the sacrament is a critical step toward redeeming God from the punitive incarnations of divine presence that permeate Constantinian Christianity in its medieval captivity. The words of institution have been used as a "warrant" — an administrative guide — for why we do what we do in this sacrament; nevertheless, they often seem to function as magical words, without which God's presence would be absence. Ironically, absence not presence is what too many services reveal. We are absent from our embodied souls, we are absent from our communal ties, and we are absent from our this-worldly ties to all of creation. Despite Calvin's significant nod to the Spirit's work in our midst, we seem to have taken Zwingli's memorial as a literal manifestation — the remembrance of a past event that has no power to change our lives here and now. This is a sacramental travesty. To commune under the notion that God is absent more often than present denies the sacramental nature of our world. We do not have to remind God why we gather, for God is the one who calls us to assemble. The God of mystery and intimacy, whose being transcends our narrow representations, is present to creation, even if we are not.

There is enough variety in eucharistic prayers up to the fourth century to attest to the absence of the institutional narrative both in the Jerusalem Prayer and in the East Syrian prayer known as the Anaphora of Saints Addai and Mari, as well as other prayers that offer only a brief reference to the same. Indeed, Bryan Spinks argues that in the context of a "theology of the Word," whatever interpretative words Jesus may have said in addition to giving thanks must be considered effective for all time (Isa. 55:10–11). Thus "when the church gathers in obedience to his Word, there can be no doubt that his word will accomplish his promise — without us having to read the words ourselves to remind him or us."[27]

God As Our Judging Companion

The communion we know as relational selves in a sacramental world is the essence of our sacramental feasts. So too is the original communion we embody as symbols of divinity within our common humanity. In the presence of God's glory, we celebrate our iconic possibilities in community. To be "friends with God" rather than enemies is to befriend ultimate mystery, to trust the beneficence revealed by Jesus, and to let holy wonder be our guide. Divine love gives birth to love. Divine love also heals. To be redeemed before God is to be liberated and healed. To speak of the "befriending" and healing power of God's love, however, is not to savor cheap grace and deny our accountability to others or our responsibility to foster well-being through concrete acts of love. Grace is never costly, but the path to well-being is, for it requires that we speak truth to power and resist the subtleties of evil that are fastened to our fears.

By its very nature, well-being implies accountability. We are to do unto others as we wish they would do unto us. We also love as God loves us. When love judges, it judges for the sake of healing and well-being. Despite Moses' ascription of vengeance to God — "vengeance is mine" (Deut. 32:35) — retribution is not in God's nature. The enactment of vengeance is human nature at its worst. Divine mercy, in contrast, always seeks to redeem the evildoer that evil might be undone. It is not up to us to "worry" whether or not God will hold "sinners" accountable in a "next-life" scenario. Thinking such as this perpetuates evil, it does not undo it. Instead, each of us must attend to our own unjust actions here and now. Those who act unjustly do so for many complex reasons, including the learned behavior of hate. Yet underneath their hatred, which extends to molecular recesses deep in their bodyminds, suffering thrives in their lack

27. Bryan D. Spinks, "The Institution Narrative in the Eucharistic Prayer," *News of Liturgy* 157 (January 1988): 4.

of communion and denial of community. Can anyone seriously doubt that these individuals live their own hell here and now?

Jesus' most profound teaching has to do with loving our enemies. In the face of terrorism and other atrocities, many of us would prefer to ignore these words and take up arms. Yet even here table-truth confronts us:

> Even though I walk through the valley of death,
> I fear no evil; for you are with me;
> your rod and your staff — they comfort me.
> *You prepare a table before me in the presence of my enemies;*
> you anoint my head with oil; my cup overflows.

Whenever we adopt a bunker mentality, a table prepared "in the presence of my enemies" consoles our weariness. Yet imagine with me the deeper truth at work here. Our enemies are at the table not to witness to our bounty but to share in it. The wonder is not that they have come but that God is the host and the star on which our hearts are staid.[28] Welcome, not vengeance, *is* the food of feasts. Difficult to imagine? Of course! A necessity of love? Yes! Compassion is not a buzz-word for being nice; it is the embodiment of love, a love that calls evil by its rightful name and meets it on God's terms, not ours.

To love kindness, to do justice, and to walk humbly with God (Mic. 6:8) are acts of love that mark the path to well-being. When these are absent, our freedom is diminished and our well-being is compromised. Love is only as good as the lover.[29] When fear orders the lover, sin abounds. When love is freed from the power of fear, grace abounds. Everyone we label as a sinner in our eyes is not a sinner in the eyes of God. Those who are — because they continue to violate their own participation in divine relationality and wound others in the course of their own evil intentions — have already felt God's judgment. They are suffering *now,* and their actions betray their own disconnected bodymind. Unlike most of us, God mourns for their return and prays for their awakening — an awakening to new life that is always a return to original communion. Our response-ability as disciples of Jesus is to love rather than hate, to heal rather than blame, to reconcile — restore relation — and to resist the disconnecting power of fear that threatens the very life of the world that God so loves.

---

28. Robert Frost, "Take Something Like a Star," in *The Poetry of Robert Frost: The Collected Poems, Complete and Unabridged,* ed. Edward Connery Lathem (New York: Henry Holt Co., 1979), 403.

29. Cited in Mary Potter Engel, "Evil, Sin, and Violation," in *Lift Every Voice: Constructing Christian Theology from the Underside,* rev. and expanded, ed. Susan Brooks Thistlethwaite and Mary Potter Engel (Maryknoll, N.Y.: Orbis Books, 1998), 168.

Re-imaging Our Rites

Table-fellowship was at the center of Jesus' ministry and remains his most profound legacy. Yet table-fellowship is more than eating and drinking in Jesus' name. Being there is one thing, being fully present to new possibilities is another. The table-fellowship of Jesus commands us to bring to the table the courage of our convictions. On the one hand, if we come with the willingness to enter the mystery of divine love, if we come with the willingness to be ambassadors of reconciliation, and if we come with the willingness to be place-setters for hope, then the openness of our hearts will be blessed. On the other hand, if we come as stiff-necked people, certain that nothing in our lives will change and wanting no more from life than what we already have, then the hardness of our hearts will confirm our preconceived notions. The act of eating with others honors biological and social needs. In contrast, table-fellowship involves risk. To share a meal with another is to risk revealing ourselves not just to our companions (those we break bread with) but to ourselves as well. Expressing one's deepest self is a risk rarely taken yet one very much needed for community and communion to flourish. In the intimacy of table-grace we welcome life larger than our own — the life that really is life within this life (1 Tim. 6:19).

The Intimacy of Grace

Western culture fears the body even as it exploits the power of sexuality and undermines intimacy. Nevertheless, true intimacy involves a depth of self, a "letting in," that few of us achieve. When fear stifles intimacy, it stifles the essence of our humanness — relationality. Such fear must not go unchallenged. Fear of intimacy may be thrust upon us by the invasiveness of others or the all-controlling presence of false gods, but if hope gives way to hopelessness on the basis of such fear, we lose more than ourselves; we abandon new possibilities for life in the midst of life.

In the immediacy of intimacy — where deep calls to deep — grace gives birth to self-transcendence. In the immediacy of a "wider fellow feeling," our awareness of being one within a larger whole makes us one with all. Self-transcendence is not about separation. When we leave our self-containing worlds and trust Jesus' imaginative openness, we immerse ourselves in the truth of our diverse lives. We come to know the presence of divinity within all of life, even our own. When we celebrate the diversity of creation and the differences among people that are represented by distinctions in race, ethnicity, class, gender, sexual orientation, and physical ability — differences that mark us as unique manifestations of the divine presence — we give glory to the mystery whose loveliness births us all.

Sharing a meal is both a social and political act. It matters with whom we eat and whom we exclude. To eat with another binds us to the other, as St. Paul warned — "You cannot partake of the table of the Lord and the table of demons" (1 Cor. 11:21b). In a world where most of us are more than eager to label others as the enemy, we never eat together without political risk. There are always people eager to judge us by the company we keep — just so with Jesus. The imperial church may have proclaimed Jesus as "one without sin," but clearly he committed sins against the religious establishment of his day and the Roman state. He was soundly criticized for eating and drinking with sinners and for healing and forgiving with "authority." These were revolutionary acts in a world constrained by dominarchal notions of privilege and power. Such acts of liturgical resistance cost him his life.

In subverting Jesus' ministry of open table-fellowship and downplaying his acts of healing, imperial Christianity turned Jesus' feast of our lives into a fast — a fast many of us still follow. Because of the forcedness of this fast, our capacity to awaken and "live out God" suffers even now.[30] Removing imperial, eschatological fear from our bodyspirits will require us to widen our table-fellowship and increase the frequency of our feasts. We will also be required to honor the imaginative bodymind of Jesus' Christ-Christa community and nourish spontaneity, imagination, and self-awareness within our own embodied souls. Where the imperial church would have us speak of the mind of Christ, can we speak of the bodymind of Christ-Christa? Where the imperial church would have us speak of the spirit as being greater than the body, can we claim our bodyspirit in Jesus' Christ-Christa community? I believe the well-being of our embodied souls — our imagination-connection with divine mystery — depends on our willingness to reclaim Jesus' table-fellowship as the feast it was meant to be. As it was in Jesus time, so it is with us: if we widen our hearts by seeking the commonwealth of God, what we need will be given.

Gathered at the welcome table of God, we can be nourished with well-being, even as the Holy One calls us to accountability for the company we fear to keep. Relying on the divine bodyspirit within him, Jesus embodied a world-expanding, relational love — a radical world openness — that sought to bring well-being to life in and through community. His vision persists . . . seeking risk-takers and truth-tellers in our time. Yet fear persists just as powerfully . . . denouncing any vision that "dwells upon the tender

30. Dorothee Sölle, *Thinking about God: An Introduction to Theology* (Philadelphia: Trinity Press International, 1990), 186.

elements in the world" or rejoices in the immediacy of a love that heals slowly and quietly through the intimacies of grace.[31] How shall we embrace such a vision in the face of such fear? How shall we turn our backs on imperial fasts? Perhaps we can do so by allowing imagination its rightful place in Holy Communion. The immanence of the world — the inflowing of creation into the depths of our being — when received by the transcendence of divine mystery within all of creation makes the impossible possible, mourning turns to joy, life overcomes death, and resurrection happens.

The Christian life lived apart from the imperial paradigm of obedient self-sacrifice is an imaginative and creative life that nurtures, explores, and incarnates the divinity within our humanity and the divinity within all of creation. In its most profound expressions of liberation, Christianity witnesses to the bodymind of Christ-Christa: the imaginative and challenging relational power that calls us to embrace a feeling for infinity in all its diverse epiphanies. The sheer inexhaustibleness of life's possibilities, the infinity, the mystery, the deep and dazzling darkness of life, allows us to find meaning for ourselves and return this meaning to God. In so doing, we impart abundant life to a faint-hearted world. This is the vision Jesus embodied. When Jesus calls us to abundant life, he calls us to experience life as a feast, a feast of meanings, a feast of opportunities, and a feast of possibilities. To be invited to such a feast is to make eucharist, to offer thanks for divine and diverse epiphanies of love that nurture us toward well-being. Would that more of us could welcome his invitation.

Practical Premises

The guiding principle for celebrations of Holy Communion at which I am privileged to preside is this: everyone is welcome, even the nonbaptized, and no one who wants to receive is ever discouraged from participating. Holy Communion is a converting rite where grace is not merely proclaimed — it is enacted![32] Many faithful Christians, choosing to keep Jesus' death central to their celebrations, will hold on to the image of Jesus' sacrifice. Likewise their eucharist will continue to speak of body and blood and use the words of institution. They will do so because this is the ritual expression in which their embodied souls are fed. At the same time those who experience victim imagery as dangerous to their sense of safety and selfhood will continue to abstain. Are differences such as these too stark

31. Alfred North Whitehead, *Process and Reality,* corrected ed., ed. David Ray Griffin and Donald W. Sherburne (New York: Free Press, Macmillan, 1978), 343.

32. John Wesley, "The Duty of Constant Communion," in *John Wesley's Sermons: An Anthology* (Nashville: Abingdon Press, 1991), 501–9.

to reconcile? In terms of sharing a common eucharist, this seems to be the case — at least in the present climate. But it need not be the case that a particular community of faith has to exclude people on either side of this theological and liturgical chasm. Two distinct liturgies could be enacted within the context of one community at separate times, if community members were made *mindful* of differing liturgical sensibilities.

Likewise, the role of children needs to be rethought, as it already has been in many congregations. Reformation churches have promoted the practice of keeping children from the Lord's Supper until they have been thoroughly taught to understand the sacrament. Unfortunately, given the way that many children were disciplined by their Reformed parents, one can imagine this type of restraint as once again symbolizing the exclusion of the "unworthy." To take the presence of Christ seriously and yet practice excommunication reveals a questionable theology. If Christ is truly present, as we believe, we should allow his saving grace to confront the worst of "sinners" and the youngest of saints and bring them to faithfulness. This view does not extend to someone who abuses the very nature of the table by disrupting the meal itself. Rather it extends to all who wish to commune because they seek the genuine healing power of Christ-Christa. All who present themselves to our tables should be encouraged to come, most of all our children. Given that "absence from communion" in the colonial period "was an offense for which some persons were chastised,"[33] we would do well to recognize the many ways in which the practice of Holy Communion has placed a punitive deity before a forgiving one. Surely we can do better.

To change our communion imagery, I believe we must change our liturgical practices. Imagine what Holy Communion could be if our congregations left behind the penitential imagery they once absorbed, including the elemental imagery of "bread and water" that many congregations still encounter. Imagine, too, if joyfulness triumphed over "dignity." All too often tight choreography leads to confusion rather than communion. Re-imaging our table-fellowship in the name of God's hospitality also means discerning whether wine or grape juice will be used, whether individuals will come forward and drink from a common cup or receive by intinction (the act of dipping the bread into the cup), or whether the congregation will remain seated and be served in their pews. My own preference is to encourage communicants to demonstrate their thanksgiving by moving to the table, if they are able. For those unable to move easily, servers can be

33. Doug Adams, *Meeting House to Camp Meeting: Toward a History of American Free Church Worship from 1620 to 1835* (Saratoga, N.Y.: Modern Liturgy Resource Publications, 1981; Austin: The Sharing Company, 1981), 81.

instructed to observe who remains seated and approach those who indicate they wish to receive.

Practicing resurrection means practicing an open table. I would rather offer a recovering alcoholic or a person allergic to wine something they can drink than use a substance that will turn them away. My point is not to advocate anything goes (such as pizza and beer or soda and pretzels), but I am concerned that what we serve does not take precedence over whom we serve. If this means two primary cups must be used, one with wine and one with grape juice, so be it. Many will disagree with the openness I espouse. Nevertheless, I am more concerned about opening a conversation on sacramental generosity than I am about celebrating the sacrament rigidly. The elements we use and the communities we gather hold symbolic power. Even so, I believe greater love resides in communicating grace than in restricting it through the use of certain elements. Sacred food has undermined sacred fellowship long enough. Taking the life-circumstances of communicants seriously within the context of table-fellowship will, I hope, transform the altar-tables of an apocalyptic future into grace-tables here and now.

Bearing Witness to the Heresy of Hope

Jesus gathered a community of disparate and often desperate individuals and charged them to live out a radical world openness, an openness that excluded no one from the table, even the nonbaptized. The disciples who attempted to embody this openness soon witnessed a different reality: generosity often became the first casualty of fear. I have argued that we can (and do) nurture openness by allowing our imaginations to be blessed by God's sacramental generosity. Embodied, compassionate love can be the measure by which redemptive communities of Christ-Christa befriend one another in faith, engage the world in hope, and bring justice to the oppressed. Through concrete acts of love we practice forgiveness and expand the Spirit's resurrecting power.

For this to be the case, especially in churches where conflict rather than compassion rules, more congregations must use imaginative images of God and humankind in their communion songs and prayers in order to increase their awareness of their feeling, thinking selves and their interdependency with all creation. If this were to happen routinely, I can imagine new possibilities for right-relation and transformation. Would that you could too! The greater journey of my life that surrounds these reflections is well aware of how difficult these possibilities have proven to be. Even so, I am encouraged to journey onward, knowing all things are possible in the company of a loving, forgiving, and challenging God. This God has taught me that

I am the mystery that is not mine, as are you! Likewise, when I claim the redemptive power of God and become love,[34] I am more than the sum of my becoming, as are you! God gifts us with the power of imagination through the communion of the Holy Spirit. As God's wellspring of generosity, Christ Jesus allows us to experience an infinite source of wonder and to feast on hope. Truly Jesus *lived for us* and now *lives with us.* In the power of the Spirit, he reminds us of truths once forgotten — God is *for us* and *with us,* not as separate selves, but as relational beings in a sacramental world, embodied and much beloved.

The feast of our lives awaits us! The vastness of God's compassionate love lies within us and before us. It is the message for which we must be the messengers in our time. The wisdom and power of the risen One call us to God's eternally present table of forgiveness. May we come with hope and claim for ourselves a more-than-human humanness. May we then go forth to offer all people a generosity worthy of Christ-Christa, whose love is *with us now!* Truly, "glad communion" is a gift worth receiving.

RSVP

It is time to let the Spirit have its way with us.
This table is set, for
sinners, lovers, dancers, and dreamers,
the dying, divorced, suffering, and fearful.
All who are weary and heavy laden,
all who work for justice,
all who seek resurrection. Come.
Be not afraid, for hope is real, love is true, and God is good.
Come, let us keep the feast!

---

34. Sölle, *Thinking about God,* 187–88; Abraham J. Heschel, *Between God and Man: An Introduction of Judaism,* ed. Fritz A. Rothschild (New York: Free Press/Macmillan, 1959), 62.

APPENDIX A

Paradigm Shifts to Encourage Well-Being

"For us to newly criticize the pervasive language of sacrifice, requiring its transformation, will be for us to newly open ourselves to transformations in the meanings of Christian worship, of the death of Christ, of Christian ethics and of the human relationship to the created world."[1] Gordon Lathrop's prophetic observation encourages my imagination to take a leap of faith worthy of Christ-Christa.

Potential Signs of a Colonized Imagination	**Potential Signs of a Liberated Imagination**
Patriarchy/dominarchy/kyriarchy	Mutuality and right-relation
Domination=subordination	Communal well-being
Imagination is evil	Imagination is our spirit connecter
Power-over	Power-with/power-within
Internalized oppression	An intact psychic integrity– "I am worthy of God's love"
Death serving ways of being	Life-enhancing ways of being
Hopelessness=depression	Hopeful zest for life
Suffering is a lesson from God	Suffering is sin's evil twin
Suffering=psychic disconnection	Labor pains are living pains
Suffering love is good	Compassionate love resists suffering
Denial of pain and distrust of emotions	Awareness of feelings and discernment of pain
Obedient self-sacrifice	Voluntary self-sacrifice, community sacrifice
Violence disconnects	Love allows life-connections
Humiliation breeds shame	Humility accepts our interdependence
Isolation breeds fear	Community supports life-connections
Sacrificial atonement=human helplessness	Original communion=the divinity of our humanity

1. Gordon W. Lathrop, "Justin, Eucharist, and 'Sacrifice': A Case of Metaphor," *Worship* 64 (January 1990): 47.

Potential Signs of a Colonized Imagination	Potential Signs of a Liberated Imagination
God imaged as our enemy/the divine punisher	God imaged as our companion/ the encourager
God is distant, beyond us	God is beyond and within simultaneously
Transcendence as beyond, over against	Transcendence as interrelatedness/among
Punishment as God's judgment	God's judgment condemns punishment
Reconciled to God by the cross	Reconciled by divine forgiveness
Forgiveness as punishment	Forgiveness as God's nature
Costliness of grace=an apocalyptic lie	Divinity of grace=a greatening power
Contrite heart=crushed spirit	Open hearts strengthen bodyspirits
Apocalyptic eschatology=future	Realizing eschatology=now
Redemption as past and future	Redemption as present possibility
Crucifixion/cross as core of faith	Cross/resurrection as core of faith
Jesus as *crucified* and risen Redeemer	Jesus as crucified and *risen* Perfecter of faith
Jesus as Lord and Savior	Christ Jesus as the icon of God's generosity
Christ as Wisdom and Power of God	Christ-Christa as Wisdom and Power of God
Jesus Christ as God's definitive incarnation	Christ Jesus and God's continuing embodiment as Christ-Christa
Wounded healer	Healing healer
Christ will come again	Christ is with us now
Focus on human sin and disobedience	Focus on social evils and our sins
Self-denial is the way of the cross	Self-forgetfulness > self-denial
Self-denial confuses grace	Self-transcendence reveals grace
Human unworthiness prevails	Human worthiness glorifies God
Grace (God) alone saves (individuals)	Grace greatens us to cocreate and heal
Our humanity is never good enough	Our humanity is a gift to be cherished

APPENDIX B

Communion Prayers

These prayers (with slight adaptations) have been used in congregational settings and received warmly. I share them by way of example. The language of body and blood is present in honor of Jesus' physicality and our own. Sacrificial imagery, however, is absent. While you are free to use them with acknowledgment,[1] I hope that these prayers encourage your own sacramental re-imaging.

Communion Prayer I, Amazed by Grace

[I prefer to print only those portions of the prayer that immediately precede a congregational response, which is set in bold type. Prayers printed in full can be educationally useful in the classroom or if requested by parishioners for their own devotional use; however, they are not liturgically necessary. Printing too many words may cause participants to be captive to the written word at the expense of the embodied Word.]

Ante Communion

I generally do not use a prayer of confession in this service, in order to avoid this rite's penitential history. In lieu of a confessional prayer, one may encourage the Exchange of Peace as a symbol of reconciliation for the community. An asterisk (*) indicates that those who are able or inspired may stand.

*The congregation remains standing, following the communion Hymn.

**The Invitation*

My friends in Christ, this table is open to all who desire to be touched by the wonder of forgiveness.

---

1. Individuals or congregations may reprint or adapt for worship and educational purposes these prayers, provided the following acknowledgment is given: from (or adapted from) *The Feast of Our Lives: Re-imaging Communion*, copyright © June Christine Goudey (Cleveland: Pilgrim Press, 2002).

Nothing can separate us from the love of God in Christ Jesus; therefore, I invite you to open your hearts to the love that you already are.

Come as you are, in the sure and certain knowledge that Jesus invites you to feast on hope. Come, for God is gracious and merciful, and abounds in steadfast love.

*God be with you.
And also with you.
Lift up your hearts.
We lift them up to God.
Let us give our God thanks and praise.
In praising God we are amazed by grace.

Celebrant continues
Gracious God, source of steadfast strength, we delight in giving you praise; with purpose and compassion you gave of yourself, created our world, and called it good. Creating creatures of every size, shape, and color, you blessed humankind with the gift of your image.

Congregation responds
As you comfort us so, too, you challenge us. You speak to us of the widow and the sojourner, the homeless and the abused. You call us to turn from evil and, in returning, you welcome us with forgiving grace. Thanks be to you, Holy One, for rolling waters of justice, ever-flowing streams of hope, and the courage to start anew.

*Sung Response

[One verse of a hymn may be used here. Where possible, choir and congregation alternate.]

[All sit as celebrant continues . . .]
Before all who rage against your truth, before all who deny your love at work even now, we offer these prayers for the sake of your world.

Intercessory Prayers

[These replace the Pastoral Prayer. Allow for silence, and invite concerns to be prayerfully named by the congregation.]

Our Father/Mother [Debts]

Celebrant:
In gratitude for the love and generosity of Jesus, we join with angels and archangels to sing your praises. . . .

*Sung Response

[Repeat previous response.]

Celebrant:
Your majestic love overwhelms us with wonder, Holy One, and the universe rejoices. Blessed indeed is the one who loves in your name.

In the power of Jesus we gather at this table, remembering all that you have given us.

We remember Jesus' healing touch, his strong compassion, his righteous anger, and his prayerful strength. Bone of our bone and flesh of our flesh, he claims us by grace.

We remember how he gathered your people, stranger and friend alike, gave thanks to you, offered them the bread of life and the cup of blessing, and proclaimed a new covenant in your name.

Remembering the wonder of his life, the agony of his death, and the resurrection of his Spirit, we unite in the friendship born of this table, giving thanks always that we are gathered in the mystery of one faith....

Christ has died,
Christ is risen,
Christ is with us now!

We ask you to send your Spirit upon us, loving God, and upon this bread and fruit of the vine, that in eating and drinking together we might strengthen our commitment to do justice, celebrate creation, and honor the human differences through which your love shines.

Bless our communion with strength and purpose, we pray, and make us a more compassionate people, through the power of your risen Christ; for we pray as one, in the communion of the Holy Spirit, giving glory and honor to you, one God now and forever. So may your people say, **AMEN.**

Breaking the Bread

The bread, which we break, symbolizes our communion in the body of Christ.
In eating this bread you and I become one.

Pouring of the Cup

The cup, which we pour, symbolizes our communion in the risen life.
In drinking this cup our lives overflow with grace.
Come, for all things are now ready.

Sharing the Bread

The deacons distribute the bread. All partake together after these words:
You are the body of Christ, become the bread of life!

Sharing the Cup

The deacons distribute after these words: Receive the risen life with joy! *All partake as they wish.*

Prayer of Thanksgiving

God of mystery and wonder, we rejoice that you have gathered us at table in the communion of your Christ, and have fed us once again with forgiving grace. Send us forth with courage renewed, and friendships strengthened, to love as we have been loved, and to heal as we have been healed, that we might forgive others as you have forgiven us. Amen.

Dismissal and Benediction

Communion Prayer II, As We Gather

(If desired this communion service can be cocelebrated by two persons. Celebrants should preside with enthusiasm and joy.)

*Those who are able or inspired may stand.

Ante Communion

(The Exchange of Peace followed by a brief hymn verse aids the transition to the table.)

**Invitation to the Table, and Prayer*

God be with you.
And also with you.
Lift up your hearts.
We lift them up as one.
Let us offer God our thanks and praise.
It is a good and joyful thing to praise the living God.

Celebrant 1
Come with open hearts to this table of resurrection!
(Silence)
God of necessary endings and new beginnings,
You who speak and shape new worlds,
You who bless and multiply life,
Receive our deep and joyful thanks for all your gifts.

Beloved Maker,
In the beginning
Your creative hands and heart
Revealed your wondrous powers,
And all of creation bowed in awe.
Created female and male in your image,
Your earth creatures delighted in Eden's possibilities.
All things seemed good,
All things seemed holy.

Celebrant 2
And yet like so much in life
It all seemed too much too soon.
We quickly learned the price of freedom,
The risk of reaching beyond our grasp,
The meaning of sin.

Together or alone
We hunger for your goodness,
Your deep communion,
Your lasting forgiveness,
Your amazing grace.

Celebrant 1
Your sweetness lingers on our tongues, Holy One,
Your faithfulness beckons us to start anew.

As deep calls to deep with gratitude and grace, we join
With all creation to sing your praise:

Glo-ri-a, glo-ri-a, in ex-cel-sis De-o! *New Century Hymnal*, 756[2]
Glo-ri-a, glo-ri-a, al-le-lu-ia, al-le-lu-ia!

Glo-ry to God, glo-ry to God, glo-ry in the high-est!
Glo-ry to God, glo-ry to God, al-le-lu-ia, al-le-lu-ia!

In word and story,
In poem and prayer,
Your hope comes.

Again and again
Jesus reveals your loving ways,
Your righteous judgments,
Your tender mercies.

---

2. *The New Century Hymnal* (Cleveland: Pilgrim Press, 1995).

Celebrant 2
He touches us like a
Brother,
Teacher,
Lover,
And friend,
Fully human, fully divine,
Beyond our reach,
Yet near at hand,
Prophet and priest,
Savior and sacrament,
Transfiguring all who accept his yoke.

Celebrant 1
As he gathered his friends at table,
He gathers us in one faith, one baptism, one hope.

We remember
How he took bread, and
Having blessed and broken it,
Gave it in the tenderest of manners, [saying]

Celebrant 2
This is my body given for you.
Do this faithfully in remembrance of me.

Celebrant 1
In the same manner, he took the cup,
And having given thanks, gave it to them in the tenderest of manners.

Celebrant 2
This cup is the new covenant
Joining our life's blood as one.
May you find forgiveness here.
In eating and drinking together we receive Jesus' love,
Transform our hearts, and imagine new futures, for

Christ has died,
Christ is risen,
Christ is with us now! [**Alleluia!** May be added in Eastertide.]

Celebrant 1
Come now, Holy Spirit; bless these prayers, this food, and our lives
That we might be a blessing to one another and to your greater glory.
Chimes

Keep us faithful to all who have gone before us
To serve your high purpose.
May we not fail them,
May we not fail you,
May we not fail one another. **Chimes**

Brooding Spirit, life-giving Truth,
Send us forth to the places we have feared to go.
Weave us into your tapestry of resurrection
And dwell with us always. **Chimes**

For in you we live and move and have our being
Now and forever. **Amen**

Celebrant 1
(Breaking bread) The bread we eat symbolizes our participation in the body of Christ.

Celebrant 2
(Pouring the cup) The fruit we taste symbolizes our participation in Christ's new creation.

Celebrant 2
Holy things for holy people, receive them in faith and be thankful.

Sharing Bread and Cup

Celebrant 2

Prayer of Thanksgiving

For love shared and hope renewed, for promises remembered, and Christs among us, for the feasts of this life and those to come, we give you thanks, O God. Send us forth to reconcile and make new, praising life in the midst of death, bearing hope on angels' wings, and giving thanks always and everywhere that life is precious beyond all telling. Alleluia and Amen.

Communion Prayer III, In the Beginning

[When possible, I suggest sung responses be included in the bulletin, so that people need not fumble around searching for the right hymn page. Again, the prayer should be spoken, not printed, except for small sections that lead into congregational responses.]

*Those who are able or inspired may stand.

Ante Communion [ends with the Exchange of Peace]

**Celebrant*
God be with you.
And also with you.
Lift up your hearts.
We lift them up as one.
Let us offer God our thanks and praise.
It is good to gather in thanksgiving. . . .

**Sung Response*

"As We Gather," verse 1 *New Century Hymnal* #332

Celebrant
Join me now in sacred silence,
Rest in wonder and breathe deeply into your life,
That is all that is asked of you.

[Silence]

In the beginning some say nothingness,
In the beginning some say chaos,
In the beginning some say wisdom,
In the beginning some say word,
Beloved Maker, receive our gratitude.

In the beginning you were, you are, and you always will be,
Stirring, shaping, transforming, creating,
Newness.
In dark night and day light,
Your creative juices flow.
Waters part and heaven appears,
Waters join and creation shouts, "Land ho."

The fruit of your labor nourishes us.
Your seasons change us.
And through it all,
Love and laughter,
Joy and sorrow,
Birthing and dying,
We remember the love.
We are wonderfully made,

Lovingly blessed,
Eternally guarded.

Stars and dust,
Waters and blood,
Soul and spirit
Pulse through our human core.
Part image,
Part mystery,
Part madness,
At times in awe,
At times at odds with life itself.
Still, you call us back to the loving...
In a heartbeat.

Sung Response

"As We Gather," verse 2 *New Century Hymnal #332*

Celebrant
In word and story,
In poem and prayer,
Your hope comes.
We call him Jesus,
To you he is son,
To us much more:
Brother, teacher,
Lover, friend,
Pioneer and perfecter of our faith.

The table is set, the time is right,
Your meal like no other claims us.
Holy memories too good to be true
Refuse to die, eternally.

In friendship and blessing Jesus calls us beloved.
Imagine!
Nourishing bread, quenching cup, ours for the asking.

He takes and blesses, breaks and pours, gives... freely.

In the joining of body and blood,
Yours to his and his to ours,
Hunger and thirst part company.

Communion happens!

Love soothes our pain, melts our anger, frees your forgiveness.
In Christ's coming and calling,
In Christ's living and dying,
Hope is tenacious and triumphant.

"Remember," you say,
"home cooking never tastes as good as soul food."

Sung Response

"As We Gather," verse 3 *New Century Hymnal* #332

Intercessory Prayers [not printed]

Receive our hopes and prayers, our dreams and aspirations, Holy One, and keep us faithful in the midst of them. Save us from sins too deep for words, from failures too painful for memory, and from our refusal to love without conditions. Embrace us and embolden us to turn again, to the living of your loving ways.

Joined in friendship and high purpose, we pray aloud or in silence
For persons and peoples near and far,
For friends and strangers alike
Who as with us have need of your care and courage. . . .

[Sustained silence for people to speak if they wish]

Pain-bearing, heart-healing Spirit, receive these prayers and heal those who offer them.
Bless this food, our lives, and this fellowship
That we might be a blessing to one another and a balm to your world.

Quicken our hearts, steady our faith,
And lead us into resurrection, for in you we live and move and have our being now and forever. Amen. . . .

Sung Response

"I Come with Joy" (verses 2 and 3 only) *New Century Hymnal* #349

Celebrant
The gifts of grace are free. Come, all things are ready.

Sharing of the Bread and Cup: Communion by Intinction

Prayer of Thanksgiving [not printed; people repeat celebrant's words]

Thanks be to you, O God,
For the blessings of this table,

For the blessings of Christ's presence,
For the blessings of this community.
May we go forth to serve you joyfully and fruitfully,
Being steadfast in faith,
Tenacious in love,
And abounding in hope.
So may it be. Amen and Amen.

Closing Hymn

"I Come with Joy" (verses 4 and 5 only) *New Century Hymnal* #349

Dismissal and Benediction

Index

Abelard, Peter, 116, 118–21, 123
absence, 3, 25, 49, 57, 115, 117, 129, 140, 149, 159, 167–68, 173
absolution, 80
abundant life, 6, 125, 147, 172
abuse
  of child, 126
  of power, 127
  sexual, 56, 124
  See also oppression; violence
accountability, 13, 168, 171
Adam, 38, 72, 116
Akedah, 74, 75
alienation, 21, 34, 110, 138, 148
Alison, James, 8n, 90, 107
anamnesis, 68
Anselm, 84, 116, 118–21, 124, 131, 132
Apocalypse, as genre, 90–95, 98, 100–104, 107, 109, 128
Apocalypse of John, 80, 98, 100–101, 103. *See also* Revelation of John
Apocalypse of Paul, 109
Apocalypse of Peter, 90, 93, 109
apocalyptic eschatology, 61, 93, 94, 96, 98, 101, 110, 144, 154, 178
apocalyptic fear, 10, 83, 85, 102, 110, 128, 135, 149, 161, 165
apocalyptic imagery, 61, 88, 90, 93, 94, 98, 103, 107, 117, 127, 143, 157
apocalyptic impulse, 140
apocalyptic judgment, 83
apocalyptic language, 95, 96, 102, 108, 109, 163
apocalyptic messenger, 72
apocalyptic symbolism, 94–95
apocalyptic thinking, 3, 65, 93–97, 100, 127, 135
Apostle's Creed, 85, 95
archeological layers, 61
Armstrong, Karen, 59
art, 5, 7n, 9, 13n, 49n, 55, 75, 78, 88, 106–7, 120
artist, 38, 47, 103
Asian theology, 5
atonement, vii, 10
  "deceiving the devil," 103n, 118, 127, 151n
  "once and for all," 17, 76, 79, 84, 103, 154, 156, 158
  penal substitution, 31, 121–23
  ransom, 115, 118, 119
  satisfaction, 84, 115–19, 121, 127, 128, 131
at-one-ment, 32, 64, 86
Augustine, 24, 30, 45, 59, 60, 89, 102, 103, 106, 114, 116, 144
Aulén, Gustaf, 116, 118, 121
autonomy, 26
awe, 14, 82, 133, 159, 183, 187

Baker, John Austin, 12
baptism, 15, 30, 31, 64, 82, 101, 116, 117, 129, 131, 132
  baptismal anointment, 155
  of repentance, 124
  second, 61, 128. *See also* penance
Baptism Eucharist and Ministry (BEM), 17, 18, 61, 64, 66–69, 84
"baptismal equality," 31
barbarians, 92
Barth, Karl, 60, 89, 123
Baxter, Richard, 79n, 83
"believers in exile," 2
Bellah, Robert, 11
"blood of Jesus," 8, 91, 107, 129, 166
"body of Christ," 14, 17, 34, 48, 67–69, 72, 76, 81, 87, 91–92, 129, 134, 147, 165
bodymind, 42, 140, 149, 168–69, 171–72

bodyspirit, 135, 140, 146–47, 149, 158–60, 164, 171, 178
bodywisdom, ix, 47
Boff, Leonardo, 29n, 113
Bonhoeffer, Dietrich, 157n
Book of Common Prayer, 83
Bradshaw, Paul, 70, 74, 105n
"bread of life," 2, 73, 74n, 85n, 181, 182
Brock, Rita Nakashima, 12n, 47n, 126, 148
broken body, 2
broken spirit, 78, 79, 157
brokenness, 13, 17, 26n, 27, 86, 89
Brown, Joanne Carlson, 22, 124
Browne, Robert, 87
Buber, Martin, 6
Bushnell, Horace, 123, 142
Bynum, Carolyn Walker, 92, 99

Calvin, John, 6, 14, 18n, 25, 76–78, 81–84, 121–25, 132, 162, 167
Campbell, McLeod, 123
Carroll, James, 51, 114
Cavanaugh, William, 41, 54n, 63, 76
censor/censoring, 54, 58, 59, 86
Charlemagne, 92
Chile, 41, 54, 76, 134
Chilton, Bruce, 71, 72
Christ, 30, 35, 158, 160, 175, 178. *See also* Jesus
Christ Jesus, viii, 30, 35, 87, 158, 160, 165, 175, 178. *See also* Jesus
Christ-Christa, 11, 12, 16, 36, 57, 58, 62, 86, 89, 152, 157–60, 171–75
Christian imagination, 7n, 9, 66, 90, 108, 128
Christus Victor, 116, 118
class, 7, 126, 170
classic, 55–58
Cochrane, Arthur C., 63, 65
collective imagination, 41, 72, 114
colonized imagination, 40, 45, 46, 137, 177
communal meal, 18, 65, 70, 105
communal relations, 3, 149
communal well-being, 7, 13, 24, 26, 28, 33, 37, 58, 79, 85, 102, 147
compassionate love, 10, 13, 33, 48, 79, 148, 152, 164, 174, 175, 177
confession, 81–82, 130–31, 164
confessional prayer, 128, 163
"conquered from within," 148, 155
consecration, 92, 166
Constantine, 3, 13, 75, 116
contrite heart, 77–79, 157, 178
contrition, 79
convergence, 17, 61, 64, 66, 67
Copernican view, 52
corporal punishment, 86, 135, 140–44
covenant, 71, 72, 98, 99, 102, 103, 153, 154
Creator God, 14, 39, 157, 165
creators, 58, 133
cross, 17–19, 50, 51, 88, 113, 124–27, 159, 161, 178
Crossan, John Dominic, 27, 71, 96, 106, 111n, 154, 155n
crucifixion, 8, 19, 31, 73, 75, 82–83, 115, 132, 156, 159, 162, 178
cup, vii, 2, 20, 65, 70–73, 79, 87, 91, 169, 173

Daly, Mary, 7, 30, 31n
Daly, Robert, 68, 74, 75, 77n, 104n
Damasio, Antonio, 44n, 138n, 139
Davies, Horton, 73, 74n, 84, 85
death, 9, 19, 51, 65, 117–25, 161, 166
"defecting in place," 5
demonic, 21, 119
demons, 80, 124, 171
depression, 21, 140, 141, 177
devil, 21, 104, 110, 118–20, 128, 137, 141
Dillistone, F. W., 19, 86, 87n, 120n, 121n
discernment, 85, 178
disconnection, 14, 28, 48, 53, 114, 133, 169, 178

divine companion(ship), 26, 79, 157, 160, 165, 168, 178
divine forgiveness, 88, 103, 121, 122, 127, 154, 158, 175, 178
divine grace, 6, 16, 26, 88, 131, 133, 142, 157
divine judgment, 108–9, 149, 169, 178
divine justice, 24, 35, 110, 117, 119, 149
divine love, 12, 29, 33, 38, 42, 126, 137–38, 156–57, 161, 168, 170
divine presence, 12, 19, 30, 45, 53, 57–58, 82, 115, 126, 158, 167, 171
divine punishment, 27, 81, 107, 116, 121, 127, 173, 178
divine revelation, 46, 108
domestic violence, 124, 140–41
dominarchy, 11, 13, 22, 23, 26, 33–36, 56, 58, 60, 79, 177
dominators, 41
dominology, 23
Donnelly, Doris, 57
Driver, Tom, 21, 158n

earth, 14, 25, 39, 52, 67, 90, 96, 101–2, 109, 112, 132–33, 162
earth-creature, 132, 183
earthly communion, 8, 85
Eastern Orthodox, 30
ecumenism, 66, 67
elect, 123
Eliot, T. S., 13–14
embodied soul, 134–52, 153, 157, 167, 171–72
embodiment, 31, 160, 161, 169, 178
emotion, 6, 135, 138
emotional integrity, 43–44
empathy, 26, 131, 141, 147
emperor, 12–13, 22, 29, 92, 113, 120, 150, 158–59
enactment, 7, 54, 62, 121, 127, 164, 168
enemy, 1, 41, 55–56, 85, 115–17, 119, 123, 135, 137, 168–69, 171, 178
epiclesis, 166
erosion, 18, 94, 135, 145–47
eschatology, 93–96
eternal punishment, 69, 98, 103, 112, 149
eucharist, 8, 16–18, 27, 29, 30–38, 58, 61–72, 88–89, 103–7, 131–32, 157. *See also* Holy Communion; Lord's Supper
eucharistic prayer, 12, 16, 66, 153, 160, 166, 167, 168, 179–89
Everett, William Johnson, 23, 24, 30n
evil, 3, 5, 33, 90, 118–19, 130, 147–52, 168, 169, 177
excommunication, 8, 128, 129, 133, 173

Fackre, Gabriel, 68
"family of origin," 24
Farley, Wendy, 18n, 33, 126, 127, 146n, 150n, 152
fear of God, 69, 133, 153, 159
fears, 1, 3, 16, 20–21, 40, 54, 81, 111, 150, 162, 168, 170
feast, vii, 63, 66, 67, 83, 85, 86, 104, 107, 148, 153
  of judgment, 85
  of the lamb, 37, 84, 88, 104, 162
  of our lives, 89, 152, 162, 171, 172, 175
feelings, 22, 24, 42, 139–42, 151, 177
feminism, 11
"fencing the table," 2, 82, 160
Fisher, M. K., 13–14
forgiveness, 2, 20, 27, 82, 123, 128, 148, 156–58, 161, 174
  and Jesus, 61, 113, 131, 154, 156
  of sin, 69, 87, 99, 103, 115, 119, 120, 123, 132, 148, 155, 166
Forsyth, P. T., 87n
freedom, 3–4, 10, 28, 32, 42–43, 47, 55, 115–17, 125–26, 142, 146, 158
Freud, Sigmund, 60
Frost, Robert, 169
"fruit of the spirit," 6, 89

Galileo, 52
gender, 5–8, 10, 25, 170
George, Timothy, 9, 111n, 121n, 122n, 123n
Gloria Patri, 1
god-representations, 60, 135–36, 139, 159
good and evil, 59, 85, 96, 127, 147, 150–52
grace, 11, 20, 29, 90, 148, 158. *See also* divine grace
Greven, Philip, 10, 99–101, 134n, 140, 141, 143, 144
Grey, Mary, 29
grief, 41, 151
guilt, vii, 9, 53, 65, 88, 89, 114–16, 142, 149, 151

Hall, Douglas John, 144n, 150n
Handel, G. F., 120
hard-heartedness, 38
Harrison Beverly, 24, 29
hatred, 11, 22, 56, 121, 143, 168
Hazelton, Roger, viii, 29n, 45n, 49
heart-mind, 6, 62
heaven, 3, 7, 10, 90, 94–96, 104, 107–9, 141, 155, 166, 186
heavenly banquet, 87
Hebrews, 74, 77, 98–107, 122, 144, 154, 156, 161
hell, 21, 85, 93, 103, 107–12, 140–45, 161
heresy, 3, 4, 8, 13, 129, 151
Heschel, Abraham, 14n, 117n, 133, 175n
Heyward, Carter, 149n, 150, 164n
high priest, 68, 99, 101, 103, 156
Hitler, Adolf, 54
Holy Communion, vii, 3, 8, 19, 63, 103, 153–75, 179–89
Holy Spirit, 6, 25, 46, 60, 67, 69, 70, 82, 89, 158, 165, 175
hope, vii, 1, 3–5, 15, 48, 85, 133–35, 147, 158–60, 174, 175
hopelessness, 42, 45, 58, 137, 159, 170, 177
horizon, 7, 35, 53–54, 58, 61, 114, 133, 135, 151, 162
hospitality, 8, 48, 84, 173
human experience, 20–21, 28–29, 37, 45, 47, 49, 60, 150
human imagination, vii, 6, 25, 35, 39, 86, 94, 123, 144
humiliation, 44, 86, 88, 89, 99, 128, 131–33, 140, 152, 177
humility, 44, 132, 133, 177

imagination, 37–62
imaginative feeling, 14, 159, 162
imago Dei, 45, 46, 59
immanence, 25, 38, 52, 172
immune system, 40, 41
incarnation, 3, 8, 11–13, 31, 45, 123, 126, 146, 152, 156, 160, 167, 178
injustice, 7, 23, 36, 67, 102, 127, 135, 143, 151, 157
"inner disposition," 17, 68, 75, 77–79
institutional narratives, 167. *See also* words of institution
interdependence, 42, 164, 177
internalized oppression, 22, 41, 155
interpretation, 2, 9, 17, 45, 50–51, 61, 66, 68–70, 72–76, 114–16, 146, 154
intimacy, 43, 80, 167, 170
Irenaeus, 119, 14
Isaiah, 85, 96n, 97, 112, 120

Jennings, Theodore, 94
Jeremiah, 32, 85, 154
Jeremias, Joachim, 73
Jesus
  death of, 17–19, 32, 51, 68, 88, 91, 98, 113, 125, 166, 172
  ministry of, 8, 128, 156, 159, 164, 170–71
  prayer of, 17, 67, 71n
  return of, 65–66, 73, 94–95, 99
  suffering of, 8, 18, 33, 80, 88, 113, 124, 145
John Paul II, Pope, 50

Jordan, Judith, 26n, 131
Judaism, 75, 79n, 97, 156
judgment, 10, 20, 38, 53, 86, 90, 93, 97, 101, 122, 144, 154
"Judgment Day," 3, 85, 144
Jung, Carl, 16, 22n, 60, 151n
justice, 9–11, 49, 86, 96, 103–4, 164, 169, 174–75
Justin Martyr, 75

Käsemann, Ernst, 94
Kelleher, Margaret, 7, 38, 53, 54
Keller, Catherine, 18, 26n, 28n, 95n, 102n, 103n, 104n, 160n, 161
KINGAFAP, 24
"knowing good and evil," 150

lack of praise, 58, 64, 149
Lamb of God, 72, 82, 103, 122, 154
Langer, Ellen, 52, 53
Langer, Suzanne, 7n, 49n
Last Judgment, 94, 98, 107, 110, 111, 161
Last Supper, 8, 12, 63, 64, 69, 70, 72, 77, 87, 104, 106
Lathrop, Gordon, 75, 76, 177
lectionary, 88, 97
Leo X, Pope, 16
lex orandi, lex credendi, 64
liberation, 5, 15, 20, 22, 32, 58, 172
liberation theology, 15, 102
life-experience, 74, 86, 140
life-work, 10, 32, 89, 158–59
liturgical renewal movement, 4
liturgical theology, 35, 57, 163n
liturgy, 5–7, 15, 20–22, 36–37, 45, 54, 58, 62–63, 84, 86, 120
"lived-experience, 30, 39, 48, 51–52, 61, 88, 94, 101–2, 109, 117
Lombard, Peter, 30
Lord's Supper, 8, 63–64, 70n, 74, 77, 82–84, 94, 173. *See also* eucharist; Holy Communion
love, 9–10, 19, 37, 40, 43, 89, 115, 119–21, 138, 142, 148–49, 168–69. *See also* compassionate love; suffering love
loveliness, 133, 148, 171
Luther, Martin, 33, 50, 76–78, 80–81, 103, 110–11, 114, 121–23, 125, 132, 144, 161–62

Marxsen, Willi, 70n, 72, 74
McFague, Sallie, 24n, 49n, 87
"meal of Melchizedek," 103
medieval captivity, vii, 120, 167
memorial meal, 63
memorial, 65, 67, 68, 77, 81, 154, 167
Mercersburg tradition, 83, 84
messianic banquet, 61, 64, 84, 85, 90
metaphor, 5, 24, 26, 49, 68, 76, 87, 103, 118, 123, 162, 177n
metaphorical imagery, 23, 25, 75, 84
Middle Ages, 9, 92, 103, 109, 128n, 129n
Miles, Jack, 59
Miles, Margaret, 103n
mindfulness, 51–53
mindlessness, 48, 51, 52, 64, 103, 126, 129
misogyny, 11, 102, 104
Moltmann, Jürgen, 95, 110, 124
mujerista theology, 5
mutuality, 23, 26, 27, 29, 36, 147, 148, 150, 152, 164, 178
mysterion, 29, 30

Neville, Robert C., viii, 6, 26n, 39n, 43n, 47n, 55n, 148n, 160n
Nicene Creed, 85, 95
Noddings, Nel, 26n, 130, 152n

oppression, 9, 11, 29, 32, 50–51, 76, 102, 114, 126, 150–51, 177. *See also* torture; tyranny; violence
orans, 79
original communion, 17, 53, 168, 169, 177
original sin, 45, 106, 116

orthodoxy, 3, 4, 12
orthopraxy, 11
orthopathema, 146

Pagels, Elaine, 3n, 16n, 114n, 115n, 116n, 151n
panentheism, 25, 39
pantheism, 25n
Paris de Grassi, 16
Parker, Rebecca, 22, 124
parousia, 105, 106
Passover, 64, 65, 68, 69, 70, 73, 74, 88, 91
patriarchy, 22, 126, 177
Paul, Apostle, 65, 69, 72, 73, 79, 91, 108, 117, 118, 140, 171
Paul, Robert S., 86n, 87n, 121n, 122n, 123n
Pelagius, 16, 116
penance, 27, 30, 61, 113–14, 119, 121, 128–32, 160, 165
penitential eucharists, 9–10, 18–19, 21, 80, 103, 162, 163
penitential practices, viii, 9, 112, 128, 134, 156
Penitentials, 130–31
personal salvation, 18, 91, 103, 127, 129
phantasy, 42, 48
physical integrity, 44
physical senses, 39, 42
"picture of grace," vii, 9, 10, 113, 161, 162
piety, 68, 82, 83, 131, 143
Pinochet, Augusto, 41, 54, 66
power
  from-within, 28, 177
  of fear, 114, 116
  of guilt, 114–15
  of imagination, 46–47, 146, 175
  of praise, 56–58
  of ritual, vii, 35, 84, 114
  of shame, 114, 127
  over, 23, 79, 126, 130, 177
  with, 28
praise, 1, 13, 38, 45, 60, 82, 159, 165, 180, 182–83, 186
"praise and thanksgiving," 38, 56–58, 79, 165
praxis, 9, 15, 17, 22–23, 63, 75, 79, 87–88, 146n
prayers, 22, 30, 64, 65, 73, 79, 81, 87, 105, 121, 131, 174
priest, 17, 68, 72, 74, 80, 91–93, 102–4, 122, 130, 155–56, 162, 184
process theology, 149
Procter-Smith, Marjorie, viii, 10n, 31n
prophets, 32, 45, 108
Psalms, 24, 77, 82, 120
psychic integrity, 43–44, 131, 133, 137, 146, 177
punishment, 10, 21, 26, 88, 98, 108, 109, 139, 149, 150, 155
  as atonement, 97, 117, 119, 121, 122, 124, 126, 127
  as image, 95, 99
  as penance, 127–29
punitive god-image, 3, 127, 137
Puritans, 83, 117, 119n, 123

racism, 126
Ranke-Heinemann, Uta, 112
Ray, Darby Kathleen, 113n, 118n, 126, 127, 151n
redemption, 10, 32, 51, 81, 113, 118, 120, 123, 127, 157–59, 162, 178
Redemptionism, 11
redemptive power, 33, 57, 120, 150, 175
Reformation tradition, 4, 64, 68, 77n, 103, 163, 166, 173
Reformed Judaism, 97
Reformed liturgies, vii, 4, 58, 79, 81, 166
Reformed theology, 1n, 27, 60, 84n
reformers, 4, 9, 12, 15, 17, 61, 76–77, 79, 111
relational integrity, 44
relational self, 13, 25–26, 34, 36, 79, 133, 137

representations, vii, 3, 23, 53, 59, 72, 78n, 86, 107, 138, 141, 164, 167
resistance, 5, 18, 21, 25, 31, 56, 76, 126, 134, 158, 171
Revelation of John, 80, 97, 101–3
revelation, 31, 38, 46, 55, 93, 161
Rich, Adrienne, 11n, 23n
Ricoeur, Paul, 50n
Rilke, Rainer Maria, 56n
ritual, 21–22, 24, 35, 55, 64–65, 70, 84, 103, 105, 128
"ritual of power," 128
"rituals of self-hatred," 11
Rizzuto, Ana-Maria, 60n, 135–36
rod, 100, 134, 140, 142, 144, 169
Roman Catholics, 5, 30, 120, 131
Ruether, Rosemary Radford, 22, 159

sacrament, 8, 14, 29–31, 67, 82, 120, 160–67, 173–74
  of penance, 9, 15, 61, 69, 127, 130
sacramentum, 29
sacrare, 29
sacred fellowship, 69, 72, 174
sacred food, 69, 72, 91, 174
sacrifice of praise, 67, 76–79, 103
sacrifice, 3, 17–18, 32–33, 45, 65–80, 87–92, 98–105, 115, 120–22, 134, 155–56, 177
sacrificial theories, 9, 10, 22
sacrificium laudis, 76
salus, 27
salvation, 5, 20, 27, 35, 45, 69, 141, 154, 156
salvation history, 166–67
Sanders, E. P., 97–98, 117
sarx, 72
Satan, 3, 114, 118–20, 151
Schreiter, Robert, 19, 146–47
Schüssler Fiorenza, Elisabeth, 12n, 23n, 36, 70n, 95n, 98n, 102, 113n, 140n
scripture, 5, 45, 59, 61, 140
Second Coming, 8, 65, 94, 105, 166
self-denial, 16, 86, 126, 178
self-disclosure, 30–31, 55
self-emptying, 18n, 91, 160n
self-giving love, 12, 68
self-giving, 79, 91
self-hatred, 11, 22, 56, 121
self-identity, 18, 37, 41, 55, 119
self-image, 7, 52, 57, 103
self-immolation, 75, 86
self-mutilation, 56, 134
self-reflection, 34, 58, 63, 103
self-respect, 28, 126
self-sacrifice, 17, 48, 56, 70, 124–26, 145, 172, 177
self-transcendence, 16, 26, 47–48, 57, 79, 133, 170, 178
sexism, 22, 26, 126, 161
sexuality, 20, 43, 132, 170
shame, 56, 71, 86–89, 114–15, 127, 130–33, 142, 177
Shoah, 50–51
sin and suffering, 18, 116, 126
Smith, Dennis, 70
Socrates, 114
Sölle, Dorothee, 33n, 42, 48, 171n, 175n
soma, 72
"son of man," 65, 72, 93, 96, 101, 118
soteriology, 74–75
soul, 6, 44, 46, 49, 80, 108, 113, 127
Spinks, Bryan, 12, 82–83, 168
spiritual integrity, 44
Spong, Bishop John Shelby, 2, 4
"stiff-necked," 38, 170
subordination, 8, 11, 23, 39, 177
Suchocki, Marjorie, 28, 149, 157
suffering love, 10, 33, 91, 98, 115, 117, 123–24, 128, 148, 149, 177
suffering, 17–18, 31, 33, 114, 117–18, 144–46, 148, 163, 175
symbol, 6, 9, 15–16, 22, 30, 34–35, 37–40, 46–51, 92, 139, 150, 165–66

table-fellowship, vii, 8, 18, 37–38, 90, 92, 153–55, 160, 165, 170–74
Taussig, Hal, 70

temple, 68, 72, 96, 98, 101, 115, 154–56
Tertullian, 1, 3, 30, 114, 128, 131
thanksgiving, viii, 2, 12, 14, 17, 66–67, 75, 88–89, 145, 158–59
theodicy, 149–50
Thompson, Bard, 77n, 79n–83n
Tillich, Paul, 16, 27n, 39n, 49n, 120n, 137n, 157n, 164n
torture, 19, 41–42, 50, 54, 63, 76, 110, 115, 134
Tracy, David, 36n, 55, 58
transformation, 7, 15, 21, 53, 62, 71–72, 75–76, 93–94, 125, 149, 154, 174
trauma, 3, 9, 19, 94, 111, 115, 135, 139, 141, 155
tyranny, 46, 118

victim, 8, 23, 41–42, 56, 90, 104, 107, 141, 146, 151, 156, 172
violence, 9, 23, 26, 41, 75, 107, 111, 115, 137, 146–47, 150–52, 177

Wainwright, Geoffrey, 55, 64–66, 70, 105, 107
Watts, Isaac, 123
welcome-table, 128, 171
well-being, 15, 40, 43, 54, 58, 136, 148–49
Wenig, Margaret, 75, 97
Wesley, Charles, 123
Wesley, John, 123, 142, 182
Westminster Directory, 83
White, James F., 7, 80, 82
Whitehead, Alfred North, 26, 172n
Wilder, Amos, 37, 55, 111
Williams, Daniel Day, 157
Williams, Delores, 125–26
"wisdom of the body," 135, 138n
womanist, 5, 125
womb of death, 19
wonder, 14, 44, 57, 162, 168, 175
words of institution, vii, 2, 12, 61, 63–64, 67, 69, 81, 163, 165–67, 172
Wordsworth, William, 39
World Council of Churches, 17, 66–67
worship, 4–7, 14–16, 35, 45, 52–53, 57, 62, 68, 75–76, 79, 82–83, 129
wounds of Jesus, 18

Zwingli, Ulrich, 86–87, 91, 177